MRPII: Integrating the Business

MRPII: Integrating the Business
A practical guide for managers

Martyn Luscombe

Senior Consultant
The CIM Institute, Cranfield

Butterworth-Heinemann Ltd
Linacre House, Jordan Hill, Oxford OX2 8DP

 PART OF REED INTERNATIONAL BOOKS

OXFORD   LONDON   BOSTON
MUNICH   NEW DELHI   SINGAPORE   SYDNEY
TOKYO   TORONTO   WELLINGTON

First published 1993

British Library Cataloguing in Publication Data
Luscombe, Martyn
   MRPII: Integrating the Business
   I. Title
   658.7

ISBN 0 7506 1626 1

Composition by Genesis Typesetting, Laser Quay, Rochester, Kent
Printed in England by Clays Ltd, St Ives plc

Contents

— Preface —

Compared with some of the new competitive strategies of the 1990s, manufacturing resource planning (MRPII) looks decidedly seasoned. Strategies that have come to prominence in recent years include exciting concepts like total quality management, lean production, time-based competition, world class manufacture, focused factories, concurrent engineering and competitive benchmarking, to name but a few. MRPII predates them all, its origins stretching back over a quarter of a century. So why is a new book on MRPII needed? Is MRPII still relevant in this new age of competitive manufacturing? Even if it is, can anything new be said about it?

The core technique of MRPII is material requirements planning (which can be abbreviated either to MRPI, or, as in this book, simply to MRP). According to recent surveys, over half of all UK manufacturing companies use computer-based MRP. Only 4% of engineering companies employing more than 50 people have no MRP system. More companies are intending to purchase MRP software, and many that already have it will acquire further modules in order to move towards a full MRPII environment. In 1991, some 30% of UK companies intended to invest in MRP/MRPII software over the following two years. Between 30 and 40% of companies using MRP have so far installed all the additional modules needed for MRPII operation. Around half of those still using only MRP intend eventually to progress to full MRPII.

Just how successful these investments have been depends on how one measures success. One study suggests that over 80% of the MRPII implementations in Europe have failed. In contrast, two studies in the UK found that over 50% of MRPII implementations deliver the expected benefits. Perhaps expectations were not as high as they might have been. Certainly the popular image of MRPII is not one of success. The *Financial Times* (24 September 1992) spoke of "the 'failure' of MRPII" and described it as "one of the vogue computerized systems of the 1970s."

The present situation can be summarized as follows. MRP has achieved a high penetration of manufacturing companies (including the great majority of larger ones). Investment in MRP/MRPII software is continuing at a steady rate, but success has been, at best, mixed.

Is MRPII still relevant? In view of the increasing use of MRPII software, manufacturing industry clearly believes that it is. Indeed it seems to be more relevant than ever. There is little sign of MRPII being replaced by those newer strategies that are vying with it for the attention of senior managers.

Is there anything new to be said about MRPII? The disappointing results achieved by many companies suggest that there is still much to learn. Yet there are surprisingly few recent books on the subject. There is very little balanced discussion of the strategic role of MRPII, and not much by way of practical advice for managers who are considering implementing it, or who wish to revive a failed implementation.

One reason for this lack of serious literature seems to be a perception that MRPII is not really a strategic issue. Perhaps it seems too technical for senior managers to concern themselves with. Or possibly its origins in production planning suggest that it is merely a scheduling tool. Furthermore, since it requires the use of computers, perhaps MRPII is best left to the information technology specialists. All of these views are greatly mistaken. The impact of MRPII, properly implemented, is at least as great as any of the more recent competitive business strategies that seize the headlines. Indeed, it is rarely possible to achieve the full benefits of any of these other strategies unless MRPII is also in place. MRPII brings structure, discipline and systems integration to a business. These attributes are essential whatever the strategic thrust the enterprise wishes to adopt.

MRPII is neither a piece of computer software nor simply a scheduling tool; it is a competitive business strategy. Its significance is such that all managers within manufacturing companies need to understand it. Not only those managers working in materials management or information technology, and not just those in the lower echelons of the managerial hierarchy. All managers are impacted by MRPII, and they need to understand how.

This book is aimed at the needs of practising managers. Its objective is to explain as clearly as possible what MRPII can do and what it cannot, and what is required of managers if they are to achieve the benefits that MRPII offers. It is not a prescriptive book, containing lists of dos and don'ts. Its aim is to convey an understanding of how things work within MRPII, because only then can managers really apply it properly. Inevitably there is some discussion of the technical aspects of MRPII. However this is in no greater depth than is necessary for a full understanding of the important issues that managers must address. The use of numerical examples to explain the inner workings of MRPII is avoided wherever possible, since these can be tedious to follow and tend to overemphasize the detail at the expense of the concept.

At all times this book takes a realistic view of MRPII. There is no doubt that the techniques which MRPII embraces contain questionable assumptions and simplifications. The problems that result from these shortcomings are highlighted, and ways of overcoming many of them are suggested. Neither MRPII nor any other single strategy provides a complete route to achieving and sustaining competitiveness. Many different, complementary, approaches must be combined. For most companies, MRPII will be one of those approaches.

Busy managers who want a condensed summary of what MRPII is, and what it means to them, should read Chapters 1, 4 and 7. Those who need a more rounded understanding of the subject, without delving very far into the technicalities, could miss out Chapter 2 on first reading. Any manager working in a company which is intending to introduce MRPII, or is already using it, will need to read the whole book.

Students too will find this book useful, although they may consider that in reaching its conclusions it lacks the academic rigour to which they are accustomed. Those whose ambition is to enter the ranks of management may soon have an opportunity to put into practice the lessons of this book. The value of sound experience and proven methodologies will then become apparent.

Above all, this book is about the challenges of managing complex manufacturing operations to achieve ever higher standards of excellence. Even MRPII is only a part of the total picture, and must be seen in that context. This book takes a rather wider view than that sometimes adopted by those who work exclusively within the 'MRPII industry'. MRPII is simply a mechanism for helping managers to achieve their primary objective of improving business performance. That objective is what is really important, and it is where my own interests lie. Many stimulating challenges await managers who are dedicated to improving things; I hope that this book will equip and enthuse them to pursue this demanding and rewarding goal.

Acknowledgements

This book results from 22 years' experience of working in manufacturing industry. During that time I have never been far from MRPII. Previous managerial responsibility for materials, production and information technology has ensured that I have experienced MRPII from a variety of angles. I have been involved in many implementations, undertaking the roles of analyst, user, project leader and consultant.

This experience was not gained in isolation. Much of what I have learnt has come from working with other people - colleagues, system suppliers, and even clients - on real problems. It would be quite impossible to acknowledge each of their contributions individually. Nevertheless I am grateful to all those with whom I have worked over the years for sharing their ideas and experience with me.

There are others whose advice and help I deliberately sought in writing this book. These I can, and shall, thank individually. Firstly there are Ian Glenday and David Spyer, who supplied case study material on Reckitt Pharmaceuticals and Alcad Limited respectively. Both contributed a great deal more than mere case histories, and their ideas have influenced this book in several ways. The conclusions drawn in the case studies are, however, entirely my own. Sadly, since the Alcad case study was written it has been announced that Alcad's manufacturing facility is to be closed down. Alcad's parent company was faced with over-capacity in a falling market and decided to rationalize production into a larger and more automated plant in Sweden. Even world class levels of performance are no guarantee of survival in today's tough market-places.

I am grateful for the assistance of Paul Moss, of ASK Computer Systems Limited and Rob Bloor, of Largotim Limited. Software suppliers are extremely influential in promoting and enabling the MRPII concept, so it was important that the book reflected trends and developments in that field. With backgrounds in two of the leading suppliers in the UK, Paul and Rob both gave me valuable insights into current issues and future strategies.

One of the more complex issues touched upon in this book is finite capacity scheduling. It sometimes seems that the few people who have sound understanding and practical experience of finite scheduling are greatly outnumbered by those who have strong, but unsubstantiated views on the subject. Fortunately Damian McGinn, of Davy Morris and Jon Whelan, of John Brown Systems, both of whom fall into the former category, were able to provide some practical and reasoned input on this topic.

Several colleagues at The CIM Institute reviewed the manuscript and made numerous suggestions for improving it. Dr Stephen Evans and Robin Lane provided many helpful comments on the structure and content of the book. Dr Ip Shing Fan, Dr Jeremy Busby and Lesley Jones all reviewed those parts of it where their specialist knowledge exceeds my own. Other members of staff, researchers and students at The CIM Institute have at various times stimulated thoughts and imparted pieces of information which have now found their way onto these pages. In addition I must thank Melanie Sanders, who converted my rough sketches into the diagrams that are scattered throughout this book.

Finally I must mention my wife Sandra, and Matthew and Adrian. Not just for their tolerance of my partial withdrawal from family life during the book's gestation, for they are all busy people and I suspect the hardship was less than I might like to believe. Indeed the example they invariably set in conscientiously tackling their various homeworks shamed me into doing likewise. All helped by willingly surrendering the PC when I needed it, not interrupting me (too often) when I was deep in thought, and being unfailingly enthusiastic about the whole project. My thanks, and love, to them.

Martyn Luscombe

List of abbreviations

ABC	Activity based costing
AI	Artificial intelligence
APICS	American Production and Inventory Control Society
ATP	Available to promise
CAD	Computer aided design
CAM	Computer aided manufacturing
CAPP	Computer aided process planning
CCR	Capacity constraint resource
CIM	Computer integrated manufacturing
CNC	Computer numerical control
CRP	Capacity requirements planning
DBMS	Database management system
DRP	Distribution resource planning
EBQ	Economic batch quantity
EDI	Electronic data interchange
EOQ	Economic order quantity
ERP	Enterprise resource planning
FIFO	First in first out
FMS	Flexible manufacturing system
GUI	Graphical user interface
IBS	Integrated business system
IGES	Initial Graphics Exchange Specification
ISO	International Standards Organization
IT	Information technology
ITT	Invitation to tender
JIT	Just-in-time
MAP	Manufacturing Automation Protocol
MPS	Master production schedule
MRP	Material requirements planning
OPT	Optimized Production Technology
PAC	Production activity control
PLC	Programmable logic controller
RCCP	Rough cut capacity planning
SCADA	Supervisory control and data acquisition
SFDC	Shopfloor data capture
SPC	Statistical process control
STEP	Standard for the Exchange of Product model data
TPS	Toyota Production System
TQM	Total quality management
VDU	Visual display unit

— 1 —

An introduction to MRPII

Begin here

For most readers, this book will not be their first exposure to manufacturing resource planning (MRPII). Previous experience may have been gained from working in a company which uses such a system, or from books, courses, articles, salesmen or consultants. These experiences are likely to have emphasized different aspects of MRPII, and may have been supportive of the concept or wholly opposed to it. As a result, no two readers will approach this book with exactly the same perspective of its subject matter.

The aim of this chapter is to establish a common understanding of MRPII, by reviewing briefly its historical origins and then outlining the main techniques that characterize it. The reader can assist in this process by setting aside all previous knowledge of the subject, and starting out afresh.

A brief history

It may be an over-simplification to say that MRPII originated from the computer industry's wish to sell more computers. Nevertheless, it is certainly the case that MRPII provided an application that allowed computers to move beyond the accounts department and into manufacturing management for the first time. As a result, the major computer manufacturers of the day were amongst the most active participants in the early development of MRPII theory.

The first step along the path was the development of bill of material processors. These contain software that maintains the links between a product and all the sub-assemblies, components and materials that go into its manufacture. Bill of material processors could calculate very quickly all the material quantities required to make a batch of a particular product, even if that product was made up from many thousands of different items.

The bill of material processor was developed into material requirements planning by the addition of three further functions. These were:

- netting
- batching
- time-phasing.

These functions are explained in the next section.

Material requirements planning soon became known simply as MRP. Later, when the concept of manufacturing resource planning evolved from MRP, it doubtless seemed logical to give it a name and an acronym that suggested 'MRP plus'. However, as we shall see later in this chapter, MRP and MRPII are fundamentally different, and the similarity between these two abbreviations has been the cause of much subsequent confusion.

By the end of the 1960s, MRP was becoming an established technique in the USA and was beginning to appear in Europe. As a tool for managing materials, MRP seemed to have much to offer, but it was limited by its inability to take account of capacity. This deficiency was overcome with the development of closed loop MRP, described later in this chapter. Closed loop MRP offered a complete system for managing both materials and capacity. For companies that had been struggling with ineffective manual systems, the appearance of a management tool that promised to sweep away all the uncertainty and confusion associated with batch manufacturing seemed almost too good to be true.

As the 1970s progressed, the expression manufacturing resource planning, or MRPII, began to be used, describing a concept that was now moving beyond closed loop MRP. But it was not only our understanding of the techniques of MRPII that was developing; computer technology was also advancing. An important development as the decade came to an end was a move away from batch processing in favour of on-line transaction processing.

Batch processing required that written records were made of all transactions affecting data held in the system (stock issues, order receipts, scrap notes, design changes etc). These dockets were batched by transaction type and keyed into transaction files, or stored as punched cards. At convenient intervals, sometimes daily but frequently only weekly, a batch program was run on the computer, accessing the transaction files or punched cards to update the relevant data files.

It was almost impossible to keep data accurate under these circumstances. There were no visual display units (VDU) with which to make enquiries into current status. Printed reports were the only information available, and the format of these, once programmed, could not easily be modified. Information was always late, and frequently in the wrong format.

On-line transaction processing enabled data to be entered and verified at source, and files to be updated as the data was accepted. This was a great step forward. It was this advance more than anything else that enabled MRPII to become an everyday tool for use throughout the company, rather than a specialist task for the computer department.

The 1980s saw the emergence of a new industry as a multitude of system suppliers appeared, offering software packages based upon MRPII concepts. As time passed, new functionality was added to the core processes, and an ever-wider range of peripheral modules was incorporated into the software. Computing technology advanced further, as we shall see in later chapters, adding greater flexibility in the use of these systems.

An important early influence on the use of MRPII was the American Production and Inventory Control Society (APICS). This body was quick to realize the importance of the new technology and did much to publicize its benefits in the USA, leading what became known as the 'MRP Crusade' of the early 1970s. APICS has continued to have a major influence over MRPII, particularly in the USA. Definitions of MRPII terminology established by APICS are now universally used, and APICS sets standards for MRPII software which are widely followed by software developers.

The effect of this standardization has been to ensure that a common language is spoken by those working in the MRPII industry, and that APICS-compliant software is of at least a certain minimum specification. This standardization has also had the effect of limiting innovation in the software products that are on offer. From the earliest days of MRPII there has been a rather evangelical belief amongst enthusiasts that it is universally applicable, and that the underlying concepts are immutable. This rigid approach has been one of the factors that has split much of the manufacturing world into MRPII believers or non-believers. In later chapters we shall examine how a more flexible approach, both in the design of software and in the way it is applied, might enable companies to get more out of their MRPII implementations.

Material requirements planning

We have seen that MRP developed from bill of material processors, which managed the links between a product and the sub-assemblies, components and raw materials from which it was made. The word 'item' encompasses all materials, parts and products which are identified by unique part numbers. Bill of material processors are not concerned with the physical form an item takes, only with its position, or level, in the structure of the product. The top level (level 0) is usually a finished product. Items that are used in the final assembly of the level 0 item are held at level 1 of the bill of material. These items may in turn have their own components, which are held at level 2, and so on. Figure 1.1 shows a typical bill of material structure. Any physical limit in the software on the number of levels that can be used usually far exceeds most companies' needs.

In order to evolve into MRP, bill of material processors required the addition of three essential functions: netting, batching and time-phasing; each of these functions is explained below. The terminology used in these explanations is that of engineering assembly: sub-assemblies, components, final assembly etc. This is the type of industry most commonly associated

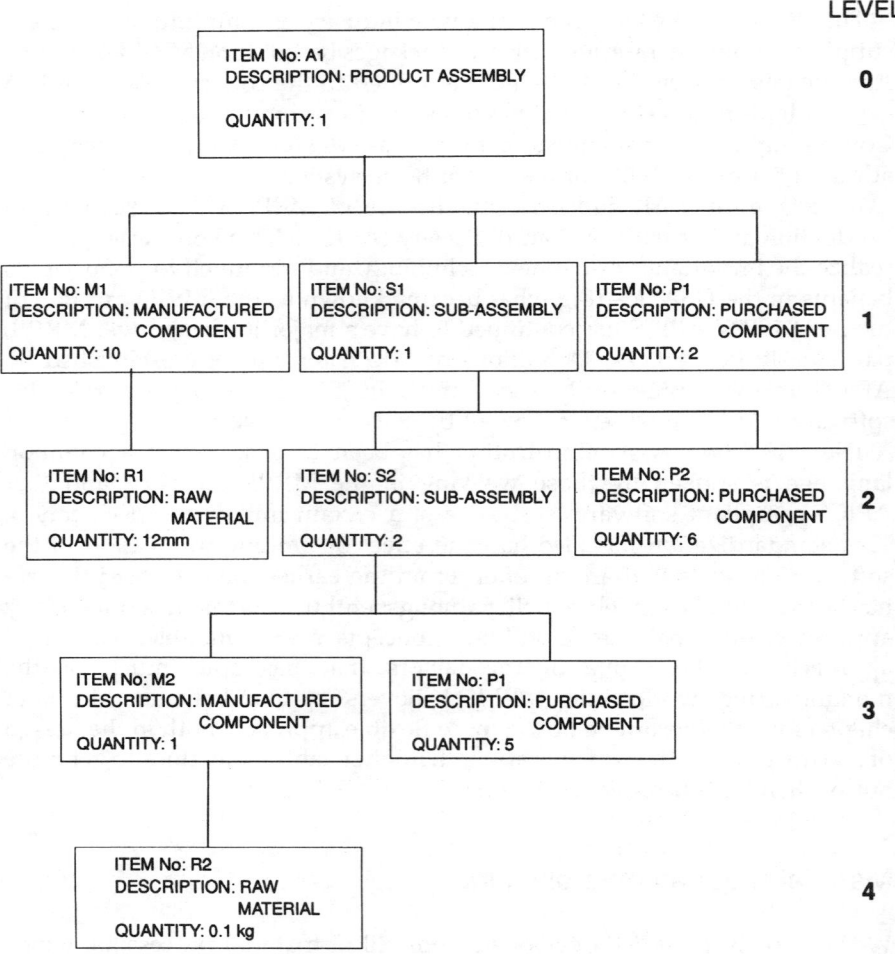

Figure 1.1   Typical bill of material structure

with MRP, but the concepts are equally applicable to the food, pharmaceutical, chemical or other industries. The terminology might vary (recipes, formulae, ingredients etc) but the approach is just the same. In general this book follows the convention of using the vocabulary of engineering assembly, but the special considerations that arise in applying MRPII in non-engineering industries are discussed in later chapters.

Netting

Netting is the process which takes account of existing inventory when calculating the sub-assemblies, components and materials required to manufacture a given quantity of a product. The first step is to deduct any stock of the product that has not already been allocated to a sales order (i.e. the free stock) from the number of products required. Then any products presently planned for assembly are also deducted. The remaining balance of products required is called the net requirement.

This net requirement is now 'exploded' into the items needed in the final assembly of the product (level 1 items), creating a gross requirement for each of them. Free stock and planned production are again deducted, leaving a net requirement for each assembly item. This net requirement is in turn exploded to the next level of the bill of material.

This process is repeated down through the bill of material, level by level, with each new level representing the preceding stage of manufacture. The process ends either at the lowest level, which in most cases is a purchased item, or when a point is reached where existing inventory will satisfy the requirement that has been passed down from the level above.

In practice, the process is slightly more complex than this because the system may need to adjust net requirements to satisfy lot sizing rules or safety stock policies applying to the item in question. If so, it is the adjusted figure that is exploded down to the next level, rather than the net requirement. The use of lot sizing rules and safety stocks is explained more fully in Chapter 2.

Batching

Often the same item appears in the bills of material of more than one product, and perhaps many. Such an item may be needed in the manufacture of several different products at the same time. It would be extremely inconvenient if MRP reported many separate net requirements for this item, one for each of the products from which requirements were being generated. Instead MRP accumulates all the requirements that are passed down from higher levels of the bill of material, regardless of the source of those requirements.

Stock and planned production are deducted from this accumulated gross requirement to calculate the net requirement for the item. If MRP attempted to keep the various requirements separately identified it would be faced with the problem of deciding which one to deduct existing stocks and planned production from first. Batching is therefore convenient both for the system and for the planner who has to deal with all the net requirements generated by MRP.

Sometimes it is important to know where a requirement has come from. For example, if material that has been ordered in response to an MRP-generated requirement is delayed, the planner will want to know which customer orders will be affected. MRP has a facility called pegging, which traces requirements back up through the bill of material to the products from which the demand originated. Pegging makes no judgements about how any existing stocks of the material should be distributed amongst the various products that need it. Instead it merely reports all of the products generating demand for that material, leaving the planner to decide the priorities. Which is, of course, exactly how it should be.

There are some particular situations in which retrospectively pegging requirements, to find out where they came from, is not enough. These situations dictate that requirements are not to be accumulated at all, and that each requirement must be manufactured as a separate batch. This may be necessary to satisfy traceability regulations, or it may be needed to enable batches to be costed to individual contracts. Whatever the reason, it is a situation with which MRP cannot readily cope.

Fortunately such situations are rare. Usually it is possible to satisfy traceability or contract costing requirements without physically separating batches. Nevertheless, companies using traceability or contract costing should assess their needs carefully before embarking upon MRP.

In carrying out batching, MRP recognizes that an item which is common to several products is unlikely to appear at the same level in the bill of material of each. In one product the item may be two levels from the top, and in another it could be three levels down from the product. The same item may also be ordered by customers as a service part, making it in effect a product in its own right, and therefore a top level (level 0) item. An item may even appear at different levels in the bill of material of a single product. In Figure 1.1, for example, purchased component P1 appears at both level 1 and level 3.

MRP follows a systematic procedure of working its way down through the bill of material, processing all the top level, or end items first, then all the level 1 items, then level 2, and so on. In so doing, it meets our common item several times and, until the very last time that item occurs, MRP cannot calculate its total requirement. MRP needs to know when it has found every instance of the item so that it can deduct stock and planned orders from the accumulated gross requirement, and explode the resulting net requirement down to its own components.

The technique MRP uses to find out when it has reached the final instance of the item is called low level coding. When a company first creates its product bill of material records, the data is examined to find the lowest level at which each item occurs on any product. This level number, the low level code, is held as part of the item record for that part number. It is maintained by the system whenever the bill of material is amended. MRP knows it is time to calculate the net requirement of any item once the level corresponding to its low level code has been reached.

Time-phasing

Clearly it is important to know not just which items will be needed, and in what quantities, but also when they will be needed. Time-phasing enables due dates to be attributed to requirements that are generated by MRP, and indeed MRP is sometimes referred to as 'time-phased material requirements planning'.

For each item in turn, MRP carries out the process of exploding demand, netting, and batching on a period-by-period basis, starting at the first time period (or time bucket) in the plan. The projected closing stock at the end of one time bucket becomes the opening stock for the next bucket. MRP makes the assumption that any existing manufacturing or purchasing orders which are due for completion during the time bucket being processed will be completed on time. The scheduled order receipts are therefore added to the projected stock.

Time buckets used in MRP can vary in length, even within one MRP run. For example, a daily bucket may be used for the first four weeks, followed by a weekly bucket for the next 12 weeks, and finishing with a monthly bucket for the remainder of the plan horizon. The issues involved in setting time buckets are discussed in Chapter 2.

This process of rolling forward through time, for each item in turn, establishes the due dates for any new manufacturing or purchasing orders that are required. To calculate the start dates for these orders, MRP uses a pre-determined lead time for each item. This lead time, which is based upon an estimate of the normal length of time to make or purchase a batch of the item in question, is held as part of the item record.

When MRP plans a new order for a finished product, it deducts the standard lead time to assemble that product from the order due date. This calculation produces a start date for the order. Since this start date is the date at which the assembly components will be needed, it becomes the due date for the requirements passed down to level 1. This process is called lead time off-setting. It continues as MRP proceeds down through the bill of material, with the start date for each stage of manufacture becoming the due date for the items made at the preceding stage. Because lead time off-setting works backwards in time, from a predetermined due date, it is described as backward scheduling.

It is important to note the significance that MRP attaches to order due dates. Component orders are planned to be completed immediately before they are needed for the next stage of manufacture. The assumption is made that orders will always be completed on time. If a company implementing MRP fails to achieve a high level of due date adherence, it can expect to run into serious difficulty.

MRP needs to take account of non-working days in carrying out lead time off-setting. It uses a shop calendar to do this. The shop calendar assigns day numbers to every working day, for as far into the future as necessary. Weekends and holidays do not have day numbers, so when MRP deducts lead times, expressed in days, from requirement due dates, it only considers working days. Day numbers are only used internally and are converted back into true calendar dates for reporting purposes.

The individual lead times of the components of a product accumulate through lead time off-setting to form aggregate lead times for each pathway down through the bill of material. The longest pathway represents the cumulative lead time for the product. This is the elapsed time from the point of raising the first purchase order to the completion date of the product. The cumulative lead time, like the item lead times that contribute to it, is a fixed period of time.

If a customer places an order for a product with a required delivery date that is within this cumulative lead time, MRP may calculate start dates for component items that are earlier than the current date. Telling the planner that a new material requirement should have been ordered already is not very helpful, but there is nothing in MRP's logic to prevent this from happening.

There are only two ways in which MRP can avoid generating new actions in past time periods. The first is to ensure that all new customer orders are dated far enough into the future to cover the accumulated lead time of the product in question. The second way is to create speculative free stock (or planned orders) of lower level components. In this way, when MRP processes the customer's requirement for the first time it finds sufficient inventory already available to prevent any new requirements arising for the lower level items. The first solution presupposes that the customer is willing to wait for the goods for the total cumulative lead time. The second solution assumes that some form of forecasting is available to enable stocks to be planned before the customer order is received.

Few companies find either of these solutions easy to achieve, and failure to cope properly with this aspect of MRP is one of the main reasons for difficulties in implementation. We shall be returning to this aspect of MRP in later chapters, to examine the techniques that are available to help.

Dynamic priority setting

Time-phasing provides the final piece in the MRP jigsaw. Bill of material explosion determines the lower level items needed to manufacture a product. Netting takes account of existing inventory. Batching allows all the requirements for an item that are needed at the same time to be accumulated into a single batch. Finally lead time offsetting establishes start dates and due dates for the resulting manufacturing and purchasing orders.

MRP plans orders to cover every requirement that it has calculated. The requirement is a demand, the planned order is a supply. MRP's task is to ensure that for every demand it identifies, a matching supply is available. In raising planned orders, MRP applies the lot sizing rules mentioned earlier, so planned orders are not necessarily mirror images of the requirements that caused them. Frequently one planned order will cover several requirements. Over the entire horizon covered by MRP, though, supply and demand will be kept in balance.

At this point it makes little difference whether the planned order is for a purchased item or a manufactured one. The order simply represents a quantity of an item that is required by a specified due date and must therefore be released (to the supplier or to production) by its start date.

Creating new planned orders is only part of MRP's role. The situation changes from one MRP run to the next, as customers place new orders or amend existing ones, events in production fail to follow the plan exactly, materials are scrapped, stocktaking reveals stock errors, and so on. Each new MRP run takes the situation as it now is, and tries to make the best of it. This means that in addition to raising new planned orders, MRP seeks to amend existing orders in response to the changed circumstances.

If MRP comes across a situation where there is insufficient supply planned to meet the current demand for an item at a point in time, it always brings forward (expedites) an existing order that is due at a later date before it raises new planned orders. If supply exceeds the demand, then MRP attempts to defer orders that are now not needed until later, or to cancel those no longer needed at all. In each case, exception reports are printed to inform the planner of the need to take action.

The role of MRP is to report the condition but leave the planner to decide whether or not to respond. In order to accept the recommendation, the planner must confirm the action back through a VDU, and possibly amend shop paperwork that has been issued to production.

This ability to review the entire plan in response to changed circumstances is called dynamic priority setting. It is one of the great strengths of MRP. It is a facility that requires very careful management, though, as it is all too easy to permit too much change from one MRP run to the next. MRP will be able to respond without difficulty, but the extent of rescheduling that results can easily become unmanageable. Either the planner becomes snowed under with too many exceptions to action, or production is subjected to severe and repeated disruption. In either case, MRP tends to get a very bad name.

Is that all there is to MRP?

It can be quite difficult now to understand why MRP made such an impact when it first appeared upon the scene. The logic involved in the process seems obvious. The bill of material is exploded to find out what items are needed to manufacture the products that are to be built. New orders are planned or existing ones rescheduled accordingly. Surely this is what planners have always done?

In fact planners rarely operate in this way without computer-based MRP systems to help them. Some companies making a small range of simple products have always been able to carry out a manual MRP process. For the majority of companies, however, the sheer volume of data to be handled and the number of calculations to be performed have ruled out this approach. In the absence of MRP, other techniques have been used. These have generally been based upon some kind of re-order point system.

Re-order point control analyzes past usage of an item to estimate the level of stock that is needed. A re-order point is calculated that will cover the period of time required to complete a replenishment order. It includes an additional element of safety stock, to allow for variations in demand during the replenishment lead time. Using statistical methods, the planner determines a re-order point that will provide the required service level (i.e. the probability of stock being available when required). Clearly, the higher the required service level, the greater the inventory needed. Service levels in excess of 95% tend to become very costly in terms of inventory, while 100% service is statistically impossible.

Re-order point systems can be extremely effective when used to control items subject to off-the-shelf demand, such as retail goods or routine service items. They are less suitable for use in planning a manufacturing operation, for the following reasons:

- Stock control theory assumes that demand (i.e. withdrawals from stock) will be at a reasonably steady and continuous rate. In a manufacturing environment stock withdrawals tend to be occasional and in bulk, as material is consumed in the irregular manufacture of production batches.
- Re-order points are calculated from past usage of the item concerned, without reference to the product(s) within which it is used. Future demand may not follow the historical trends, for a variety of reasons, including new product introductions, design changes, sales promotions and so on.
- Even in a re-order point system that is working well, a product assembled from 20 different items, each subject to a 95% service level, would have only a 36% chance of all the items being in stock when needed to assemble a batch of products (0.95^{20}). Assembly shortages under such a system are therefore to be expected, and are not an indication of failure (although they are usually treated as such, to the exasperation of the planner).
- Re-order point systems seek to hold stock of all items at all times, whereas MRP plans for materials to be available only when they are needed.

A distinction is often made between independent and dependent demand. Independent demand is typified by the retail environment, where the daily sales volume of an item is not directly determined by any single factor. Ice cream sales, for example, may be greatly influenced by the weather, but other factors such as price, competitor actions and advertising all impact upon a large numbers of potential consumers. There is no way of calculating exactly the quantity of ice cream that will be sold on any particular day.

Dependent demand is directly calculable from the known requirements for the products from which it arises. Once an ice cream factory has planned to manufacture a certain quantity of ice cream, in response to its expectations of likely demand, the requirement for the ingredients can be calculated exactly. Independent demand lends itself to the use of re-order point systems of stock control, dependent demand can be better managed by MRP.

Re-order point systems are essentially order-launching systems. They do not have MRP's dynamic priority setting capability. Once an order has been released to production there is no mechanism to review due dates, even though these will inevitably change as actual demand varies from historical patterns. Other procedures for changing priorities need to be found. Since assembly shortages are the norm, even for efficient re-order point systems, manual shortages lists usually form the basis for priority changing.

This leads to the widespread practice of expediting, in which roving expeditors each attempt to pull through the jobs needed to meet their part of the assembly schedule. All the expeditors are in competition with each other to jump their jobs to the front of the queue at each resource. The outcome usually depends more upon the strength of personality of the expeditor than on the true commercial priority. Production managers are left confused about which job they should do next, and baffled when a job not due for another two weeks suddenly takes precedence over one that is already three weeks late.

Factories that have experienced this type of control can find it very difficult to adapt to the ways of MRP, where working to due date is mandatory. Once order due dates have become discredited, the shopfloor finds it difficult to accept a new regime which stresses above all else the importance of due date adherence. In the absence of meaningful due dates, quite different criteria are used to prioritize the work. The factors taken into account may include, for example, the relative skill level of the available operator, the potential to earn a good bonus, the achievement of departmental volume output targets, the minimizing of machine change-over time, and the ease with which the material can be accessed. Less favoured jobs are only done when an expeditor becomes insistent.

Factors such as these are extremely important to those working on the shopfloor. Senior managers are often only dimly aware of these influences, or of their own role in creating them. Yet unless the realities of shopfloor life are understood, and addressed, the introduction of better planning systems will change little. Reconciling MRP's insistence on working to due dates with the existing shopfloor culture can be a major challenge for those involved in MRPII implementations. The issues arising during implementation are more fully discussed in Chapter 4.

Compared with re-order point methods, MRP represents a massive breakthrough. The simple logic of the MRP technique replaces procedures that are both more complex and less effective. This does not mean that MRP is the only satisfactory way of managing dependent demand items. For example, the use of kanbans to provide control of manufacturing inventory without the use of MRP logic is explained in Chapter 6. Nevertheless, when first introduced MRP provided planners with an important new tool, the attractions of which are still obvious.

Closed loop MRP

Whatever the merits of MRP as a means of planning material requirements, it contains no facilities for planning capacity. In a manufacturing business, a materials plan that does not take account of capacity is of limited value. There is little point in knowing what work needs to be done to complete an order on time if there is insufficient labour or machine capacity to do it. This shortcoming of MRP was soon addressed, again through the application of computer power.

Capacity requirements planning

MRP controls the process through which manufacturing orders are created and, when necessary, amended. It therefore has full visibility of all outstanding work. If the work content of each job is known, it is a simple task to calculate the overall workload. Routing records which specify, for each item, the manufacturing operations to be carried out, the resources to be used and the time required for each operation, provide the information needed to calculate workload.

Capacity requirements planning (CRP) is the process that performs this calculation. CRP analyzes each outstanding manufacturing order in turn. The quantity ordered is multiplied by the time per operation, and the resulting workload is credited to the specified resource (work centre) in the planned production period. When all orders have been processed, the total time for each work centre is summated by time bucket. The resulting workload is compared with the available capacity, typically in the form of histograms for each work centre.

As we shall see in Chapter 5, CRP is not a precise tool. The aim of CRP is not, therefore, to achieve an exact match of load to capacity in each period. Indeed it would be most unexpected if load and capacity were found to be closely matched, since the load arises as a consequence of a material plan that has been generated by MRP. The logic of MRP does not attempt to smooth workload on individual resources, so the loading on any one work centre can vary significantly from period to period.

Some interpretation of CRP output is needed, therefore, to establish whether or not the projected load is likely to be achievable once it has been smoothed. If the load is not achievable it will not be possible to meet the order due dates set by MRP. This situation is clearly not acceptable, since it is fundamental to the MRP concept that due dates are adhered to. Therefore if CRP shows that the workload is not achievable, corrective action must be taken. One option is to increase capacity to meet the peak loads, perhaps by transferring labour from under-loaded work centres, working overtime, or sub-contracting. The alternative option is to reduce the workload.

The only way to reduce workloads is to make changes to the data used in the MRP run that preceded CRP. Usually this means delaying the due dates of some of the products the company was planning to manufacture, or reducing the quantities to be made. In either case, MRP would generate smaller requirements for lower level items in the periods that had been overloaded, resulting in reduced capacity requirements. An alternative approach would be to amend safety stocks or change lot sizing rules, in order to achieve a similar outcome.

Using CRP in this way led to the concept of closed loop MRP. No longer would MRP operate as a standalone materials planning system. The output from MRP would now provide the input to CRP, which would test whether or not the workload was realistic. Should the planner decide that the resulting capacity plan was unacceptable, MRP data would be amended and the whole process repeated, thus closing the loop.

Master production scheduling

The introduction of closed loop MRP focused attention on the way in which product deliveries were scheduled. Since planned due dates or quantities of end items had to be adjusted in order to achieve a workable plan, it would clearly save time if the initial plan were as realistic as possible. This would minimize the need to repeat the MRP/CRP cycle to fine-tune capacity loadings.

Demand for end items can arise in various forms including customer orders, warehouse stock replenishment orders, inter-company transfers and sales forecasts. In addition there may be service demands for lower level items, which could be in the form of customer requirements or stock replenishment orders. All these types of demand can exist within the same organization. So long as each demand specifies the item ordered, the number needed and the delivery date required, all the information needed by MRP is available. Merely inputting all these demands into an MRP run and hoping for the best is, however, unlikely to result in an acceptable capacity plan. There is a need to manage demand, to improve the likelihood of achieving a reasonably balanced utilization of resources.

In order to manage demand, an additional step is required prior to the MRP run. This step is called master production scheduling. The objective of master production scheduling is to develop a top level plan which balances the needs of the customer with efficient operation of the production resources. The resulting master production schedule (MPS) must be acceptable to both sales and production management, an elusive target if ever there was one.

Developing a satisfactory MPS requires the use of tools with which to measure and compare different schedules. In theory it would be possible to run MRP and CRP on a selection of alternatives and select the best, but this approach is not usually very satisfactory, for reasons that are explained later under *Closing the loop*. Instead a process called rough cut capacity planning is used as an alternative to multiple MRP/CRP cycles.

Rough cut capacity planning (RCCP) calculates loadings in a similar way to CRP. There are two important differences, however. Firstly, RCCP focuses on the key resources needed to manufacture each type of product, ignoring those work centres where capacity is unlikely to be a constraint. Secondly, since RCCP precedes MRP, loadings are calculated directly from the quantity of end items required, without any adjustment being made for existing inventory, or for the lot sizing rules that MRP will apply to lower level items.

In some companies RCCP can be carried out very simply. For example, in a foundry with a limited range of products it might be enough simply to keep the number of tonnes of product planned each week to a satisfactory level. In other situations a more sophisticated approach is required. Sometimes a bill of resources is created for each product, containing summaries of the work content of that product on the key resources.

A bill of resources is different from the routing record used in CRP. The bill of resources contains details of the key operations carried out on all the components of the product, as well as in the final assembly of the product itself. In contrast the routing record for an item only contains details of the operations involved in the manufacture of that item, and is not concerned with items at a lower level in the bill of material (which have their own routing records). Furthermore, whereas the routing record includes details of every operation used in the manufacture of an item, the bill of resources usually contains details only of operations carried out in critical work centres. Clearly it is desirable for the two sets of information to be consistent, so the bill of resources should be derived automatically from information contained in the bill of material and routing records.

Using RCCP the planner can model a range of different master production schedules relatively quickly. The calculated workloads may not be as accurate as those generated by CRP, but they should be good enough to test whether the plan is workable. More accurate and detailed capacity plans can be produced later, after running MRP.

Business planning

From the point of view of top management, the MPS determines what the company will produce, the use that will be made of the company's assets and human resources, and the cash flows resulting from planned material purchases and invoiced despatches. These are not decisions that should be made by the planner alone. Top management must actively manage the process of master production scheduling. This objective is achieved in two ways. The first is through a formal signing-off of each new MPS, to indicate top management's acceptance of the plan. This procedure is essential to give the plan credibility throughout the organization. It also places necessary restrictions on top managers' own freedom of action to insist upon subsequent amendments.

The second way that top management controls the MPS is by setting ground rules which constrain the decisions that the planner can make. The task of producing a satisfactory MPS is never easy, since the requirements of the customer, as represented by the sales department, and those of efficient manufacture, which are the concern of production management, rarely coincide. There is a much greater chance of success if the process of master production scheduling is governed by a set of business policies that can direct the actions of the planner, and to which the company is committed.

These policies are established through a business planning process that defines the objectives of the organization and determines the level of resources to be available for production. Integration of business planning with master production scheduling gives the planner guidance and authority in the task of creating the MPS, and enables top management to exert both long term control and short term influence on company operations.

Business planning is generally carried out once a year, as a formal process, although the resulting plans should be kept under constant review. Business planning is a two-stage process. The first stage is the development of a strategic business plan. The strategic business plan decides issues such as:

- which products will be sold in which markets
- target sales volumes for each major product family
- capital available for investment in inventory and fixed assets
- customer service requirements, in terms of lead times and delivery performance
- new product introduction dates
- product cost targets that will enable planned margins to be achieved, taking account of likely price movements
- policy for handling products with seasonal demand (e.g. smooth production and build for stock in off-season periods, or hire and fire).

In the second stage of business planning, the strategic business plan is developed into a manufacturing and logistics plan, which covers issues including:

- changes in the production system (manufacturing technology, material flows and organization) necessary to achieve cost and lead time targets
- investment plans for new manufacturing facilities and equipment
- human resources plans, including recruitment, training and development
- time-phased production output targets, by product or product family, needed to satisfy sales projections
- finished goods stockholding policy
- distribution strategy
- purchasing strategy.

Using information generated by the strategic business plan and by the manufacturing and logistics plan, the planner can take a number of actions to update core planning data. Work centre capacity profiles can be set up covering the entire plan period, based upon capital investment and human resource plans. Finished goods stocking levels can be set. Lot sizing and safety stock policies for lower level items can be reviewed to ensure they are consistent with the manufacturing technology and material flows, and with financial targets for inventory. Manufacturing lead times can be adjusted in line with the characteristics of the production system. Purchasing lead times and schedule arrangements can be amended to reflect changes in purchasing policies.

Business planning also provides the planner with guidance in the routine task of master scheduling. Sales forecasts can be compared with plan projections, so that deviations may be investigated. Conflicting customer requirements can be prioritized in accordance with marketing strategy. New products can be phased in smoothly, and superseded products phased out with only enough residual inventory for on-going service requirements. Sales department demands for ever higher finished goods stock levels, and production management demands for ever larger batch quantities can be deflected by reference to the appropriate management policies.

As stated earlier, it is not enough for top management to set the business plan once a year and assume it will provide a sound basis for guiding operations for the following twelve months. Circumstances change, and the plan must be amended accordingly. Some companies hold a formal monthly plan review, usually called Sales and Operations Planning, to keep the business plan current. Other companies prefer to review the plan on an as-required basis. Whichever approach is used, top managers must ensure that the constraints and direction they apply to master production scheduling are always meaningful and current.

Closing the loop

Business planning is the final element of closed loop MRP. Figure 1.2 shows how the various aspects of closed loop MRP come together to form a planning system that extends from top management strategy making through to the planning and rescheduling of individual production and purchase orders.

The arrows on the right hand side of the diagram represent feedback from the execution of the plan. Feedback is essential to enable each stage in the planning process to take account of the existing situation. Strategic business planning must recognize the limitations imposed by existing products, production facilities and capabilities. Manufacturing and logistics plans need to take account of the current master production schedule, which may extend many months into the future. Deviations from the plan on the shopfloor affect planned material availability and capacity loadings, while changes in short term resource levels (e.g. through machine breakdowns) affect actual plant capacity. These changes must be taken into account in future master production schedules. An effective and timely feedback system is required to ensure that at each stage the loop is closed and the planning function is integrated.

Ironically the one aspect of Figure 1.2 where the closed loop process is of limited usefulness is the MRP/CRP cycle from which the closed loop MRP concept originated. It is not really practical to keep repeating the cycle until the results are satisfactory, for three reasons. Firstly the whole process is time-consuming, so important ordering and rescheduling actions are delayed. Secondly there is no guarantee that a new attempt will be better than the last, since there is no mechanism for convergence. If the problem is that a single work centre is over-loaded in a particular time period, then pegging could be used to track the demand back to the customer order causing it. The usual situation, however, is a complex mixture of over- and

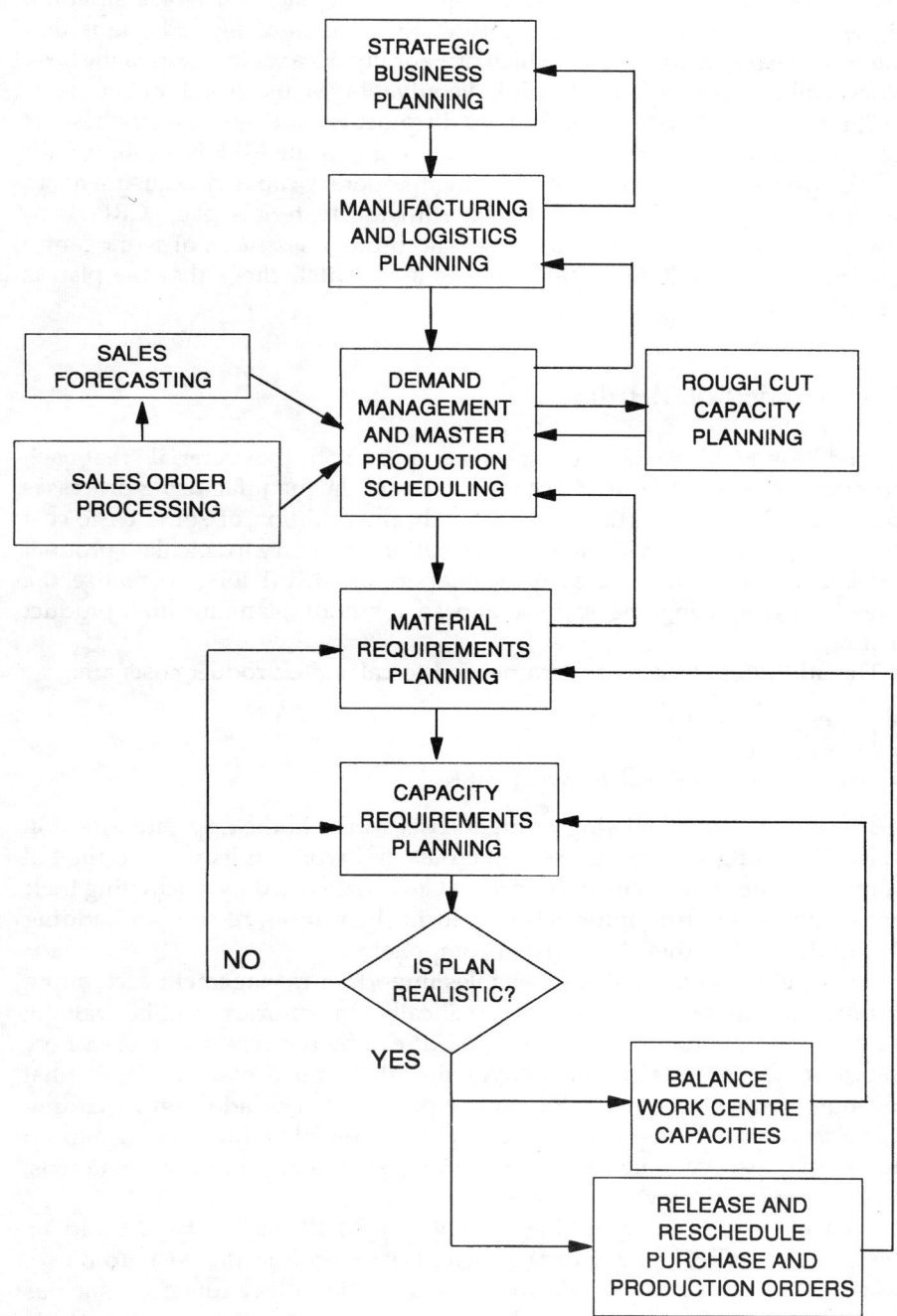

Figure 1.2   Closed loop MRP

under-loads on different work centres in different periods. Attempting to resolve any one of them through pegging might lead to a worse situation elsewhere. The third reason the MRP/CRP cycle is of limited use is that there is no easy way to decide which of a variety of capacity plans is the best. None will be ideal, and each will have advantages and disadvantages.

The MRP/CRP cycle is rarely used in practice, and greater emphasis is now placed on RCCP as the tool for ensuring that the MPS is feasible. CRP is used primarily as a means of planning temporary capacity adjustments in order to bring capacity into balance with the materials plan. CRP does, however, give a far more detailed and accurate assessment of work centre loadings than RCCP, so it still provides a last-ditch check that the plan is feasible.

The essence of MRPII

Closed loop MRP needs a full specification of both the materials that each product is made from (the bill of material) and the manufacturing processes involved in making it (the routing). Only the addition of some basic cost data is required to provide all the information necessary to calculate product costs. It did not take the early developers of MRPII long to realize the advantages of using the same database for both planning and product costing.

The additional basic cost data needed to calculate product costs are:

● prices of purchased items
● labour cost rates
● work centre overhead recovery rates.

The routine for calculating product costs works in the opposite direction to MRP, starting with purchased materials and working its way up the bill of material. Items at each bill of material level are costed by calculating their production costs from information held in the routing record, and adding this to the cost of their lower level components.

The availability of item costs enables important management accounting information to be generated automatically. Inventories can be valued, purchase requirements arising from MRP can be converted into cash flow forecasts, actual costs can be compared with planned costs, and potential revenue arising from the MPS can be predicted. The addition of costing transforms closed loop MRP from a production planning system into an integrated operations management system capable of controlling materials, capacity and cash flow.

Such a system, incorporating closed loop MRP and costing, could be described as MRPII, and probably would have been in the past. To do so, however, would be to exclude from the definition other functions such as invoicing, vendor selection, and management and financial accounting. These omissions would be contrary to the general perception of MRPII, and also somewhat arbitrary in view of the obvious links between these functions and those contained in Figure 1.2. On the other hand it is perfectly possible to have a successful MRPII implementation that excludes some of these peripheral functions.

To define MRPII it is not really necessary to specify which business functions are included and which are not. The vital ingredient of MRPII is closed loop material and capacity planning. MRPII is dependent upon computer software, but the software alone does not produce MRPII. Only the determination of top managers to run their business in accordance with the logic of closed loop MRP will make MRPII a reality.

If a definition is required, it is this. MRPII is a structured approach to manufacturing management in which a suite of integrated computer software covering the main operational business functions is used to assist in the closed loop planning of materials, manufacturing capacity and cash flow, in accordance with company policy, to meet customer delivery requirements.

To make the distinction between the concept of MRPII and the computer systems that support it, the expression MRPII system is avoided in this book. Instead the term integrated business system (IBS) is used to describe the software, while MRPII signifies the overall management philosophy.

It is sometimes suggested that MRPII is possible without MRP. Certainly many companies have implemented an IBS without using the modules involved in MRP. Using an IBS in this way is perfectly valid, if for some reason MRP is unsuited to the business in question. But the result is not MRPII. Above all, MRPII is concerned with planning, and without MRP an IBS has no mechanism for projecting business plans into the future. An IBS is an operational tool, the modules of which can be applied selectively; MRPII is a total approach to managing a business.

Class A MRPII

Companies implementing MRPII need to know how well they are doing. Unfortunately it is not always easy to tell. The definition of MRPII does not give precise guidelines on which software modules should be implemented, which options in those modules should be applied, or what new management initiatives may be required. So a company that feels it is doing well has no absolute scale against which to confirm its progress; a company whose MRPII implementation is losing momentum may not know where to focus its resources in order to make the break-through.

The Oliver Wight Organization, which specializes in MRPII education and consultancy, developed the ABCD checklist in order to provide a universal measure of success in MRPII implementation. The original ABCD checklist was a questionnaire covering some of what the Oliver Wight Organization considered to be the key aspects of MRPII. Areas covered by the checklist included the functionality of the software being used, the accuracy of data held within the system, the way in which management was using the system, the extent of the training programme undertaken, and a selection of operational performance measures. A grade was awarded to the company depending upon the answers given. The ultimate accolade was to achieve Class A status, Oliver Wight's sign of excellence in MRPII implementation.

The ABCD checklist has become in effect an unofficial MRPII certification process. The value of achieving the certificate should not be overstated, however. Just as BS5750/ISO9000 certification ensures the existence of a comprehensive quality system, but does not guarantee the quality of the goods being produced, so Class A MRPII is more concerned with how an organization measures up against a set of subjective questions than whether the business is meeting its potential.

Nevertheless, for many companies a stated intention to achieve Class A status provides a target for their implementation efforts and a clear demonstration of their commitment to MRPII. The motivational effects of this challenge can flow through the organization, providing a real boost to the implementation process. If only for this reason, the ABCD checklist is an important innovation.

The ABCD checklist has been amended over the years, and in its most recent form has moved beyond the definition of MRPII given here. The checklist now seeks to provide a complete measure of manufacturing excellence. It does this by including targets on the use of just-in-time and total quality techniques, in addition to the expected MRPII-related measures.

If Class A status were the only measure of MRPII excellence, overall success rates would be desperately low. Only a few hundred companies worldwide have been certified as Class A by the Oliver Wight organization, out of some tens of thousands which use MRP-based software. This does not, of course, represent the reality of the situation. No doubt there are companies that have reached Class A performance but have not applied for certification. There are many others that have been more interested in achieving success by their own standards than in meeting criteria set by an external body. Even so, there are far too many companies that have fallen short of what could be achieved, and of what they set out to do.

These companies can improve their performance, but doing so is hard work. True success only comes from really understanding MRPII, so that it becomes an integral part of the way in which the business is run. No-one should delude themselves that the key to success is simply working to get the right answers to a certification checklist, no matter how well the questions have been thought out. Similarly, there is no off-the-shelf implementation methodology that will do the work for them. Managers who truly wish to use MRPII to steer their business must learn for themselves which levers to pull and which buttons to press. The half-hearted are doomed to failure.

2

Tools, techniques and choices

Choices for managers

Over the years MRPII has accumulated a set of tools and techniques that help make things run a little more smoothly in companies which know how to use them. Often these tools and techniques offer choices that allow the planning and control systems to be configured in a way that matches as closely as possible the characteristics of the business.

This chapter describes some of these tools and techniques, and examines the choices that they offer to managers implementing MRPII. Readers who are interested only in gaining a broad understanding of MRPII may choose to miss out this chapter. Those who do, however, should remember that there are important configuration choices to be made, and that the wrong decisions could significantly reduce the chances of a successful implementation.

Configuring the system does not mean modifying software, nor does it mean deviating from MRPII concepts. No two businesses are identical in the way they operate, and there is sufficient flexibility within the MRPII concept to allow companies to select the techniques that suit their circumstances. To configure a system properly it is necessary to understand in depth the options that are available within the system. Only then is it possible to decide how those options might best be applied to the organization in question.

Some configuration decisions are made when the IBS is first installed. The user is asked to select options and set parameters across a whole range of system features. Since these configuration routines need to be run at a very early point in the MRPII implementation process, the user may not fully understand the implications of the choices being made. Once the system has been configured, the decision process tends not to be revisited. This is partly because the existence of the dormant options tends to be forgotten and partly because some decisions are difficult to reverse once the system is live.

Other configuration decisions are made by system users setting up the initial data, and responding to alternatives offered by the system during the course of day to day operations. These decisions can have a major impact on the success of the system, and should only be taken within the context of clear guidelines that set out how the system is to operate.

It is essential that senior managers involve themselves fully in the configuration process, and this means making the effort to understand the issues involved. Responsibility for configuring the system cannot be delegated to junior members of staff, even if they are more familiar with the details of the tools and techniques available. What they lack is the overview of the business objectives that the system is intended to address.

The tools and techniques described in this chapter are not just of concern to the technician, planner or other specialist system user. They are of critical importance to top managers who do not want to treat their planning and control system as some kind of black box that is beyond their control or understanding. A willingness to become involved in system configuration is the top manager's first demonstration of commitment to managing the business through MRPII.

Master production scheduling

Master production scheduling is the most critical element of the entire closed loop MRP process. MRP rigorously plans all the dependent demands that arise from the MPS that it is given. If for any reason the MPS is not valid, the whole material plan is useless. There are several techniques that can be used in constructing an MPS, and it is essential that the most suitable ones are chosen for the particular business environment of the company concerned.

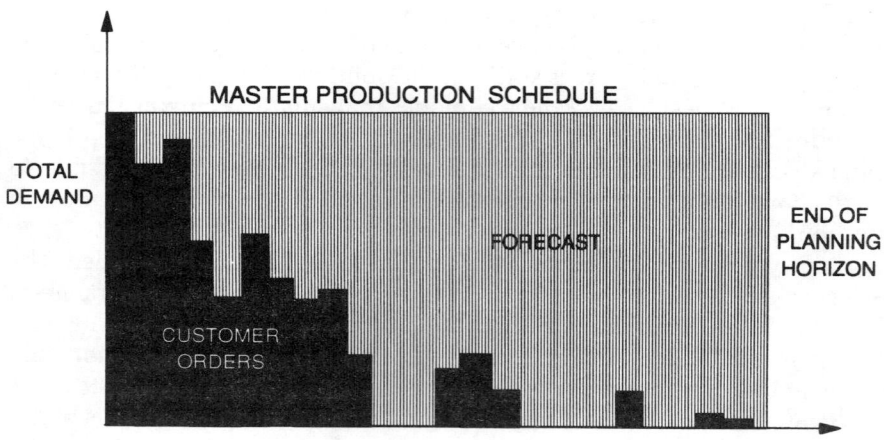

Figure 2.1   Consumption of the forecast for a product by customer orders

The MPS is a statement of the products that the company plans to manufacture over the planning horizon. This planning horizon needs to extend at least as far into the future as the cumulative lead time of the products contained in the plan. If the company wishes to give its suppliers some visibility beyond the current purchase order, or if a longer view of capacity requirements is needed, an even greater horizon must be used. Planning horizons can be two years or more in some industries, and one year is quite common.

Few companies are lucky enough to have a firm order book stretching that far into the future, so it is usual for the MPS to be based at least in part on a forecast of future demand. As customer orders are received they replace (or consume) the forecast, and the plan becomes steadily firmer as the planned assembly date approaches. Figure 2.1 shows how this process of forecast being consumed by incoming customer orders works. The quantity of each product included in the MPS remains unchanged as the forecast element is gradually replaced by customer orders. That, at least, is the theory. In practice things are a little more complex, for a variety of reasons:

- **Product variants.** Companies often produce so many different variants of their products that the quantity sold of any one variant is very small, making forecasting impossible.
- **Schedule stability.** Forecasts may be revised many times as time rolls forward. MRP can always provide the rescheduling messages needed to re-establish the balance between supply and demand, but these re-scheduling actions could cause considerable disruption to production. Some method of ensuring reasonable stability in the MPS is needed.
- **Forecast and order reconciliation.** Even if the forecast is regularly revised, incoming customer orders will differ to some extent from the forecasted products included in the MPS. It is necessary to reconcile forecasts and orders that do not match up.
- **Assembly flexibility.** Where possible it is better to assemble the products the customer has actually ordered rather than the ones in the MPS, if these are not required. This can only be done if surplus assembly components are available to provide the necessary flexibility.

There are many techniques for dealing with these complexities. Some of the most important are described below.

Product variants

Some products contain so much variety within the basic design that the number of variants which could be produced can run into thousands, or even millions. The motor car is an example that is often quoted. Colour, engine capacity, manual or automatic transmission, and four- or five-door body are amongst the features that the customer can choose. In addition there are many options that the customer may specify, such as air conditioning, sunroof or fog lights. Features and options are different types of variation. With a feature the choice is between two or more alternatives (the car has to be painted some colour), whereas an option is something without which the product is still viable.

In cases such as the motor car it would be quite impossible to forecast all the variants that are theoretically possible, so a different approach is needed. One thing that can be forecasted is the demand for the product family as a whole, ignoring the problem of variants. After all, no-one would launch a product without having any idea of how many they were going to sell. It is usually possible to forecast other things as well. Let us continue with the example of the car. If there were a choice of, say, 1600cc or 1800cc engine, it should be possible to establish the proportion in which these are normally chosen. Perhaps 30% of customers choose 1600cc engines, whilst the remaining 70% prefer the 1800cc unit. We might also find that 60% of the cars are sold with five-door bodies, and the remainder with four doors.

Analysis of historical trends, together with market research, tells us we can expect that about 15% of our customers will want sunroofs. We do not know which engine they will choose, nor whether they will want four- or five-door bodies, but this does not matter. We have enough information to set up a bill of material that will allow us to plan all the materials that we need. This bill of material is shown in Figure 2.2.

The top level item is the product family, in this case the model range of the car that we wish to plan. We have a forecast for the total sales of this model,

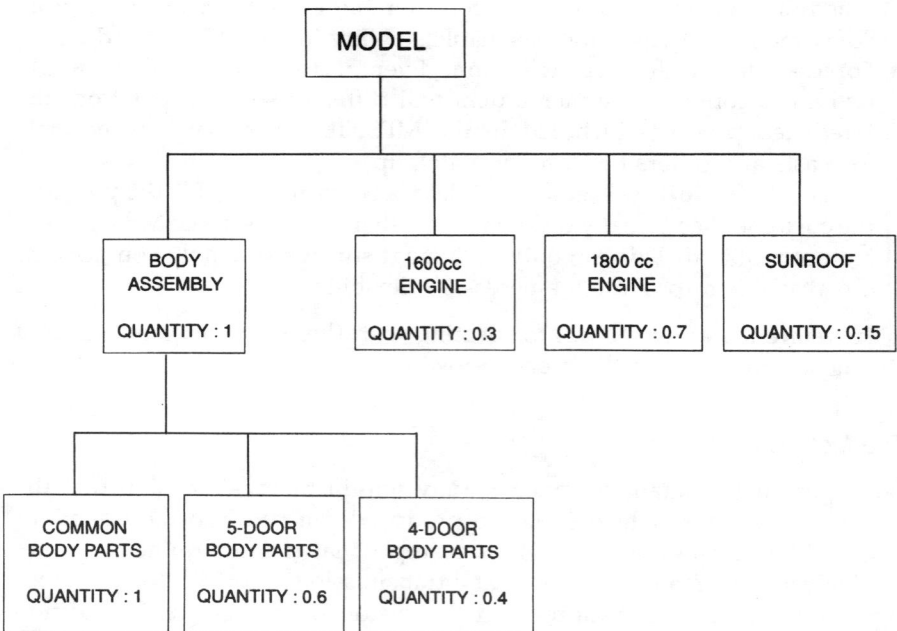

Figure 2.2   Example of a planning bill for a motor car

which can be exploded down to the next level. The first item in the next level is the body assembly, and we know that every car will need one of these, so the quantity per vehicle is one. There are many body components that are common to both the five-door and the four-door version, so every body we assemble will require a set of these components. These are contained in the common body parts module.

A module is, in effect, a bill of material within another bill of material. The top level of this particular module is an item number representing the kit of common body parts. The parts themselves are linked to the module item number at lower levels within the bill of material. For convenience, Figure 2.2 does not show the lower level items within the module. In many ways, a module is similar to a sub-assembly. The difference is that a module represents a logical product feature or option that is not necessarily capable of being assembled into a physical unit. A sub-assembly is an intermediate stage of manufacture that can exist as a separate item.

Figure 2.2 shows that the body common parts module is a component of the body assembly, with a quantity of one per body. The two other components of the body assembly are modules specific to the four-door and five-door bodies. Since 60% of cars are to be built with five doors, this module has a quantity of 0.6 per body assembly. The four-door body is used in the remaining 40% of the cars, so the quantity is 0.4. Using these relationships, a forecast entered against the model will explode down to generate the correct body components to meet the expected demand.

Moving to the next leg of the bill of material, we find modules representing the engine. These modules could be structured in the same way as the body assembly, with a single engine number made up from one module of common parts and two modules containing the parts specific to the two engine sizes. However, the engines are ordered from a separate plant which delivers assembled units, not modules. The type of structure used for the body assembly would not therefore be appropriate. Figure 2.2 shows that the 1600cc engine has a quantity of 0.3 per car, and the 1800cc engine 0.7 per car, in accordance with the forecast.

The engine and the body are features – every car needs one of each – so however many types of engine or body are on offer, the forecasted proportions in the bill of material amount in total to one engine and one body. In contrast the sunroof is an option, and the quantity per car can take any value up to and including one. In Figure 2.2, the quantity per car is 0.15, in line with the sales forecast.

For our admittedly simple car, with its narrow range of features and options, we now have a bill of material that will enable us to plan all the materials that are needed, using forecast information that is relatively easy to obtain and reasonably accurate.

There is, however, a drawback with the bill of material shown in Figure 2.2. It may be ideal for planning, but it is no use whatsoever for manufacturing the car. It is based upon modules, like the common body parts, that cannot be assembled. Furthermore, quantities such as 0.15 of a sunroof are quite meaningless to production. If we are to use this bill of material for planning, we shall need a separate bill for manufacturing purposes.

The bill of material shown in Figure 2.2 is called a planning bill; the bill of material used for manufacture is called an engineering bill. The particular form of planning bill discussed here, where the top level is a composite product containing elements of all possible variants, is called a super bill. There are other, less common, types of planning bill which could be more applicable in different circumstances. Choosing the right form of bill for planning is one of the most important configuration tasks that management must undertake.

Schedule stability

Forecasts need to be revised regularly, typically monthly, in order that they reflect the latest knowledge about future demand. In compiling the MPS it is naturally very important to take account of the latest forecast, but there are other factors to be considered as well. One such factor is capacity. The MPS must not be increased to a level where production capacity would be overloaded, just because the forecast has increased, even though the temptation to do so may be great.

A second factor to be considered is the extent to which change is feasible. Some stability is essential in a production schedule, if efficient production is to be maintained. MRP can calculate all the changes needed to deal with any new MPS, without difficulty. But if these reschedules are likely to involve major disruptions to production, it would be wiser to reduce the extent of change within the MPS. In the case of purchased items it may be impossible to gain the supplier's agreement to last minute schedule changes.

One way of achieving stability is to set time fences which dictate the permissible amount of change to the MPS. The first time fence may be, say, one week into the plan. The rule might be no changes at all to the MPS within that time fence. A second time fence may be set two weeks later. Here the rule could be that between time fences one and two the quantity of any product may be changed by up to 10%, but no new product could be added. Subsequent time fences would permit progressively larger changes, further into the future. Of course, any changes would still be subject to the overall feasibility of the MPS being confirmed through RCCP.

The use of time fences brings discipline to the management of demand, and ensures a degree of stability for production. Unfortunately there is no analytical method for deciding either the position of the time fences or the rules which should apply to them. Achieving the right balance between satisfying the customer and achieving efficient production will always be a matter of judgement. This is not a reason not to use time fences. Rather it is an argument for senior managers to give careful attention to this issue, possibly using trial and error to ensure that the right balance is obtained for their company.

Time fences for products that use common lower level materials and components can be much less restrictive than those for products built from unique components. Delaying the introduction of variety until the last minute adds flexibility and improves customer service, a fact that product designers and development engineers should always remember.

Forecast and order reconciliation

Figure 2.1 shows how customer orders consume the forecast for a product. A problem arises when incoming orders do not match the forecast. We then find that unconsumed forecast still remains when the time to assemble the product is reached, while customer orders for different products are being deferred to later periods.

The first problem to deal with is the left over forecast. There are three options:

● Assemble the forecasted product and put it into stock until a customer order is received.
● Cancel the forecast, leaving some assembly capacity unused and putting into stock those components that have already been produced.
● Cancel the forecast and assemble something different that there is a customer order for. This option assumes that the necessary components are available. We shall see under *Assembly flexibility* how this might be achieved.

There is not a do-nothing option. Unused forecast must not be allowed to drift into arrears as time rolls forward, since it would continue to generate material requirements that were not required.

Having unconsumed forecast in the MPS means that customer orders can be accepted at any time up to the point where the final assembly schedule is set. The products that are available, and the dates when they are due to be completed, are shown in an analysis called the available to promise, or ATP. The ATP is a projection through time of the forecasted products (or modules) that are included in the MPS and have not yet been consumed by customer orders. When customers make delivery enquiries the ATP shows exactly what is available, and when.

The ATP is not only used to give customers an accurate delivery date for new orders. It also provides the possibility of offering alternatives that are available earlier. Using the ATP in this way may seem to be contrary to the customer-led approach that manufacturing industry has been adopting in recent years. Surely we should be supplying the customer with the right product at the right time, not trying to sell what we are planning to make? As an ideal, this is certainly true, but most companies are still some way from achieving this degree of responsiveness, and many never will. It is much better to offer alternatives than to turn business away or, worse, promise a delivery that is impossible without disrupting other customers' orders.

Assembly flexibility

We have seen that final assembly may be scheduled differently from the MPS, to take account of the actual customer orders that have been received. Indeed, where modular planning bills are used there is no assumed final assembly schedule in the MPS, since specific end products are not planned. Ideally the final assembly schedule should be decided as close as possible to the date when assembly is due to start. The later the final assembly schedule is set, the more chance there is of being able to assemble to order, rather than speculatively building for stock. Deviating from the MPS is only possible, however, if there are suitable materials available. This assumes that some kind of stocking policy is in operation.

One approach is to use safety stocks, a subject that is discussed later in this chapter. When using planning bills, however, a better way of providing flexibility in the final assembly schedule is through a technique called overplanning.

Overplanning is based on the idea that since no forecast is exactly right, it is much more sensible to forecast a range of likely values than a single figure. In our example of the car with a sunroof option, a more realistic forecast than the single figure of 15% might be between 12 and 18%. Forecasts for the features might be as follows:

- **Five-door body.** Minimum: 54%; maximum: 65%
- **Four-door body.** Minimum: 35%; maximum: 46%
- **1600cc engine.** Minimum: 27%; maximum: 32%
- **1800cc engine.** Minimum: 68%; maximum: 73%

If the quantities of each module in the planning bill shown in Figure 2.2 are changed to the maximum forecast, rather than the most likely value, there will be enough material for all possible outcomes. Figure 2.3 shows the planning bill modified in this way. Using this bill, the composite car that is the end item of the bill contains:

$$0.32 + 0.73 = 1.05 \text{ engines,}$$
$$\text{and } 0.65 + 0.46 = 1.11 \text{ bodies.}$$

This is where the expression overplanning originates. A planning bill set up in this way provisions materials in excess of the number of products contained in the MPS. At first glance it may seem that the surplus materials will simply build up over time until the whole factory is packed with spare engines and bodies. In practice, of course, this cannot happen. Surplus materials will be netted off future demand by MRP, and a stable position will be reached.

Overplanning, like safety stock, ensures that there are surplus materials in the supply chain to provide flexibility at final assembly. The advantage of overplanning is that as forecasts change it is not necessary to amend large numbers of computer records, as is generally the case when safety stocks are used.

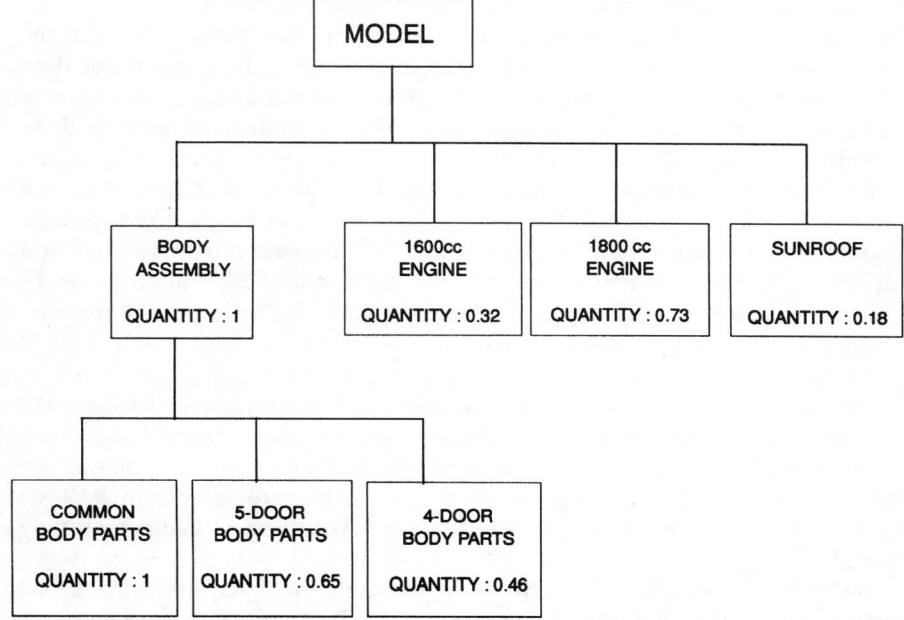

Figure 2.3 Example of a planning bill with overplanning

On closer examination of Figure 2.3, it can be seen that we are not quite provisioning 1.11 bodies for every car. The common body parts are only ordered in the quantity needed to satisfy the MPS. That is why these items were separated out into their own module. The same could not be done with the common engine parts because the engine plant needs to assemble complete engines to ship to the assembly plant.

As is always the case with any form of stocking policy, there is a trade-off between inventory costs and customer service. With overplanning it can be difficult to see how much inventory a particular overplan factor may create, once the stock levels have settled down. It may be necessary to carry out some simulation to find the best balance.

Why master production scheduling techniques are important

The importance of selecting the right techniques for master production scheduling cannot be over-emphasized. If MRPII is to succeed, top managers must use it to manage their businesses. Without doubt the MPS is the most important weapon in their armoury. Careful study of the techniques of master production scheduling at an early stage of an MRPII project, and certainly before any software is selected, is essential.

Software selection and configuration is not the only issue, however. Master production scheduling is the aspect of closed loop MRP that is most demanding of skilful human intervention. The planner performing this function has a pivotal position in the organization, but cannot carry out the role successfully if the support of top management is anything other than whole-hearted. Unless the master production scheduling approach that is to be used is thoroughly understood and accepted, this support will be lacking.

The master production scheduling techniques discussed here may not seem relevant to companies that only make to order, or only make for stock. The reason for neglecting the former is that they are very few in number, and for them master production scheduling is a relatively straightforward process of matching demand to available capacity. By definition, there is no provisioning of materials until the order is received, so the complexities of forecasting do not arise.

Companies that only make for stock do need to forecast, but since they invariably manufacture whatever the forecast specifies, they are not faced with the problems of forecast consumption. Neither are product variants a problem, since each individual product has to be forecastable in its own right. For these reasons, master production scheduling is again relatively straightforward.

Making for stock is only justified when customers require such a fast response to their orders that the goods have to be available before an order is received. Companies presently making for stock should consider whether the use of techniques such as modular planning bills and ATP could enable them to satisfy their customers' delivery expectations by assembling to order. In so doing they might achieve a significant reduction in inventory. MRPII will not bring benefits unless it is allowed to change things. This might be a good place to start.

More about MRP

Deciding the best approach to master production scheduling is not the end of the configuration issue. MRPII offers many more choices which managers need to understand if they are to avoid committing their organizations to inappropriate ways of working.

This section explores MRP logic in a little more depth, to see what choices there are in the way that requirements are generated.

Safety stocks

The use of safety stocks to provide protection against unexpected demands is a long-established technique of materials management. Wherever there is uncertainty about likely requirements the most obvious solution has always been to hold some extra inventory. There is now, however, much less acceptance of the idea of using safety stocks than was once the case. Greater emphasis is now placed upon the ability to respond quickly to variable demand without the use of inventory buffers. Nevertheless there are still times when safety stocks are required, and MRP is able to apply them.

When using MRP there should not, in theory, be any unexpected demand as the MPS which drives it is carefully managed to provide stability. The task of MRP is to calculate the dependent demand arising from the MPS, and to reschedule production accordingly; any uncertainty should have been dealt with in constructing the MPS. All that MRP needs to do is inform the planner of the detailed actions needed in response to the controlled changes in the MPS.

In practice, however, uncertainty can still arise. We have already seen how it may be necessary for the assembly schedule to differ from the MPS, to allow some last-minute flexibility in satisfying customer requirements. This flexibility requires parts to be provisioned that are surplus to expected output, and we have seen how this can be achieved through overplanning. Maintaining safety stocks of items used in assembly is an alternative method of providing assembly flexibility.

In addition to protecting against variability in demand, safety stocks can also protect against uncertainty in the supply of materials. Variability in supply may arise through the rejection of batches of material for quality reasons, or through late delivery of goods by suppliers or at earlier stages of the internal production system.

MRP provides two ways of handling safety stock. The first method is simply to specify, for each individual item, a level of stock that MRP should seek to maintain at all times. MRP subtracts this safety stock quantity from the actual inventory before carrying out the normal netting operation. In other words, it treats the safety stock as if it were not there at all. MRP never makes use of safety stock in balancing supply and demand; it always provisions additional materials instead. This means that the safety stock is always available to deal with unexpected peaks in demand, or shortfalls in supply.

The second method used by MRP is safety lead time. In this case MRP plans items to be delivered into stock earlier than they are actually needed. The role of safety lead time is primarily to provide protection against uncertainty in timing. For example, it would protect against late supply, by providing some hidden padding in the planned due date. Similarly, safety lead time provides protection against customer orders being received earlier than expected.

In theory, therefore, safety stock protects against volume fluctuations and safety lead time protects against timing variations. Often both forms of uncertainty are present simultaneously, so it is not obvious which technique should be used. Since both techniques provide surplus stock that can be used to handle whatever situation may arise, the choice of technique is not really critical. Usually safety lead time is preferable to safety stock because it adjusts itself automatically to the level of demand. Fixed safety stocks need to be reviewed regularly, a daunting task if many items are involved.

Safety lead times are less suited to items where demand is patchy, particularly in cases where the time between requirements can exceed the safety lead time. When this happens there will be periods when stock falls to zero, and there is no protection against unexpected demands. A compromise approach is to use a safety stock which is calculated from the average usage of an item over a specified safety lead time. This calculation can be repeated automatically at regular intervals, keeping the safety stock levels valid.

When using safety stocks or safety lead times it is important to be clear about the uncertainty that needs to be buffered. It is a big mistake to scatter safety stocks across all items, simply because the previous system depended upon carrying stock of every item all the time. There is an old wives' tale of MRP which says that after initial implementation, inventory will go up before it goes down. This idea arose because re-order points used in the old system were carried across into the new MRP-based system as safety stocks. The difference was that MRP was much better at keeping items at their planned level than was the previous system. All under-stocked items were immediately replenished, increasing overall inventory. Reductions in over-stocking of other items took longer to work through, so it was a while before inventory fell again.

In setting safety stocks it is important to be aware of the structure of the bill of material. Holding safety stocks at different levels of the bill can result in several layers of inventory all buffering against the same risk. The rule is to hold safety stocks at the lowest level of the bill of material at which they will provide the required flexibility. That way, they have the lowest added value and the highest potential to be turned into different finished items.

There are two final points to remember about safety stocks. The first is that safety stock and safety lead time both undermine the basic MRP concept of time-phasing, in which items are planned to be available immediately before they are required. This is a very important discipline for production to accept. Once due dates are seen not to relate to the timing of requirements, the likelihood of production keeping to schedule is dramatically reduced.

The second point is that although safety stocks may protect against uncertainty, they do not protect against disruption. The availability in stock of items unexpectedly required enables customers to be satisfied, but the result so far as MRP is concerned is a mismatch between supply and demand. Once stock falls below the safety stock level, MRP plans immediate action to restore the situation. A problem that has already been resolved can then lead to the expediting of a replenishment order for items for which there is no immediate demand.

Scrap allowance

One of the types of uncertainty that safety stock can protect against is production wastage through scrap or process loss. An alternative to using safety stock in this situation is to specify an average scrap or yield percentage on items that are subject to such wastage. This factor is used by MRP to provision an additional quantity to cover the expected loss.

Building in a scrap allowance is only sensible if the losses occur regularly on every batch. For example, scrap may be produced while setting up a machine or while a process stabilizes. Or there may be an off-cut at the end of every bar or coil of raw material that cannot be used. In other situations, however, an average scrap rate of, say, 2% could actually mean that one entire batch in every fifty is scrapped. No realistic scrap percentage could protect against this type of loss.

As with safety stocks, scrap allowances should be used sparingly, and should only be considered when all efforts to prevent the losses have been exhausted. Using scrap percentages tends to institutionalize the loss, rather than expose it as a source of wastage that needs addressing. When standard costs are calculated, the scrap percentage is considered part of normal material usage, and is included in the standard. This can lead to the somewhat bizarre situation in which production are congratulated for achieving a favourable material variance because less material was scrapped than normal. This situation is hardly appropriate in companies committed to a regime of total quality!

Lot sizing

When MRP plans a new order, it adjusts the quantity required (the net requirement) to comply with whatever lot sizing rules have been specified for that item. There are several techniques for calculating lot sizes, the most common ones being:

- **Lot for lot.** In this policy the lot size is equal to the net requirement calculated by MRP. In other words, there is no rounding up of quantity required.
- **Economic order quantity (EOQ).** Also referred to as the economic batch quantity, or EBQ. This technique is based upon a calculation that attempts to balance inventory costs with order-raising or set-up costs. The underlying theory has been thoroughly discredited for many years, but EOQ shows a disturbing reluctance to disappear.
- **Multiple order quantity.** The lot size must be a multiple of a specified quantity. Typically this quantity would be either the capacity of the container used to transport or store the items, or the quantity produced from a complete unit of raw material.
- **Minimum order quantity.** The order must be no less than a specified quantity, but can take any value greater than that. This policy is intended to prevent unacceptably small batches from being released to production (or to an outside supplier).
- **Fixed order period.** This policy looks ahead for the specified number of periods and plans an order quantity large enough to cover all the requirements in that horizon. The intention of this policy is to prevent orders being released too close together.

● **Part period balancing.** Using similar logic to the EOQ approach, this technique does at least take account of future requirements planned by MRP, whereas the EOQ is based solely upon historical usage.

Ideally the lot for lot method should be used wherever possible, because this is the only lot sizing technique that does not result in more components being produced than are immediately required. Batch sizes that are larger than necessary are undesirable for all the usual reasons associated with excess stocks. They tie up capital, require storage and handling, obscure quality problems, and they may well become obsolete if the item is superseded. In addition to all of this, there is the problem that large batches introduce lumpiness into production schedules.

Lumpiness occurs when an MPS that has been carefully balanced to smooth the overall workload is converted by MRP into a series of large, sporadic orders for lower level components. These orders in turn trigger off further large, sporadic orders for their own components, and this process is continued right down through the bill of material. Subsequent small changes to the MPS can cause extensive rescheduling of several large orders, a phenomenon that is referred to as nervousness.

In spite of the advantages of lot for lot, there are occasions when this rule cannot be applied. A common reason is that lot for lot would result in orders for the same item being planned too close together. In most factories, a new order for the same item every day would be quite unmanageable. In this case the fixed order period technique can be used to force orders to be planned at acceptable intervals. Similar logic applies to purchase orders. If weekly deliveries are required, a fixed period of five days will ensure that MRP only plans one order in any week.

Other lot sizing techniques should be used extremely sparingly. Multiple order quantity may be used if there are physical constraints that make other quantities particularly difficult to handle. The multiple quantity, however, should not be greatly in excess of a typical weekly requirement. Minimum order quantity can be used to prevent very small orders being planned for a process that requires a significant set-up time, although a better approach would be to shorten the set-up. Again care should be taken that the minimum quantity is not excessive in comparison with normal levels of demand.

Time buckets

As we saw in Chapter 1, MRP processes each item by rolling forward in time from one time period, or bucket, to the next. MRP is not too concerned about the length of each time bucket; whether it is a day or a month, MRP treats it just the same. It is only after processing has been completed that the time buckets are converted back into calendar dates, to allow the actions planned to be expressed in meaningful terms.

In early systems it was assumed that the time buckets would be weeks or months, and no provision was made for shorter buckets. Modern systems recognize that many companies need greater precision, and have been designed to operate with buckets of one day. These systems are often referred to as bucketless systems, but there is no real difference in the logic they use, only in the length of the bucket they can work with.

If MRP is processing an MPS with a planning horizon of several months, daily buckets cannot sensibly be used for the entire period. Firstly the demand information further into the future is rarely that accurate, and secondly the resulting action reports would be even more massive than they need be. Instead variable bucket lengths can be specified, becoming longer the further into the future they extend.

Care must be taken not to induce another form of lumpiness into detailed production schedules. If monthly time buckets are used to manage demands that are some way off, these demands will be satisfied by MRP planning a corresponding supply to be available at the beginning of the month in question. All the month's replenishment supplies are therefore planned for completion on the same day. This may not be important if the period is well into the future, and all that is needed is a coarse measure of likely activity levels. If, however, cumulative lead times are long, a requirement for a finished product many weeks in the future can trigger off immediate actions for lower level items. The fact that the current period is expressed in time buckets of one day will do nothing to smooth out the aggregated requirements that MRP has assumed will all be needed on the first day of that month.

This situation can be avoided only through awareness of total cumulative lead times. A pattern of time buckets may then be selected for MRP that will not create lumpy demand in the period during which orders planned by MRP will actually be executed.

Regenerative and net change MRP

A full recalculation of requirements that explodes the entire MPS down through the bill of material is referred to as regenerative MRP. Processing times for regenerative MRP can be quite long, because even items for which there has been no change in circumstance since the previous run are re-analyzed. On-line access to the entire system is usually impossible during a regenerative MRP run, because so many records need to be used and updated. These runs are almost invariably carried out overnight or at weekends, to prevent interference with normal access to the system.

In early systems, MRP runs often occupied most of the weekend, but as they were typically only carried out once a month this was not really a problem. Run times are now much shorter, but still significant.

In order to speed up processing times, an alternative approach called net change MRP was developed. Between MRP runs the system notes any transactions that might affect the supply/demand profile of an item. The item concerned is flagged, so that when a net change run is initiated only those items that have been flagged, together with their lower level components, are processed. Assuming that net change runs are carried out at regular intervals, the amount of processing is far less than would be the case with regenerative MRP.

When using net change MRP there is no practical restriction on the frequency of runs. Some systems offer on-line MRP, which analyzes the effects of all changes as they arise.

Regenerative and net change MRP runs should result in similar, or identical action reports. Regenerative MRP may access more items, but it only prints messages for those where there has been a change. However, the possibility exists with net change MRP that an obscure event, or combination of events, might from time to time change a supply/demand profile without setting the appropriate flag. It is usual for net change users to carry out an occasional regenerative run to ensure that everything is brought back into balance.

Since there is no technical restriction on the frequency with which MRP runs can be carried out, companies must choose the frequency that is most suited to their environment. Generally speaking, the faster the response expected by customers, the more often requirements should be reviewed. The degree of stability and accuracy of the sales forecast should also be taken into account. A question linked to how frequently MRP should be run is how often the MPS should be updated. This issue is discussed further in Chapter 7. Nevertheless, successive MRP runs can produce different results even if they use the same MPS. This could be, for example, because materials have been scrapped, or an engineering change has been made to a bill of material since the previous run.

Most companies seem to take a fairly conservative approach to MRP run frequency. A weekly run often produces so many recommendations that it keeps the planners busy for most of the following week. More frequent runs might be preferable. They need not produce much extra work, but would ensure that the MRP recommendations being reviewed at the end of the week were not already out of date. Unfortunately there is no definitive technique for deciding the best MRP frequency for a given environment, so it is necessary to resort to trial and error tactics.

Although many companies could certainly benefit from more frequent MRP runs, there is some evidence that it is possible to be too responsive. Some of the random events that occur in dynamic production systems tend to counterbalance each other over a period of time. Responding to every change as it happens can cause excessive volatility, with reschedules being generated that are subsequently reversed. MRP run frequency is an important operational decision, and one that requires management attention. The way of working that the planning department finds most convenient may not be the best method for the company.

Order management

The purpose of MRP is to create replenishment orders for manufactured and purchased items, and to reschedule them as necessary. These orders are the means by which the planner informs the internal or external supplier which items are required, how many are needed, and the date they must be available. In the case of manufactured items, the order also conveys information on the materials to be used in making the item, and the operations to be performed in carrying out the work.

In addition to providing work instructions, orders also provide a means of collecting information about the progress of the work. In particular, orders for manufactured items can be used to monitor movements of material and to record details of work done and operations completed.

Many tools and techniques are available to assist with the management of orders and the associated material movements.

Firm planned orders

Each MRP run generates new planned orders and reschedules (or cancels) existing orders. The aim is to make whatever adjustments are needed to keep supply and demand in balance. Sometimes the planner might decide to override a recommendation made by MRP, and change the start date or due date of a planned order (perhaps both), or to vary the quantity. If the next MRP run is not to undo the changes that have been made, a mechanism is needed to protect the amended order. This is done by designating it a firm planned order. Only manual intervention can change a firm planned order; no matter what changes arise in the supply and demand balance, MRP will not change a firm planned order.

The reason for using firm planned orders is to impose reality upon the assumptions that drive MRP. An example is the situation where a customer order has been accepted with a delivery date that is inside the normal lead time for that product. A decision has been taken that on this occasion the work can be completed more quickly than usual, but MRP does not know this. As a result, new orders for lower level components of the product are planned with start dates, and possibly due dates, earlier than the current date. The planner can override these dates, substituting meaningful dates based upon the shortened lead times that are to be used on this occasion. The orders affected are given firm planned status, so that they will not be changed back by MRP.

A second example of the use of firm planned orders is in resolving a supply problem, rather than a demand problem. Here a supplier has informed the company that a purchase order is going to be delivered late. The planner uses pegging to find out what this material in needed for, and decides that the ultimate customer order(s) can still be despatched on time, so long as the manufactured components are made more quickly than usual. The purchase order due date is deferred, in line with the supplier's new delivery promise, and the start dates of the manufacturing orders using this material are amended accordingly. These orders are given firm planned status, so that MRP does not report the resulting lead time violations.

Firm planned orders introduce a distortion into the logic MRP uses in balancing supply and demand, and should only be used in situations of importance. Since firm planned orders can only be amended by the planner, the number in use must not exceed the planner's ability to manage and keep up to date.

Works orders

Before orders planned by MRP can initiate material supply activities, they must be converted into scheduled receipts. This transformation is achieved through a process of order approval, in which ownership of the order is accepted by the planner. Once an order has been approved it becomes a scheduled receipt, which means that it is now an intention to manufacture or purchase. In contrast to planned orders, which can be adjusted automatically by future MRP runs, scheduled receipts cannot be re-scheduled directly by MRP. Instead MRP prints action messages recom-mending that the planner takes appropriate rescheduling action.

Planned orders are usually reviewed by start date. There is no point in approving orders that are too far into the future, since subsequent MRP runs may need to reschedule them. Furthermore, decisions are taken during order approval that are best left until near the time the order is due for release.

Approving orders usually requires the planner to confirm each one individually, which can be a time-consuming task. The planner can accept the order, change the date or quantity, or ignore it. In a properly implemented system, the planner should be able to accept the great majority of planned orders without change. If this is not the case, there is something seriously wrong. On the other hand, few people would be happy to accept all the orders planned by a computer system, without reviewing them first. There are times when lot sizing rules produce undesirable results, or data errors cause ridiculous requirements, and the role of the planner is to filter out the discrepancies before they go any further.

Up to the point where orders are approved, there is no real difference between orders for purchased items and those for manufactured items. From order approval onwards, procedures for processing the two types of order are markedly different. The remainder of this section is concerned only with managing orders for manufactured items. The issues affecting purchase orders are considered in Chapter 5.

Creating a works order

Approving a planned order for a manufactured item creates what is usually referred to as a works order. During this process a unique record is constructed of the materials that will be used in executing the order and the manufacturing operations that will need to be carried out. Normally the materials are those contained in the bill of material, one level below the item on order, and the operations are those held in the item's routing record. All this information is automatically transferred to the works order record, creating a separate bill of material and routing specifically for that order.

The planner has the option of amending this record, perhaps replacing a material that is unavailable with one of a higher specification. Or perhaps changing an operation from a machine that is undergoing repair to a less efficient alternative. The works order retains these changes to its one-time bill and routing record throughout its life.

In future MRP runs, it is the materials in the one-time bill that are exploded down to their own lower level items, not the standard components contained in the bill of material. Capacity plans are based upon the one-time routing, not on the standard routing record. Capacity planning reports usually distinguish between loads arising from planned orders and loads arising from scheduled receipts (i.e. works orders).

Works order release
After a works order has been approved, the next stage in its life is order release. This is the time when materials are allocated and the shop paperwork is printed. Order release can be triggered automatically, just before the order start date, or it can be controlled manually. Sometimes order release is combined with order approval.

Before orders are released it is necessary to check that material is available, to prevent orders with shortages being passed to the material stores. Material availability checking is carried out through a process called trial kitting. Selected orders are put through a simulated material issue process, and any order for which there is insufficient material available is highlighted. Where materials are common to many orders, the sequence in which these orders are submitted to trial kitting can affect the outcome. Care is needed, therefore, to ensure that urgent orders are not held up while scarce material is consumed by less critical orders.

Once material availability checking has shown that there are sufficient materials in stock, the order is released and the materials allocated to it. These allocated materials are not considered when future trial kitting checks are carried out. Allocations are cancelled automatically when the materials are issued to the order.

Material issuing
When materials required for a works order have been picked in the material stores, their inventory records must be updated by issue transactions. There are two ways of doing this. The first is by processing each item in the one-time bill individually, recording the actual quantity of material issued in each case. The second method is to use a single pick complete transaction, in which the system assumes that all items are issued in the exact quantity specified in the one-time bill. The second method is much faster, but cannot be used if there are differences between the actual quantity issued and the quantity specified. This might arise, for example, if part of a coil of strip steel is required for an order. The material stores would issue the entire coil, the unused balance of which would be returned later.

Sometimes low value, frequently used items such as fasteners are not issued to individual orders, but are issued in bulk to top up stocks kept on the shopfloor. As long as the system is informed that these items are handled in this way, it will not assume that they need to be issued to individual works orders. Picking lists printed by the system should not show bulk issue items, and pick complete transactions must not create material issues for them.

In some situations there is no material stores controlling the issue of materials to works orders. Materials are consumed as required from a pool of floor stocks, or from bulk storage tanks. To handle these situations a different form of material issue transaction is used, called backflushing. In this case materials are assumed by the system to have been issued when the order is closed and the completed items booked back into stock. Material issue transactions are generated automatically for all the items on the one-time bill of that works order, based upon the quantity of finished items received into stock.

A slightly more sophisticated variant of backflushing is pull-through. Here each material in the one-time bill is linked to a particular operation number. As the order is reported to have passed that operation, a material issue transaction is generated automatically. Unlike backflushing, pull-through allows material usage to be recorded close to the time at which the material has actually been consumed. It is dependent upon a system for recording the movement of orders from one operation to the next, and this is not always present in the type of fast moving, flow production environment in which backflushing tends to be used.

The main difficulty with backflushing (and pull-through) arises when materials are scrapped. Since the operators can readily replace any reject materials from the floor stock pool, it is difficult to establish a discipline whereby individual scrap transactions are raised. Yet if this is not done, backflushing will assume that the specified quantity only was used. If regular stock adjustments are not carried out there will be an apparent growth in the pool stock, and some red faces at the annual stocktake when the stock loss is revealed.

Scrap recording can become quite complex in a backflushing environment when complete assemblies are rejected. If a works order for 100 assemblies is closed after only 95 have been booked as completed, what has happened to the remaining five? If they were rejected on final test and thrown into the scrap bin, issue transactions for an additional five sets of components should be raised. If, on the other hand, the assembler miscounted and only assembled 95, no stock adjustment is needed. A third possibility is that five assemblies were rejected on final test, but were dismantled, with some components being scrapped and others returned to the pool stock. In this case only the scrapped components need to be issued from floor stock.

If all material movements are into and out of a controlled store, there is much less scope for confusion and error in maintaining stock records. It is for this reason that the introduction of MRPII is often associated with secure stores and rigorous procedures for controlling material movements. This is an issue we shall return to later.

Coherent material control

Combining works order control and stock recording in an integrated system creates a whole new dimension to inventory control. Materials can be tracked in a coherent manner throughout the manufacturing process, not just while they are in stores. In a properly designed and implemented system the main material movement transactions are always double-sided. Materials that are issued from material stores are added by the same transaction to a works order record. When the works order is closed, these materials (now processed to form their parent, higher level, item) are simultaneously added to finished parts stock. This process is repeated as this finished item in turn is issued to another works order at the next level of manufacture.

There is therefore complete continuity and consistency in the flow of materials through the business. There are no black holes, no lack of material visibility to confuse the MRP process or frustrate the accountants. It is not even essential for transactions to be processed at the precise time that the material movement occurs, since the balancing issuing and receiving actions are always concurrent. Of course there may be other reasons for movement reporting to be carried out speedily. In particular, stock checking can be very difficult if there is a delay between material movement and reporting.

There is an exception to this picture of integrity and consistency, and that is the process of bulk issuing described earlier. Here the double-sided transaction is broken. Materials are issued in bulk before the order is picked, and they disappear from sight. MRP is unaware of the supply of bulk issue items held in the assembly department, and consequently provisions additional stocks. Companies using bulk issuing take the view that since the items concerned cost very little, and are quickly consumed, a little over-stocking is well worth the reduction in handling that bulk issuing permits.

This conclusion is probably valid so long as a careful eye is kept on the situation. Bulk issuing is such an attractively simple technique that the number of items handled in this way can surreptitiously grow. The effects of this expansion are not readily visible, since floor stocks of bulk issue items are not part of computer inventory. Indeed, the view may be taken that since these items are supposed to be low value, it is not even worth counting them at the annual stocktake. When the problem is finally spotted, a very large inventory of largely obsolete items might be revealed.

Bill of material management

The importance of the bill of material in MRPII should by now be very apparent. Bill of material explosion is the fundamental technique upon which MRP is based, while planning bills are an important concept in the management of the MPS. Furthermore, one-time bills in work orders, used to control the movement of materials through the factory, are derived from the master bill of material. Later the essential contribution of the bill of material to the calculation of product costs will be explained. It is clear that the bill of material is of fundamental importance. Bill of material records must be properly set up and maintained if MRPII is to function correctly.

This section examines some of the tools and techniques, and choices, that are available to assist in the management of bills of material.

Structuring the bill of material

For all but the very simplest products the relationship between a product and its components can be set up, or structured, in a variety of ways. The simplest approach is to link all the purchased materials directly to the finished product, ignoring any intermediate components and sub-assemblies that are manufactured in-house. This type of structure is called a flat bill. At the other extreme, a bill might contain multiple levels. Sometimes levels are included containing items which are not real stages of production; this can happen if, for example, the design office has found it convenient to produce a drawing of a particular collection of items, and allocate it a part number.

When deciding how to structure the main, engineering bill of material, there is a golden rule that must be followed. **The bill must reflect the way in which the product is actually made.**

The importance of this rule can be illustrated through the example shown in Figure 2.4. This shows a very simple manufacturing process, in which a product is assembled from two components, A and B, which are manufactured in-house, together with a purchased item, C. Components A and B are produced in the machine shop from a single raw material held in the material store. A works order for component A controls the issue of the raw material and enables A to be received into the component store. A second works order for B operates in a similar manner. An assembly works order for the finished product controls the issue of A, B and C from the component store, and the receipt of the product into the finished goods warehouse.

In this example, the three works orders control the entire manufacturing process, while the works order issue and receipt transactions manage the physical flow of material. The bill of material structure needed to operate in this way is shown in Figure 2.5.

Now assume that this company does not understand the principles of MRPII. The bill of material structure used is the one shown in Figure 2.6. This structure has been adopted because during assembly A and B are assembled together before C is added. A and B are used in this way in other products, with different purchased items added subsequently. It is therefore convenient for the design office to use a single drawing to cover the common first assembly stage. Also the accounts department wants to know the cost up to that point, to make it easier to estimate the costs of new variants. Introducing a sub-assembly X into the bill of material satisfies both these requirements.

When MRP processes this bill of material, it plans orders for A, B and X, in addition to the order needed to assemble C and X to make the finished

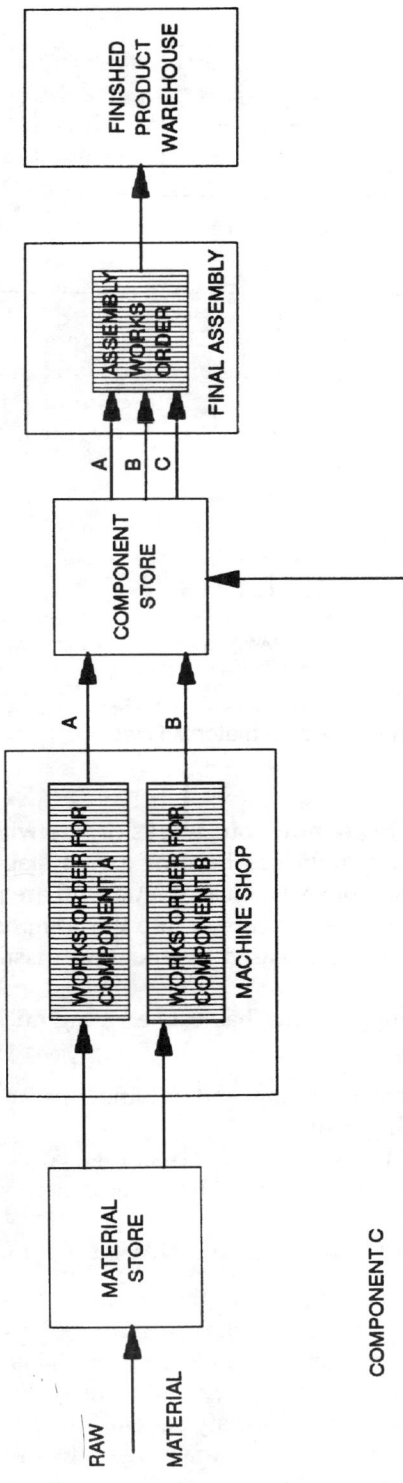

Figure 2.4 A simple material flow controlled by works orders

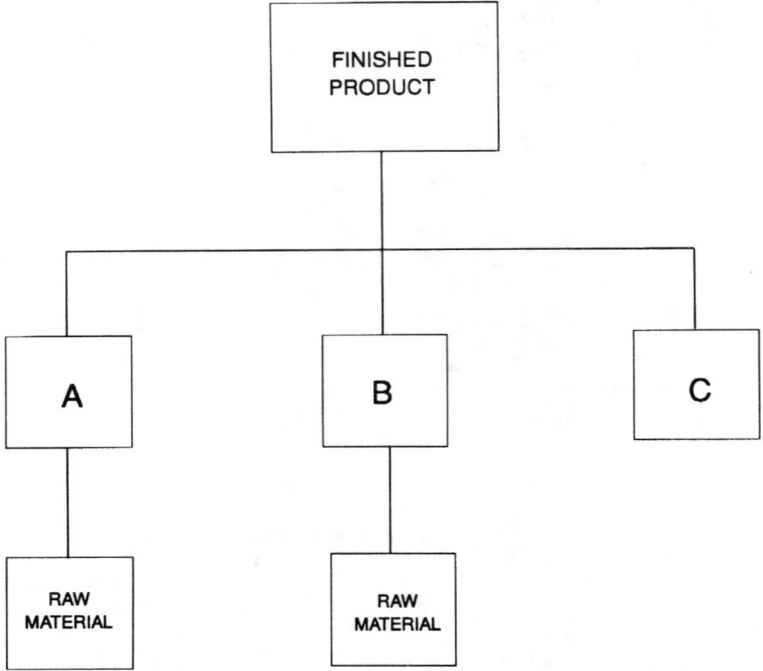

Figure 2.5   Bill of material based on material flows

product. Therefore there are now four works orders where only three were needed before. Final assembly has become a two stage process. First the works order to sub-assemble X is released. A and B are issued to this order. When it is completed, X is received back into the component store. Now the final assembly order can be released. C and X are issued to this, and the product is completed.

Structuring the bill in this way has caused a significant increase in cost and complexity. It has:

- introduced additional receiving and issuing operations, increasing the risk of stock recording error
- increased handling, transportation and storage costs
- created the need for an additional works order, with the associated administration cost
- destroyed the flow of material, and increased manufacturing lead time.

This example may seem trivial, but the situation described here exists in many, many manufacturing companies. It may be less visible when large numbers of complex products are involved, but it is there nevertheless, causing an enormous loss of efficiency and reduction in customer service. The bill of material may need to satisfy several different requirements, but its main purpose is to control the manufacture of the product. In structuring the bill, other objectives must be subordinated to this overriding rule.

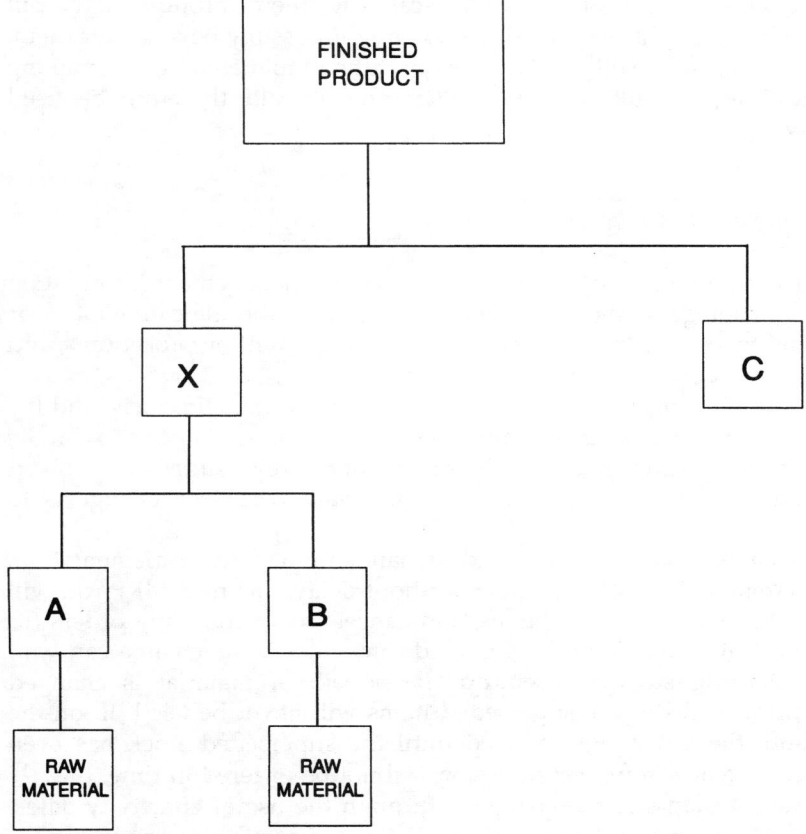

Figure 2.6 Bill of material with intermediate step in the assembly process

Phantom parts

Some of the conflicting demands upon the bill of material structure can be reconciled by the use of phantom parts. Phantom, or blow-through, parts are items in the bill which MRP effectively ignores. Requirements passed down to a phantom during the MRP process do not cause a works order to be planned. Instead they are merely passed on to the phantom's components. The only exception is if MRP finds that the phantom already has some stock, in which case this stock will be set against the requirement.

If, in Figure 2.6, X was classified as a phantom, the bill would operate in the same way as the bill in Figure 2.5. As a phantom, X would be invisible to MRP, and no orders for it would be planned. The design office would be happy because they would have a common-stage item, and the accounts department would have the intermediate cost, so all objectives would be satisfied.

Not all bill structuring conflicts can be resolved quite this easily, but phantoms are without doubt a useful tool in the right circumstances. It is easy to overdo the use of phantoms, scattering them throughout the bill wherever it is thought that one day there might possibly be a use for them. This can clutter up the bill, making it very difficult to maintain, and making user enquiries difficult to follow. Phantoms should therefore be used sparingly.

Engineering change control

The bill of material is a vital part of a company's management information systems. Its integrity should be ensured through the allocation of clear responsibility for data maintenance, comprehensive written procedures, and tight system security.

Engineering changes are a part of the life cycle of most products, and the procedures for authorizing and approving them must be integrated with the bill of material maintenance procedures. One of the key issues to be resolved when planning engineering changes is the date when the change is to become effective.

If the change is safety-critical, and demands immediate implementation, the bill of material must be changed without delay. The next MRP run will then plan orders for the new items, and cancel any outstanding orders for the components that are no longer used. But what if the change can wait until all existing stock is used up? If the bill of material is changed immediately, stocks of the superseded items will never be used. If, on the other hand, the bill is not changed until the superseded stock has been consumed, the new replacement items will not be ordered in time.

One way of planning the change is through the use of effectivity dates. The planner estimates a date by when existing stock will finally be used up (by studying the latest MRP information). This date becomes the engineering finish date of the superseded items. The replacement components are added to the bill of material immediately, with an engineering start date of the day after the finish date of the superseded items. As MRP rolls forward in time, it will use the old part numbers up until their end date, and then transfer the requirement to the replacement parts. Orders for these new items are therefore planned to be available by the effectivity date. The superseded part numbers can stay on the bill of material indefinitely, if required, to provide an audit trail of changes carried out to the product.

If usage does not go according to plan, the planner may need to amend the effectivity date to ensure the timing coincides with the exhaustion of the stock. The final fine tuning can be done by amending the one-time bill of the transition order, at the time of order approval.

Some IBS products are able to manage engineering change to coincide precisely with the exhaustion of stock of the superseded part. This facility can be very useful with simple changes, but when several items are being superseded simultaneously it is most unlikely that their stock cover will be identical. In this situation the decision on when to make the change reverts to the planner.

Not all software has an automatic facility to use up superseded stock, but the same result can be achieved by using a simple bill of material structuring technique. The superseded item is made into a phantom, and the replacement item is structured to it as its only component. MRP uses up the remaining stock of the superseded phantom item, but passes any additional requirements down to the next level, which is the replacement item. The old item can be deleted from the bill at a convenient time after the change has been implemented.

The trouble with using this approach is that it can cause distortions elsewhere. For example, if standard costs are recalculated there is a danger of including the cost of both the old and the new items in the product cost. Using phantoms to control engineering change is one example of ingenious use of MRPII tools to do things that they were not intended for. There are many other examples. Such techniques should only be used if all the possible implications of the proposed actions are understood. Otherwise the apparent solution to one problem may become the cause of several new ones.

Product configuration

Earlier in this chapter the use of planning bills was described. Planning bills enable products which are available in a wide range of variants to be forecasted without the need for individual end item forecasts. Planning bills need to be separate from engineering bills since they are based upon modules that do not reflect the way the product is actually built.

The engineering bills for these products could be structured in the conventional manner, one bill for each product variant. Where the number of potential product variants is very great, however, this form of structuring involves maintaining many separate bills, which is time-consuming and costly. The alternative is to set up engineering bills which have modules, rather than finished products, as the top level items.

The modules used in the engineering bill may not be identical to those in the planning bill, because they need to be manufacturable. In the case of the motor car example used earlier, the two engine modules would form perfectly acceptable engineering bill modules, because each specifies the manufacture of a complete engine. The five-door body parts module, on the other hand, could not be used in the engineering bill. Instead each body module would need to contain all the items needed to make a particular style of body shell, including the common parts.

Since there are no item numbers representing the finished products, the specific product required must be configured at the time of sales order entry. Instead of selecting a product item number from the sales catalogue, the customer specifies the model range and the particular features and options required. These features and options determine the modules to be selected from the engineering bill and brought together into the customer-specified product.

This process should be assisted by software that ensures the specification is complete and does not violate any rules laid down by the sales engineering department. For example, one rule could be that a rear windscreen wiper may be specified on a five-door, but not on a four-door body.

The bill of material resulting from this procedure is incorporated in a works order that controls material movements through the assembly process. In this respect it is no different from an end item bill. The bill for the configured product, however, is unique to that sales order. An identical product may never again be made. If it were, it would be configured through exactly the same process. The company may never know, and does not need to know, how many of any particular variant it has produced.

What to put in the bill

It is not always obvious which items should be included in a product's bill of material. This is particularly true in the case of materials such as paints, greases and adhesives, where it is difficult to calculate accurately the quantity used on the product. The easy answer is to exclude such items from the bill, and treat them as consumables. But even consumables have to be provisioned, and if they are not planned by MRP then a less accurate re-order point system will have to be used. Furthermore, items such as paint can represent a significant element of the cost of some products. If these costs are recovered as a part of general overheads, rather than being charged directly to the product, precision will be lost.

Usually it is worth including items such as these on the bill of material so long as the usage can be estimated with sufficient accuracy for the accumulated requirements calculated by MRP to be meaningful. If the orders planned by MRP bear little relationship to the quantities actually used, then including the item on the bill is achieving nothing, and may even be distorting product costs.

All kinds of unexpected items can be found on bills of material, often for very good reasons. A manufacturer of industrial batteries included the electricity used to activate the plates and charge the cells. Fortunately we do not yet have to order electricity in advance, but for this company the additional precision in cost calculation justified the inclusion of electricity usage.

In some companies the bill of material is used to plan resources other than materials. One example is in the engineering to order environment, where a product needs some form of customized design work to satisfy the customer requirement. A phoney item representing the design task could be created, given a suitable lead time, and added to the bill as a component of the item which required the design resource. MRP would then calculate a start date and a due date for the development activity, ensuring that it was not overlooked when the time came.

Applying a little ingenuity in the use of bills of material can provide useful results, but is not advised for the beginner. Just as the use of phantoms in engineering change control needs to be handled with care, so any other novel use of the bill of material must be fully thought through. When using integrated systems, the unforeseen side-effects of such actions have a tendency to materialize in the most unlikely places.

Costing

Costing is an important aspect of MRPII, since costs are used to evaluate inventory, measure output, assess production efficiency and calculate profit margins. Once costs were regarded as the only meaningful measure of production activity; now there is an acceptance that non-cost measures, such as delivery performance, are equally important indicators of the health of the business. Nevertheless, costs still form an important part of most managers' targets and objectives, and it is essential that costing methods are accurate and consistent with the manufacturing data.

MRPII works with two types of cost, standard (or planned) costs and actual costs. It is important to understand how these costs are generated and used.

Standard costs

Standard product costs are calculated by a process known as cost build, or roll-up. This process starts with the purchased items, which are at the lowest level of the bill of material, and works its way progressively up the bill. Costs calculated at each level are rolled up to the parent item, or items, at the next level up.

For purchased items the only element of cost is the purchase price. The cost of a manufactured item is the cost of its components, together with the labour and overhead cost incurred in its manufacture. Labour costs are derived from the allowed (or standard) time for each manufacturing operation. This time, which is generally referred to as the run time, is held in the item routing record. The run time is multiplied by the hourly labour rate for that work centre to calculate the cost of labour used. The total labour cost for the part is simply the total of the labour costs at each operation.

Overhead costs are usually calculated from the operation run times, using the overhead recovery rate specified for the work centre concerned. Sometimes several overhead buckets are available, each able to hold recovery rates representing different elements of overhead cost. These buckets are often user-defined. Labour hourly rates and overhead recovery rates for each work centre are contained in its work centre record.

Operation times can include a set-up time in addition to the run time. Since set-up time does not vary with batch size, the set-up cost per item is dependent upon its lot sizing rules. A special costing lot size, held as part of the item details for each manufactured item, is used to spread the set-up cost across the normal quantity produced.

The cost of each manufactured item is rolled up to the next level of the bill of material, becoming a material cost for its parent parts. Eventually the costs roll up to the top level of the bill to give the total product costs.

Costs calculated in this way are referred to as standard costs. There are different types of standard cost, however. This is because different values of material prices, labour rates and overhead recovery rates can be used to calculate them. Each purchased item can have more than one price, and each labour rate and overhead recovery rate can have more than one value. For example, budget prices and rates are often set at the beginning of the year at the expected average value for the whole year. Then there are the current prices and rates, which change throughout the year. Other values can be created for 'what if' analyses, to simulate different business situations. Cost roll-ups based upon different types of base costs satisfy different costing requirements. The main types of cost roll-up are:

- **Frozen standard.** The frozen standard cost is the benchmark against which performance is measured. It is usually fixed for the entire financial year, to provide consistency in the evaluation of inventory, output, cost variances etc. Frozen standard costs are based upon standard (or budget) material prices, labour rates and overhead recovery rates.
- **Current-at-standard.** If new products are introduced during the financial year, or if major changes are made in the design of existing ones or in their method of manufacture, frozen standard costs will either not exist or will be invalid. Current-at-standard shows what the cost would have been if these changes had been in place when the frozen standard costs were rolled up at the beginning of the year.
- **Current.** The difference between current-at-standard and current is that the former is based upon the standard (or budget) material prices, labour rates and overhead rates that were used to calculate the frozen standard, whilst current is based on current prices and rates. Current cost is the expected cost of an item if manufactured today.
- **Simulated.** Simulated costs can be used to model the costing implications of different business strategies, by setting the appropriate prices and rates. One important application is the modelling and acceptance of next year's frozen standard, before the previous frozen standard is overwritten.

The base data for each of these cost roll-ups is summarized in Figure 2.7. Ideally all these costs types should be available simultaneously, and software should enable one cost type to be rolled over into another, either by individual item or for all items. For example, the current-at-standard cost for a new item should be rolled across to the frozen standard, so that inventory of that item can be evaluated.

Next year's frozen costs need to be rolled over from the simulated cost fields, where they have been modelled, into the frozen cost fields on the first day of the new year. A clean stock revaluation may then be achieved. Rolling these costs over eliminates the need to re-key the new standard material

TYPE OF COST	BILL OF MATERIAL AND ROUTING		LABOUR HOURLY RATES, OVERHEAD RECOVERY RATES AND MATERIAL PRICES		
	AT START OF YEAR	CURRENT	STANDARD	CURRENT	SIMULATED
Frozen standard	X		X		
Current-at-standard		X	X		
Current		X		X	
Simulated		X			X

Figure 2.7 Source data for different types of cost roll-up

costs, which have already been entered into the simulated cost fields, into the standard cost fields.

Where a product has undergone significant change in design or in manufacturing methods, its current-at-standard cost can be rolled over into the frozen cost field in order to maintain a realistic benchmark for measuring production performance. Changing the frozen standard in this way causes an automatic revaluation of any existing stocks, and may distort company-wide variance reporting. The accounts department must monitor the build variance arising from any mid-year change to a frozen standard, if the integrity of the management accounts is to be retained for the remainder of the financial year.

Current-at-standard, current and simulated costs all can be rolled up at any time. In the case of current-at-standard, there should be a review at no greater than monthly intervals, to ensure that costs are created for any new items. Frozen costs should never be rolled up in mid-year, or the benchmark costs will be overwritten and lost.

Actual costs

Actual costs calculations are quite different from standard costs. Whereas standard costing attempts to predict what the cost of a product should be, actual costing calculates what it really was. Actual costing enables the difference between the planned level of costs and the costs actually incurred to be measured, and variances reported.

Whenever purchased items are delivered, the difference between the invoiced (actual) price and the standard price can readily be calculated and used as a measure of purchasing performance. Manufacturing efficiency is measured by collecting actual cost data for each works order. The quantity of material issued to the order is readily available, and may be costed at the actual material price. Labour bookings at each operation enable the actual time taken to be monitored. This time may be converted into labour cost by applying the actual labour rate of the operator who carried out the work. Overhead costs such as set-up cost and consumable materials can be charged at actual usage to the works order in question.

When the works order is closed, all these actual costs can be accumulated and divided by the quantity of finished items booked into stores, to give an actual unit cost of the item. Order variances can also be produced, for material, labour and overhead. These in turn can be divided into usage (or efficiency) and price (or rate) variances. A wealth of information is generated for the production manager and the accountant.

Some practical points to be considered before using actual costing are as follows:

- Complete labour bookings must be made for every single operation carried out. If this is not done the actual costing system assumes that the labour was not used, and incorrectly calculates a favourable variance. Since for minor operations the cost of collecting the data may approach the cost of performing the operation, this may not be a cost-effective prospect.
- All material issues must be booked to the correct order. Any surplus material must be returned to stores from the order, rather than being treated as a miscellaneous receipt or simply used up on the next order, otherwise actual costing will assume all the material originally issued was used. Very tight shopfloor disciplines are needed to achieve this standard of booking accuracy.
- The cost of any scrap or reworking is hidden in the overall variances, rather than being highlighted and attributed to the operation at which it arose. Variances therefore provide limited help in tracking down the cause or even the location of scrap.
- Since every order for an item produces a different actual unit cost, a convention for valuing both inventory and issues to works orders must be adopted. Average costs or first in first out (FIFO) costings are often used. Since these conventions are quite arbitrary, the idea that actual costs are 'real' costs is undermined.

Managers considering using actual costing should consider carefully whether the benefits justify the work involved. In an engineering-to-order environment, where job costing is the normal method of confirming (or otherwise) the cost estimates used to price the contract, the disciplines and administration needed for actual costing are likely to be in place. Such companies can use actual costing in the same way as a job costing system, although they will need to find a way of aggregating individual works order costs by customer contract.

Companies engaged in repetitive manufacture probably have less to gain from the information produced by actual costing. Cost variances may excite the accountants but to most production people they are something to be explained away, rather than a means of improving performance. The one piece of information that could really be useful in focusing improvement effort - the cost and source of scrap - is hidden in a morass of variance data. Some fundamental questions concerning the relevance and use of traditional management accounting techniques are addressed in Chapter 7.

Summary

This chapter has presented, in a fairly concentrated manner, some of the most important tools and techniques that are contained within MRPII. Companies all too frequently embark upon MRPII implementations with little understanding of these tools and techniques, or of the system configuration choices that they offer. In the absence of any positive guidance from senior managers on system configuration, decisions are taken based on past practice, or are left to the system supplier, who may have little understanding of the company's business needs.

Configuration can help to customize the way a company uses MRPII, but it should not be used simply as a means of reproducing previous working practices. There is no point in installing an IBS just to keep on doing things the same way as before. MRPII means finding better ways. Successful implementation depends upon forming a very clear picture, at an early stage, of what MRPII will mean to the organization. This requires that senior managers carry out a fundamental business redesign process. The objective of this process is to decide how the company will operate in the future, and to determine the role of MRPII in realizing this vision. In other words, the organization must adapt itself to suit MRPII.

Only when this business redesign process has generated a vision of how the company will operate can software be chosen which will support that vision. Although the techniques described in this chapter are standard MRPII features, it would be most unwise to assume that all software systems on the market contain the facilities described. It is important firstly to form the vision, and then to select software that is capable of supporting it. The way to do this is described in the next chapter.

3

Computers and systems

The medium, not the message

Without computers and computer systems, MRPII would not exist. The enormous number of calculations involved in MRP, CRP and other functions could not be performed without computer assistance, and the opportunity for different departments within a business to base their work on shared data would not arise. Yet when companies run into difficulties implementing MRPII it is rarely a problem with the computer system that is the primary cause. Failures by senior managers to understand the role of MRPII, to design a suitable implementation process, to educate the workforce, and to change the culture of the organization cause far more failures than inappropriate system selection. It is with management concerns such as these, rather than issues of information technology, that this book is mainly concerned.

Nevertheless, computers and systems cannot be ignored. System selection, whilst it should not be allowed to dominate an MRPII project, is an important task. This chapter explains the issues which managers selecting systems need to understand, and describes how to go about making the best choice. Subsequent chapters discuss what managers need to do if they are successfully to turn their investment in computer systems into MRPII.

The role of system suppliers

Software developers have played a major role in breathing life into the MRPII concept. They have also influenced the way companies have implemented MRPII, through the education and training they provide, and through the innovations they have included in their software.

Developing a suite of integrated software that will support the MRPII concept is a major undertaking. In the early days, when simple batch processing systems were used, some companies designed their own software. Very few companies would contemplate such a step in these days of complex on-line processing and well established software packages. Indeed, one would have to question the judgement of any that do, in view of the cost, delay and risk involved.

Package software is now the almost universal approach, and there are some very competent products on the market. In fact the choice is now so large that it is almost impossible for a company to survey thoroughly the entire market-place before making a selection. In this competitive environment, suppliers struggle to differentiate their products. In truth, the differences between systems are often very small. The variations in detail can be important, however, particularly in areas such as master production scheduling, where a range of approaches is needed to cater for the varying demand management environments that are found.

In Chapter 1 a convention was established whereby the term integrated business system (IBS) would be used when discussing software. Some system suppliers use this expression to describe their products, although others prefer integrated manufacturing system or manufacturing control system. While some suppliers are keen to stress the MRPII capability of their products, others see marketing advantage in playing down the MRPII factor, and instead emphasize the advantages of systems integration.

Figure 3.1 shows a representation of the modules contained in a typical IBS. These modules support all the major operational tasks involved in running a manufacturing company. Some suppliers offer even more modules, in an attempt to give their product a competitive edge. Such systems are certainly business systems, rather than just manufacturing

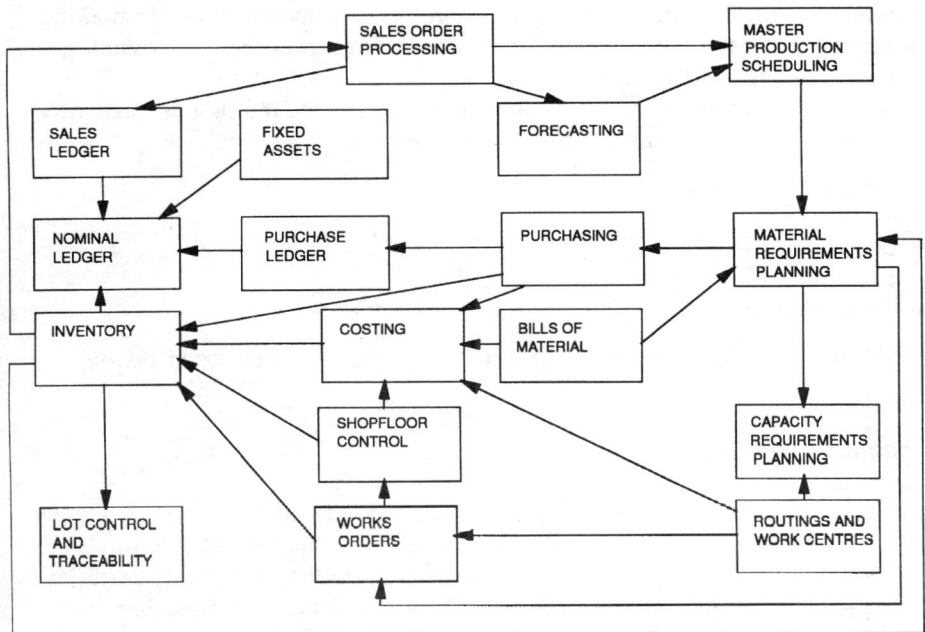

Figure 3.1 Schematic of a typical integrated business system

systems, and they are used by many companies whose business is not in manufacturing. Of course, for the majority of non-manufacturing companies operating these systems the closed loop MRP concept is not applicable. These companies cannot therefore be regarded as MRPII users.

Many manufacturing companies also fall short of achieving MRPII, in spite of implementing an IBS. Such companies either fail to implement the modules associated with MRP, or attempt to use them without any appreciation of the closed loop concept. In either case these companies are not getting the benefit they should from their considerable systems investment.

A look at computer technology

We are used to living in a world where computer technology advances at a formidable rate. This does not mean, however, that an IBS has a short shelf life. It is true that there is a steady flow onto the market of new packages, and of enhancements to existing ones, but generally change tends to be evolutionary rather than revolutionary. The cost of developing a completely new suite of software, together with the need to continue supporting existing users, create a strong preference amongst system suppliers for incremental change.

As a result, managers who are looking for a new system are often in the position of choosing between mature software that has good support, a great deal of functionality, but is based on rather dated technology, or a modern but unproven system with a more limited specification. In making this choice, it is necessary to understand what are the practical advantages of more modern technology.

There are five main areas in which computer technology is presently providing new opportunities for system users:

- integrated software
- downsizing
- user interfaces
- customizing
- open systems.

The implications of each of these developments are discussed below.

Integrated software

Until quite recently many of the software products that were sold as integrated systems were rather less integrated than might have been supposed. Often items of data used by different modules were duplicated in the system. The different records were reconciled either by regular batch updates, or sometimes by manually keying the same data into different sub-systems.

In early systems, integration was not a major issue. Processing was carried out in batch mode, so records only needed to be consistent at the time of each batch update. The introduction of on-line systems has created a much more dynamic environment. Now it is important that data is always consistent, and is readily accessible for both routine processing needs and for ad hoc enquiries.

Modern systems satisfy this requirement by using database management systems (DBMS). The role of the DBMS is to manage all the data used by the IBS, eliminating the need for duplication. The data is available when needed, not only to the various programs contained within the IBS, but to other business applications as well.

Systems are still available that fall between the old batch concepts and the modern database techniques. Whilst operating mainly in on-line mode, these systems hold data in large numbers of separate files. In everyday use there is little apparent difference between file-based systems and those which use a DBMS. Inbuilt procedures ensure that any inconsistencies are hidden from the routine user. The differences show, however, when data is needed for other purposes. This point will be explored further when discussing customizing.

Even in modern systems which are based upon a DBMS, integration may still be found to be lacking. The usual cause is that the software is actually a combination of two or more separate systems. These marriages of convenience occur when a supplier whose expertise lies primarily in manufacturing decides to offer a wider range of modules. Rather than develop these modules in-house, the supplier interfaces its products with specialist software developed by other suppliers. Examples of systems that are frequently bolted on in this way are financial ledgers, finite scheduling systems, shopfloor data capture systems, and even sales order processing systems.

The interfaces between these separate systems usually consist of regular batch updates which transfer data from one system to the other. This lack of integration can cause operational difficulties, although this is not always the case. Many companies, for example, actually prefer to keep their financial ledgers at arm's length from the manufacturing system. Full integration of financial systems can mean that every time a storekeeper transacts a material movement, the system immediately updates the general ledger. It can take some accountants quite a while to adjust to this degree of immediacy.

At the other extreme there are systems where the integration between the manufacturing and financial elements is almost non-existent. At best there may be batch transfer of sales invoice details to the sales ledger, and possibly some attempt to match purchase invoices in the purchase ledger with goods received records. Where integration is this loose, it is usually the case that the general ledger inventory is maintained quite separately from the manufacturing system's inventory control module. Systems operating in this way cannot really be described as integrated; they merely have a facility for limited data transfer.

When selecting a system, searching questions need to be asked of the supplier to uncover any areas where integration is lacking. The system may not be ruled out of contention because of a batch interface between modules, but it is as well to find out about it before purchasing the software rather than afterwards.

Downsizing

The most obvious change in computers over the years is the way they have reduced in size while increasing in performance. It is now possible to purchase high specification IBS products that are capable of running on networked personal computers (PC). These systems are capable of supporting quite large numbers of workstations and handling considerable volumes of data.

PC-based systems can be significantly less expensive than those using the more conventional central processor, particularly when a step-by-step approach is taken to implementation. Additional PCs can be added to the network, and new software modules purchased, as money becomes available. This approach is often very attractive to small companies which would be unable to afford the high initial cost of a multi-user system.

The availability of low-cost IBSs is clearly of enormous importance in providing small companies with MRPII capability. It is important to realize, however, that there is no such thing as cheap MRPII. The implementation of MRPII cannot be achieved without considerable expenditure in activities such as education and training, and setting up accurate product and process data. Whilst a successful implementation amply repays this investment, penny-pinching implementations rarely achieve the potential returns.

User interfaces

An additional advantage of PC-based systems is that there is now a very large pool of people working in industry who are familiar with PCs, mostly through exposure to spreadsheet and word processing applications. Using a PC-based IBS is a natural extension of this work, building upon the skills already acquired. System suppliers are beginning to respond to this type of user by building graphical user interfaces (features such as windows, icons and pull-down menus) into their products. This trend is likely to continue, utilizing the capabilities of the personal workstation to provide users with a much more attractive and manageable interface with their systems.

The attractions of graphical user interfaces (GUI) are such that this trend will not be restricted to PC-based systems. GUIs will increasingly become available on mid-range machines too.

Customizing

Many managers feel that their company is quite unlike any other, and that it needs unique solutions to its particular problems. How, then, can standard package software be of any use? In reality every manufacturing business has to undertake similar processes, such as entering customer orders, managing inventory, placing purchase orders and producing accounts. There are only so many different ways of doing these things, and a good software package will contain enough options to account for most of them.

That is not the same as saying that package software should enable companies to carry on doing things just as they always have. Increasingly companies are opting to change their ways of working to suit the software, rather than modifying the software to match the way they work. A policy of no system modifications is now quite common.

One reason for this change in approach is the realization that software modifications can cause far more problems than they solve. Modifications are expensive, and frequently fail to work as intended. Worse still, large scale modifications often result in the software supplier withdrawing maintenance support. New software releases cannot be taken up, even though they contain useful new facilities, because the cost of re-applying the modifications would be too great.

Some companies whose modified software has been overtaken by successive new software releases have decided to abandon their modifications and return to the latest release of the mainstream product. In a few cases this decision has been taken because the software now contains as standard the very enhancements that the company previously commissioned.

A second reason why companies now tend to be more willing to use standard software is the availability of advanced query languages. These languages are sometimes referred to as 4GLs (fourth generation languages), because they are considered to represent the fourth major advance in computer programming. The advantage of a 4GL is that it enables additional functionality to be built in to a system without actually changing the core software. Query languages have been around for a long time, but early ones were difficult to use, and often did little more than permit simple reports to be generated from one file of data at a time. If they were used at all, they tended to be the property of programming staff, rather than users.

The introduction of DBMS has changed all this. There are different types of database structure, but the form generally considered to be most suited for use with an IBS is the relational database. One reason for preferring relational databases is that they are very flexible in handling changing needs. New fields of data can easily be added without affecting the data structure already developed. A second advantage is the ease with which data can be retrieved and manipulated by a 4GL query language. Complex sub-systems can be developed relatively easily, enabling package software to be customized without impairing the core software. Furthermore, the use of relational databases provides the ability to access data from within many different applications used in the business. Relational databases and 4GLs therefore represent an important enabling technology for the introduction of computer integrated manufacturing (CIM).

Open systems

Selecting and implementing an IBS is a major undertaking for any company, and one that its managers would not wish to repeat very often. If the job has been done properly, it is unlikely that the company's business needs will change so extensively that the system will become inappropriate. Nevertheless there will be a need for evolutionary change, to reflect shifts in business focus, and also because users invariably seek further facilities as the system becomes more established.

It should be possible to grow the system in response to these requirements through a combination of three approaches. Firstly, reputable software suppliers provide regular upgrades that progressively add new facilities. The decision on what facilities should be added next is often based upon the recommendations of user groups, and on direct contacts with individual users, so there are opportunities to influence the supplier. Secondly, if suitable upgrades are not forthcoming, bespoke enhancements that do not affect core programs can be developed. Thirdly, links to other business applications that are beyond the scope of the IBS can be created. We have already seen how the second and third approaches are much more straightforward if the IBS is based upon a relational database.

Complete replacement of an IBS is, therefore, a task that should not need to be undertaken very frequently. Imagine, then, the frustration that is caused if a change in software is forced upon a company through hardware-related factors. Perhaps the use of the system has grown to such an extent that a bigger computer is needed. The present machine is the top model in the range, and an upgrade involves a change to a machine that is not software-compatible. Alternatively the existing computer may be old and unreliable, and the replacement model is again incompatible. Or perhaps there is a change in ownership of the company. The new owner insists on a change to its own preferred hardware supplier, but the existing IBS will not operate on the nominated machine. In each case the company is faced with the cost and upheaval of implementing a completely new IBS that may be no better, and perhaps less suitable, than the existing system.

The concept of open systems is intended to overcome this problem. In a world of open systems, application software would be totally portable between different computers. Whilst the computers themselves may operate in quite different ways, all would have an interface with the outside world that would make them appear the same to the application software. The open systems concept is yet to be fully realized, but sound progress is being made.

The most significant step towards open systems that IBS suppliers can take is to adopt the Unix operating system. An IBS that operates under Unix is not tied to any one particular make of computer, unlike those systems that are based upon proprietary operating systems. At present there are different versions of Unix, so there can still be some problems in moving between hardware supplied by manufacturers whose implementations of Unix are not identical. These problems, however, should not hide the very important benefits that Unix offers.

Software portability is only one aspect of open systems. The open systems concept is also concerned with overcoming the difficulties that arise in integrating different computer applications. The key issues to be tackled here are the means of communication between computers, the ability of different applications to share data, and the need for common user interfaces. The open systems movement aims to set internationally acceptable standards in all these areas.

In the case of communication between computers, the need for open standards is addressed through the International Standards Organization's (ISO) reference model for open systems interconnection. This model is widely referred to as 'the OSI model'. It identifies seven sets of activities, or layers, that are involved in the communication process. The tasks to be carried out in each layer are defined, but the specific protocols to be used are not. Different implementations of the seven layer model are therefore possible. One of the better known ones is the Manufacturing Automation Protocol (MAP).

Although the OSI model is well established, it has taken a long time for practical implementations such as MAP to become widely used. Without doubt OSI will become increasingly important as suppliers develop new generations of products, and users become aware of the advantages of open systems in a CIM environment. In the meantime, however, most computer communications are based upon the use of proprietary systems.

Openness in the sharing of data is approached through the use of relational databases, together with a standard query language. The query language SQL, which started out as a proprietary system, has since become an ISO standard. Like Unix, SQL achieved openness through its widespread use and acceptability. Open standards often originate from proprietary products. They may not meet all the criteria of a true open standard, but a working product that achieves much of what is required is better than any theoretical standard that has not yet been implemented.

As GUIs become more common there is an opportunity for software suppliers to develop IBS products, and other business applications, that operate within standard windowing environments. This would allow system users to move between the IBS and other applications simply by manipulating icons. Applications that are written around a standard GUI can be given a similar look and feel, so that users do not need to learn different ways of addressing each application.

In summary, the open systems movement is still evolving, and new standards are appearing at a steady rate. Practice is trailing some way behind theory, as can be seen by the limited use at present of OSI-based communications. The four main open systems issues that should be considered by managers involved in the selection of an IBS are:

- **System portability.** The Unix operating system provides an assurance that the IBS would be portable to a different manufacturer's hardware, if necessary. Unix is not the only operating system for which this is true (both Pick and MS-DOS can claim to provide an operating environment that offers portability), but it is the only one that is closely linked with the open systems movement.

- **Communication (Interconnection).** OSI-based communications will become increasingly important as a means of linking computers. At present, however, proprietary systems remain dominant. One example is a networking protocol commonly associated with Unix, called TCP/IP. This protocol is not OSI-compliant, but it has acquired the status of an industry standard.

- **Data sharing (Interworking).** The use of relational databases, together with the query language SQL, enables data contained in different applications (such as, for example, a personnel database, or a preventive maintenance system) to be shared with the IBS. Some of the issues to be resolved when linking different applications together are discussed in later chapters.

- **Standard user interface.** The trend towards GUIs will continue. The adoption of standards in this area allows users to move readily between different applications, being presented with the same appearance and 'feel'. User training can focus upon what each application does, rather than how to use it.

Is computer technology really important?

The question asked earlier in this chapter still stands. How does a company choose between a mature system that has a comprehensive specification, but is based on dated technology, and a Unix-based, relational database system which is as yet less well developed and relatively unproven?

The starting point is to decide those key facilities that must be available to meet the particular needs of the company. For example, is master production scheduling to be carried out through the use of modular planning bills, with products configured to the customer's order through the selection of features and options? If so, the software must be able to provide these facilities. There is simply no point in acquiring software that is incapable of carrying out the necessary tasks. The implementation of such a system cannot succeed, and any thoughts of future portability or of integration with other systems become irrelevant. If, on the other hand, a choice of software packages is available that meet the essential business needs, then technology becomes an important factor to take into account during the decision process.

Should the final choice lie between suppliers whose systems are not open, it is well worth investigating the commitment of each to the open systems concept. Some suppliers might be enthusiastic in principle, but are presently trapped in older technology for historical reasons. Others may be more lukewarm, although few suppliers will admit to not having an open systems strategy. Managers probing the extent of a supplier's commitment should ask:

- When will a Unix-based, and/or relational database version of the software be available?

- What arrangements will be made to enable users of the existing system to migrate to the Unix version?
- Which version of Unix will be adopted, and which hardware suppliers support that version?
- What Unix expertise is there currently within the supplier's organization?
- Are there any communication facilities incorporated into the system (e.g. links with shopfloor devices)? Are these compatible with OSI standards?
- Will the supplier continue to market proprietary products after open products have been launched?

Technology is only as important as the added facilities that it makes available to a business. If a system supplier offers what appears to be wonderful new technology but is unable to explain its advantages in everyday language, the benefits of that technology should be regarded as dubious. On the other hand, the technology of open systems *is* important, as a secondary factor, after functionality issues have been resolved. It would be unwise to ignore the implications of open systems when selecting an IBS.

Trends in package software

As system suppliers offer ever more facilities in their IBS products, the need to produce bespoke software or to carry out modifications to packages decreases. There are now very few companies that could not find a system capable of meeting their essential needs. This continuing drive to expand system functionality has resulted in some discernible trends. Some of the more significant enhancements that many suppliers are now providing are described in the following sections.

Flow-based manufacturing

One aspect of MRPII that severely limited its applicability in the past is the use of works orders to schedule production and to control material movements through the factory. In many companies the use of works orders is not appropriate, because work is not processed in physical batches that can be associated with specific orders. The types of production in which works orders are not applicable are:

- **Continuous process manufacture.** A continuous process is one in which a finished product flows continuously from the manufacturing facility. Changeovers to different products, if they happen at all, are very infrequent. Examples of continuous process manufacture are oil refineries and steel works.
- **Repetitive manufacture.** In repetitive manufacture, changeovers are again infrequent or non-existent. In this case, however, a succession of

discrete products leaves the end of the manufacturing process. Examples are the assembly of washing machines and television sets.

- **Levelled schedule manufacture.** One of the techniques commonly associated with just-in-time (JIT) manufacture is level scheduling. The objective of level scheduling is to smooth production by making a constant quantity of each product every day. This approach can involve mixed model production, in which a production facility makes some of every product every day. Since daily output matches average daily demand, inventory is minimized. JIT techniques, including level scheduling, are examined in greater detail in Chapter 6.

The characteristic that all these forms of production have in common is that they are flow-based rather than batch-based. Some system suppliers offer modules that address the needs of flow-based production. Sometimes these modules are targeted mainly at repetitive and JIT manufacture, in other cases they are extended into full process industry versions of the software.

The basic requirement of flow-based control systems is that they use rate scheduling instead of works orders. In rate scheduling daily production targets are set, based upon normal output rates. There is no works order to release and to close. Instead production is tracked by item number, production line and day. Over- or under-production at the end of each day can be carried over to the next day, or written off, as required. The system tracks cumulative actual output against plan throughout each production period.

Material usage is usually post-deducted by backflushing reported production, or by pulling through the materials used at each reported operation (see Chapter 2). Some systems provide an electronic kanban facility to place replenishment orders for components and raw materials. Scrap or yield is reported daily, and also cumulatively from the start of the production period.

Rate scheduling is of great importance to the three types of flow-based production defined above. In the case of process industries, such as chemicals, pharmaceuticals and food manufacture, there are several other ways in which systems based upon batch engineering concepts are inappropriate. Systems aimed specifically at process industries should be able to address the following issues:

- **By-products.** The manufacture of one product sometimes results in by-products being produced. Systems that are not specifically designed to handle by-products are likely to have difficulty with costing and inventory control.
- **Co-products.** Sometimes two similar products are scheduled to be produced together, to make more efficient use of process plant. These co-products must be treated as if they were a single product for scheduling purposes, whilst retaining individual identities for other purposes.
- **Clean-down cycle.** Production often needs to be scheduled in pre-determined cycles. For example, paints and dyes are cycled from light

colours to progressively darker ones. At the end of the cycle a complete clean-down is needed before the next cycle can begin. A similar situation arises in food manufacture, where mild flavours are followed by increasingly strong ones.

- **Recipes.** Sometimes several alternative recipes or formulae can be used to manufacture a product. The recipe used for a particular batch depends upon the cost and availability of ingredients at the time. Systems designed primarily for engineering companies assume that each product only has one (current) bill of material.
- **Production and process data.** In engineering-based systems the creation of the bill of material is often regarded as a separate activity from the preparation of the manufacturing routing. In process industries these two activities need to be tied closely together, since process decisions are inseparable from product specification decisions.
- **Shelf life.** Many ingredients used in process industries, and the products that are produced, are subject to limited shelf lives. Expiry dates need to be tracked by the inventory control system, so that materials can be used by earliest date, and quarantined should they exceed the date specified.

Very few process companies operate exclusively in continuous process mode. Many start off with continuous manufacture of a core product, but then become progressively batch-oriented. Often the transition is most noticeable at the packing stage, where products manufactured in bulk are enclosed in a variety of sizes and types of packaging. Customer-specified packs and differing national labelling requirements often lead to a seemingly endless variety of finished products, manufactured in relatively small batches. Process industry software that cannot cater for batch production and flow production within the same system is unlikely to be suitable in this environment.

Quality support

In the early days, MRPII's only active interest in quality was the provision of scrap or yield percentages. This facility merely ensured that whatever the expected scrap rate, MRP would plan enough material to cover it. Things have moved on since then, and quality is now recognized as fundamental to all business activities. Facilities now available in some IBS products that offer support to quality management include the following.

Process documentation

The routing record contains details of every operation to be carried out in the manufacture of an item. Usually only a brief description of the work to be performed is displayed in the routing record, but in some systems this is backed up by a full process definition to which machine setters and operators can refer. In this way nothing is left to chance, and updating of process documentation is prompted when the routing is changed.

Lot traceability

In some industries, such as food, pharmaceuticals, defence, and aerospace, it is essential to be able to trace particular lot numbers of raw materials right through the production process. Many systems now offer a traceability facility, although the practical difficulties in applying it mean that relatively few companies have working implementations. The problem is not the software, but the difficulty in maintaining the physical identity of specific lots on the shopfloor.

Scrap reporting

Standard works order reporting methods allow scrap to be recorded at each operation, but this often achieves very little. The main objective is to allow quantities of materials leaving each operation to be balanced with the quantity arriving. So if 100 items were recorded as completing operation one, and 95 items completed operation two, the system would expect to receive a scrap report for the remaining five. If no such transaction is received, a discrepancy report would be printed.

Costs of scrap and rectification are rarely calculated from these operation bookings. Instead they are hidden in works order material usage and labour efficiency variances. These cost variances are deduced by comparing total actual usage of material and labour on the works order with standard usage. As the figures are not extracted from scrap reports, nor are they reconciled with those reports, it is impossible to establish where and why the scrap was created.

Some systems now offer additional quality analyses. Works order reporting data is analyzed to produce management reports highlighting precisely the level of scrap produced and the operation at which it occurred. With this information, managers can focus quality improvement efforts where they are most needed.

In process industries it is generally yield rather than scrap which needs to be measured. Yield is often the most critical aspect of production efficiency, so accurate and detailed reporting is vital.

Supply chain management

Supply chain management is concerned with improving the flow of materials from the source of the raw material through to the delivery of finished products to the customer. If material flows are to be effective, there needs to be a flow of information between customer, distribution network, manufacturer and supplier, at all stages in the supply chain. Within the manufacturing organization, MRPII manages the information flows. The information system that carries out a similar function in the distribution network is called distribution resource planning (DRP).

DRP uses techniques similar to those used by MPS and MRP to schedule material movements within the distribution system. The main application of DRP is in multi-stocking point distribution networks, such as those where regional warehouses service local depots which in turn supply goods to a wide geographical spread of customers. Without DRP, each stocking point would have independent stock control systems generating replenishment orders at unpredictable intervals. The unfortunate tendency of this fragmented method of inventory control to turn a steady end-user demand into a sporadic, lumpy loading on the production facility is well known. Christopher (1986) provides an effective illustration of this phenomenon.

DRP overcomes this problem by extending the concept of dependent demand into the supply chain. Only the final stocking points are subject to independent demand, while all preceding stages in the supply chain experience dependent demand. Customer requirements at each depot should therefore be forecasted, and time-phased stock replenishment orders planned to satisfy the forecasts. DRP aggregates these orders at the preceding stage of the distribution network (e.g. a regional warehouse which supplies the depots) in order to calculate the dependent demand at that point. Existing warehouse stocks are then netted off, to produce the next level of time-phased requirements. This process is repeated back through the distribution network until the factory is reached. At this point the aggregated requirements provide the input to the factory's master production scheduling process.

DRP is able to monitor stock in transit as well as stock physically located in a warehouse or depot, so there is consistent visibility of inventory at all times. Often DRP systems are able to recommend the movement of stock between stocking points, where this action would be a cost-effective method of satisfying customer orders.

Clearly there is considerable merit in the DRP system and the IBS being fully integrated and compatible. Many system suppliers now offer DRP modules within their IBS products that provide this integration.

An alternative form of distribution is that in which a manufacturer supplies its customers direct. Here the customer places an order, or call-off schedule, and the supplier delivers the goods at the required time. No intermediate stocking points are required. In this type of distribution, delays, errors and excessive costs can arise both in raising the paperwork and posting or faxing it to the supplier, and in order interpretation and entry at the receiving company. Electronic data interchange (EDI) is being used increasingly to eliminate these problems.

In its most basic form, EDI is concerned with the electronic transmission of purchase requirements in such a way that they can be input directly to the supplier's systems. To achieve this, standards for the presentation and communication of data must be agreed. Often the pressure to move to EDI comes from large, powerful customers who can generally dictate their preferred standards. Smaller suppliers are then left having to cope with a variety of standards imposed by different customers.

Some advanced users of EDI give visibility of their finished goods inventory, and even their final assembly schedules, to their customers. Orders can then be placed directly, and stock allocated, without the need to make telephoned delivery enquiries. EDI can also be used to transfer funds in settlement of accounts, and for providing product technical information to customers. As the use and importance of EDI grows, it is essential that IBS suppliers keep abreast of the latest developments, and provide appropriate support in their software.

Shopfloor scheduling

Although MRP determines works order start dates and due dates, and keeps them current as circumstances change, these dates alone are not always sufficient for detailed scheduling of production processes. Many system suppliers now provide additional tools for scheduling, as separate system modules. These modules take works orders planned by MRP and build up a detailed work schedule that takes account of the finite availability of resources. Chapter 6 examines the reasons for using shopfloor scheduling systems, and explores the issues involved in their selection and use.

The higher-level scheduling activities involved in master production scheduling are also beginning to receive further attention from some system suppliers. Creating the MPS is one of the most complex tasks in a manufacturing business, and one that inevitably involves trade-offs being made. MPS and RCCP modules enable alternative schedules to be modelled, but they neither provide a means to evaluate and compare the results nor suggest how to make improvements. The planner is left to rely upon job knowledge to construct the MPS, with no way of proving to sceptics that the end result is the best possible solution. Under these circumstances it can be difficult for managers to accept the compromises implicit in the MPS.

Master scheduling decision support systems are beginning to appear that are built upon knowledge-based systems methodologies. By providing a simulation, or 'what if' facility these systems have the potential to provide the planner with some real help in optimizing the MPS. Since an MPS that fully satisfies the criteria laid down by top management has the best chance of being accepted by all concerned, these systems may prove extremely valuable.

System selection

Choosing the right IBS is an important and time-consuming process. There are many good systems available, and the differences between them are often not all that great. But those differences can be significant. Implementing MRPII is a difficult task, and starting off with software that is less suitable than it could be is an unnecessary handicap.

One problem is that this important decision has to be taken early on in the course of an MRPII implementation project, often before the managers within the company are fully aware of all the issues involved. Decisions tend to be either taken on the basis of superficial factors, or left to an external consultant. Both approaches are less than ideal. The only sure route to the selection of the most appropriate system is the following systematic process.

Awareness tutorial

The right starting point for an MRPII project is a decision by the top managers of a company to invest a day of their time in finding out how MRPII could help them run their business. Some of the managers may already have experience of MRPII, and indeed the company may already have elements of an IBS. Even so, a day in which the top management team builds a shared understanding of what MRPII is, and what will have to be done within their company to implement it, is indispensable.

This awareness tutorial should be led by someone from outside the company. There may be insiders with the necessary expertise, but they are often too junior to convey the message with sufficient authority. Furthermore, any insider will be associated with a functional department, and therefore deemed by others to be lacking in objectivity.

At the conclusion of the awareness tutorial, the top management team should have a clear idea of the benefits of implementing MRPII, and also an understanding of the commitment to change that it will demand of them.

Feasibility study

An MRPII project involves significant capital investment so, before proceeding, the company must satisfy itself (and possibly its parent company, shareholders or bankers) that the money will be well spent. The next step, therefore, is to carry out a feasibility study. No matter how much evangelical zeal fills the top managers after their awareness tutorial, there may be hidden difficulties or more urgent priorities that only become apparent when a detailed analysis is made. The feasibility study should put the proposed investment into the context of the company's business plans, and enable it to be assessed against other calls on the company's capital and managerial resources.

It is impossible to carry out a feasibility study properly without creating a vision of how the company would operate once MRPII had been implemented. To create this vision, the top managers must undertake the initial stage of a business redesign process. In this stage of the process, top managers agree the changes that introducing MRPII would require of the company, and of themselves. Perhaps there are existing company policies that are incompatible with MRPII, and must therefore be revised. Perhaps organizational restructuring will be needed. Far-reaching changes in the way the company carries out its business may be possible, such as moving from a make-for-stock to an assemble-to-order company. By building and agreeing this picture, top managers ensure that costs and benefits arising from the implementation of MRPII can be identified and evaluated.

The vision created by this process has a value that extends beyond the feasibility study. It is important, therefore, to draw up a formal vision statement. Chapter 4 explains how this vision statement is used to drive later stages of the business redesign process. The vision statement can act as a beacon throughout the difficult times that most MRPII implementations experience at some stage. It should include specific, quantifiable performance goals that can be used in monitoring progress as the project proceeds.

The feasibility study should conclude with a report containing the following information:

- vision statement and project objectives
- estimated costs of the project, both one-off charges associated with the implementation, and on-going costs
- likely benefits arising from the project, including intangible benefits such as improvements in customer service, as well as financial ones
- implications arising from the implementation of the project, such as changes in management style or organization structure
- alternative projects considered, and reasons for rejecting them
- an outline description of the computer system required, and the main functions it would perform
- recommendations, including an outline implementation timetable and cash flows.

At this stage both costs and benefits would be very approximate. Capital costs should include system costs (hardware and software), cabling and installation, and initial data preparation and entry (or conversion from existing systems). To these costs must be added an allowance for education, training and outside assistance. As a guide, this allowance should be calculated as 50% of the system costs. A lower assumption would create the possibility of unpleasant surprises later on.

Benefits should be conservatively estimated. The main quantifiable financial saving usually arises from a reduction in inventory, although increased production efficiency, higher output rates and reduced purchasing costs could also be expected from a successful implementation. Overhead costs should fall as the benefits of shared data and integrated systems are achieved. Intangible benefits could include reduced lead time, improved delivery performance, fewer order acknowledgement and invoicing errors, and faster response to customer enquiries. These intangible benefits may well result in increased sales, but it is very difficult to predict the extent of any such improvement. It is also difficult to assess subsequently whether the predicted benefit actually occurred, since variations in order intake can be caused by so many factors.

Verifying that anticipated benefits are in fact achieved is an important task. It very easy to forget about the anticipated benefits once the company moves into the excitement of MRPII implementation. Yet the predicted benefits should become targets against which the success of the project is assessed. All too often implementation becomes an end in itself, and the benefits are taken for granted. In reality, savings rarely drop out automatically. Managers have to go looking for them, and the use of targets provides the impetus to do so.

Project launch

Once the feasibility study has been completed, and its recommendations accepted, top management must appoint a project leader and select a core implementation team. This team will have responsibility for seeing through the entire MRPII project. Project management structure will be discussed in more detail in the next chapter.

The core team must receive initial MRPII education, to prepare them for the next stage in the project: drawing up the system specification. This education is one of the most neglected areas in MRPII implementations. Even companies that are prepared to spend large amounts of money training staff after the system has been selected and installed often neglect education prior to system specification.

If the people responsible for the specification do not fully understand the options that are open to them, the specification will contain only trivia. Many system specifications are no more than a set of unco-ordinated wish lists gleaned from middle-managers who themselves do not understand MRPII. The thrust of such specifications is to describe the existing ways of doing things, rather than to contain a vision of how things should be in the future. The manager who specifies the need for automatic printing of daily shortage lists has not begun to understand how MRPII eliminates the need not only for shortage lists, but for expeditors as well.

Once the core team has received adequate MRPII education it is in a position formally to launch the project. This event should incorporate as much razzmatazz as the company can muster. Newsletters, posters, team briefings and all the other means of communication open to the company should be used to inform all employees that something is starting that will impact upon every single one of them. MRPII is an all-embracing business strategy. The earlier the company's employees realize that something big is about to happen, the more chance they will have to adapt to the changes that are coming.

System specification

The system specification is not a technical document that only information technology (IT) specialists can understand. It is a statement of the functions that the system will need to perform in order to support an MRPII implementation within the company. The specification is sometimes referred to as either a functional or a user specification.

The difficult in writing a user specification is that to specify fully all the required functions is an enormous task. Some specifications attempt to do this, and the result is a checklist of many hundreds or even thousands of required features. Almost certainly there will be no one package system that satisfies all these needs, so judgement is required to select the system that seems to offer the best fit.

In a specification prepared in this way, probably about 80% of the contents are standard features that any reputable system could satisfy. They are therefore irrelevant to the selection process. Other questions are, of necessity, expressed with such brevity that alternative interpretations are possible. A supplier responding to such questions will naturally assume an interpretation that can be satisfied rather than one that cannot, and so record a positive response.

The outcome is that the company is faced with several alternative products, each of which achieves a high percentage correlation with the specification, but none of which satisfies it exactly. The decision process has not moved forward at all. Often the selection is then based on other grounds, such as price, and the whole costly process of preparing the specification has achieved nothing.

A better approach to system specification is as follows:

- **Build upon the vision statement.** The business redesign process developed a vision statement of how the company will operate in the future. The core team, using their new knowledge about the workings of MRPII, must identify the key software features that this vision implies. Armed with this information, they must work with the managers concerned, jointly to agree a specification that meets future, rather than existing needs.
- **Understand the options.** The core team should research the package software market, and identify a number of possible suppliers. By examining the suppliers' product specifications, asking a few questions, and attending a few demonstrations, it will become clear which features are universally available, and which are not.
- **Focus on the exceptions.** The written specification may then be prepared, describing in some detail those features which are critical to the successful operation of the system, and particularly those which are less commonly found. Standard features can be specified in much more general terms.
- **Specify what, not how.** It is frequently the case that software suppliers have developed different ways of achieving a particular end result. A specification that concentrates on how things should be done, rather than on the result to be achieved, may rule out a perfectly acceptable system.
- **Explain the issues thoroughly.** The specification should help the supplier to understand the unique characteristics of the company, and how they are to be managed. The use of abbreviated notes and obscure jargon terms should be avoided.

Invitation to tender

The system specification is the main element of the invitation to tender (ITT), but other requirements also need to be specified. Typically the ITT might include the following sections:

- **Company background.** An outline of the company's business, reasons for implementing the proposed system, and a description of any existing computer applications.
- **System specification.** This is the detailed user specification. Tendering organizations should be asked to respond in detail to all points covered by the specification.
- **Hardware configuration.** This section would specify:
  - the number of VDUs (including any at remote locations)
  - the number of printers, together with speed and quality requirements
  - backing-up facilities, such as tape streamers.
- **System sizing information.** Suppliers submitting tenders need information that will enable them to calculate data handling and storage requirements. Estimates should be provided of likely transaction volumes and file sizes. The following list gives an idea of the kind of information that should be included:
  - number of items (part numbers)
  - number of bill of material links
  - number of routing records, and average number of operations per routing
  - number of suppliers
  - number of customers
  - number of inventory transactions daily (and peak rate, if not spread evenly across the day)
  - number of ledger postings daily
  - number of sales orders daily, and average number of lines per order
  - number of purchase orders daily
  - number of works orders raised daily
  - number of works order bookings daily
  - number of live sales orders, purchase orders and works orders.

  Estimates should be provided both at current volumes and at projected volumes in two to three years' time. The ITT should require tendering companies to state the point at which an upgrade to the proposed hardware would be required, and to provide details of what that upgrade would involve.
- **Operational requirements.** This section will either specify, or ask for information on, a range of items such as:
  - compliance with open systems (Unix, relational databases, query languages, OSI)
  - environmental conditions (e.g. will a dust-free, air-conditioned room be required?)
  - recovery procedure from system failure (e.g. is recovery up to the last back-up, or up to the last completed transaction?)
  - interfacing and communication requirements with existing systems, or externally (e.g. through EDI networks).
- **Support.** The system supplier should be able to offer full system documentation, user training, hotline telephone support, and hardware

maintenance. The availability of these services must be confirmed by tendering organizations, and costs provided. Maximum response times for reacting to problems should also be specified.

- **Contractual requirements.** Requirements concerning the terms and conditions of any resulting contract would be specified in this section. Delivery timescales and acceptance testing procedures would also be included. A point to be clarified is ownership of the source code of the system. Source code means the computer programs which make up the system in readable, maintainable form. System suppliers frequently supply only the object code, which enables the system to run but which cannot be modified. If source code is not to be supplied, there should be arrangements whereby ownership of the source code would pass to the user in the event of the supplier going out of business. This is called an escrow agreement.
- **Other information.** This section provides the opportunity to request tendering organizations to include any other information that might help the decision process. Examples are:
  - information about the ownership and financial status of the supplier
  - number of existing users of the system, and details of reference sites
  - details of any modifications to the standard software that the supplier is proposing to carry out in order to satisfy the system specification
  - details of any part of the proposed system that is to be provided by a third party
  - recommendations on the specialist support staff needed for satisfactory operation of the proposed computer system.

The ITT should be sent to no more than about six suppliers, all of which should have already been investigated and found likely to be able to comply with the specification. Each supplier would have been asked to confirm its willingness to respond. There is no point in sending out large numbers of unannounced tenders, since many suppliers would simply not bother to reply. Those that did could well be the ones most desperately in need of an order. The busy, successful suppliers are perhaps the ones least likely to regard the ITT as serious.

The assumption has been made that new computer hardware will be required. Any existing computer would almost certainly require a major upgrade if it is to run a full IBS, rather than (or in addition to) whatever went before. There will be a period when both systems, old and new, are installed on the machine together, so the capacity of the computer would have to be sufficient for that peak loading. Upgrading the existing machine may be nearly as expensive as purchasing a new one, and may have the disadvantage of restricting the choice of software. It is usually better to choose the most suitable software, even if it does mean a change of hardware.

A further assumption is that a single supplier will be responsible for providing both hardware and software. This is by far the most common practice. It is very much in the interests of the purchasing company, which can expect the supplier to take full responsibility for a turnkey installation. Where more complex requirements have been specified, particularly involving integration with other systems, the supplier may propose using a third party for the integration work. Any contract entered into must make it very clear who is the prime contractor, and precisely what they are responsible for.

Suppliers should be allowed reasonable, but not excessive time to respond to the ITT; about three to four weeks should be adequate. Failure to achieve the specified time would not necessarily rule a supplier out, but should be regarded as a possible sign of inadequate commitment and reliability.

Tender assessment

Since each tender contains a large amount of information, comparing them is a difficult task. One approach is to decide a weighting to be given to each section of the tender (system specification, operational requirements, support etc), and to define a system for allocating marks to each item within the sections. Ranking the tenders then becomes a simple matter of adding up the scores. The main advantage of this approach is that so long as the marking scheme is decided before the tenders are received, ranking becomes a totally objective process. If there is a need to demonstrate impartiality in the way the decision is made, a scoring system is difficult to beat.

However, scoring systems have little to recommend them when demonstrable impartiality is not an issue. Any marking system is quite arbitrary, and different weightings can lead to very different results. Any one feature can only be allocated a relatively small proportion of the total marks, whatever the weightings used, yet in practice there will be several items which are of very great importance. A system that failed to satisfy two or three such requirements might be a very poor choice, even if it achieved a high overall score.

In this type of situation, human capacity for intuitive assessment is vastly preferably to mathematical logic. The best method of ranking tenders is for the core project team members each to study the tenders, and then agree in open debate on an order of ranking. This method not only leads to the best results, it also ensures the commitment of the core team to the eventual choice.

The extent to which cost affects the decision will depend upon the attitude of the company concerned. Some companies choose the system that is the best match to their requirements, almost without regard for price; others operate within a tight budget. In the latter case, only suppliers whose products are likely to fall into an acceptable price range should be invited to tender, or a great deal of time will be wasted on both sides.

When analyzing the costs quoted in the tenders, care should be taken to ensure that like is being compared with like. An apparently low quoted cost could mean that the supplier has missed out an essential item of equipment, or made an arithmetic error. The best approach is to draw up a table of all items of software, hardware and services that are required, enter the costs each supplier has quoted for each item, and build up a comparable cost for each supplier.

Although the one-off costs are the most significant, on-going charges for hardware and software maintenance contracts should not be ignored. Of even greater importance is the size of any specialist support staff that might be required to operate the computer.

There are several danger signals for which tender assessors should be on the alert. These include the following, although there are probably other variations:

- promises that a required feature will be available in the next software release (it probably will not)
- proposals to supply hardware that is at, or near, the top of the range (successful users always need to move to a larger machine much earlier than they expected)
- tenders specifying smaller, less powerful (and therefore lower-cost) computer hardware than comparable tenders. Explanations claiming that "our software is more efficient" should be treated with caution
- proposals to convert a system to run on a different computer, or under a different operating system, from the one that it has previously used
- failure to respond to any specific points raised in the ITT
- over-emphasis on supposedly superior technical features not mentioned in the ITT
- unwillingness to supply reference sites (some suppliers will provide a complete list of all users of their system).

The output from the tender assessment stage is a ranked list of suppliers. The differences between the top two or three are unlikely to be so great that the final choice is obvious. Even if there is a strong front runner, it is still too early to make a final choice.

Shortlist investigation

The next stage in the selection process is for the top ranking two or three suppliers to move onto a final shortlist, for further investigation. No more than three companies should be included, because this stage is quite time-consuming. It is best to choose only two, keeping a third in reserve. If one of the favoured two suppliers is later ruled out, the reserve can be brought into play. In that way it is always possible to make comparisons.

Shortlist investigation should include the following activities:

- formal presentations by each supplier
- visits to selected user sites
- telephone survey of other reference sites
- demonstrations of the software
- hands-on use of the system at the supplier's premises
- examination of user documentation supplied with the system.

This stage of the project has four objectives. The first is to learn from the experience of other users. Questions to ask at reference sites include:

- which modules are you using? (sometimes reference sites are found to be using only a few basic elements of the system)
- does the software work properly, or does it contain 'bugs'?
- was the tender document accurate, in particular:
  - was the equipment quoted adequate for the task?
  - did the software perform as stated?
  - were the costings provided accurate?
  - was the system delivered within the lead time stated?
- how well was training carried out?
- has the supplier responded quickly and effectively to requests for help?

The second objective of the shortlist investigation is to find out if a good working relationship is possible with the supplier. If individuals within the user's organization and the supplier's cannot establish a reasonable rapport, it is likely that friction will arise when the going gets harder. The shortlist investigation throws people from the two companies together, and provides early warning of any possible problems. For this process to work properly it is important to get beyond the salesman, and to make contact with the people who would provide implementation support and training.

Thirdly, the shortlist investigation is an opportunity to examine the software at first hand. Care should be taken not to place too much emphasis on this activity. It is all too easy to let the appearance of the system override far more important criteria. Attractive screen layout, effective use of colour and graphical displays are very seductive, but also much less important than system functionality, supplier support and training provision.

Furthermore, appearances can be very deceptive. For example, a system that has simple, uncluttered screen displays may in fact provide too little information for serious users. Similarly a system that has an apparently clear and logical hierarchy of menus may prove very slow in practice, when moving from one transaction to another. On the other hand, a system which enables users to key a code number (or hit a function key) to access the screen needed for the next transaction may look more complicated, but could prove much faster. Regular users will soon remember the codes they use routinely.

Some systems allow screen displays to be customized without the need to change the software. This can be useful if the data presented on the standard screen displays is not what is needed, or if the company is anxious to retain its own terminology for particular types of data.

The final objective of the shortlist investigation is to expose the system to as many people within the company as possible. The people who will eventually use the system should be allowed to provide some input to the decision process, even if they do not yet fully understand how the system will work. They may nevertheless come up with some very practical questions that the experts had overlooked, and they will certainly appreciate being asked for their opinion.

At the conclusion of the shortlist investigation, the core implementation team must review all the information and opinions that they have gathered, and decide on their preferred supplier. The team must then put their recommendation to the company's top management team for approval.

Negotiation

The final stage in system selection is the negotiation of the contract. This should not be regarded as simply an opportunity for the company to see how big a discount can be extracted from the preferred supplier. There are substantive issues yet to be resolved. Most tenders contain options and alternatives. The company now has to decide exactly what it needs to purchase.

Care must be taken over the details of the contract, to ensure that they are reasonable and acceptable. No matter what promises, estimates, suggestions and guarantees the tender may contain, the contract is the only document to which the supplier can be held accountable. Whilst no purchaser would wish the contract to end up in dispute, it is important to be certain that if it should, the interests of the company are protected.

This stage of the selection process is the final chance for the company to satisfy itself of the viability of the preferred supplier. This is not a stable market, and there are many small suppliers competing for business. The continued existence of any one supplier should not be taken for granted.

Professional help

Buying a computer system without professional help is rather like buying a house without using an estate agent, surveyor or solicitor. It can be done, and it might save some money, but it is very risky and could end up costing a great deal more. Some companies go to the other extreme, expecting outside consultants to select systems for them. This, also, is not a good idea.

An experienced consultant should be able to guide and advise during the selection process, without actually taking on responsibility for making the decision. Particular areas where outside expertise is valuable are as follows:

- **Awareness tutorial.** This can only be led satisfactorily by an external adviser. The necessary expertise in MRPII is unlikely to be available internally. Objectivity is also essential at this point, if top managers are to be convinced of the advantages of MRPII. Insiders are unlikely to be perceived as being totally free of bias.
- **Feasibility study.** A consultant would provide experience in identifying likely benefits and costs, an outsider's view of changes needed within the business, and a knowledge of potential alternative projects that should be considered.

- **Project launch.** The consultant would advise on the structure and membership of the core implementation team. People appointed to the team would require MRPII education, which the consultant would be able to provide.
- **System specification.** A thorough understanding of the alternative approaches available within the MRPII concept is needed when preparing the system specification. The consultant would guide the company through the key issues to be addressed, ensuring that decisions were taken based upon a real understanding of those issues. As system requirements became clearer, the consultant would advise on which were unusual, and so required emphasis in the specification, and which were routine.
- **ITT.** The consultant would be experienced at collecting the information needed in the ITT, and would be able to identify suitable suppliers to which the document should be sent.
- **Tender assessment.** Expertise may be required in evaluating technical matters raised by suppliers in their tenders. Highlighting differences between tenders and restating costs on a comparable basis both require a certain amount of interpretation of technical information. An experienced consultant carrying out this work would also be able to spot any danger signals appearing in a tender.
- **Shortlist investigation.** This activity must be carried out by people from the company selecting the system. It opens up the decision process to a larger group of people, and exposes them to the shortlisted systems and to the suppliers' personnel. The consultant's role is to ensure that the company is not distracted from the main decision criteria by trivia, or by suppliers' sales talk.

At the conclusion of this process, the company is quite entitled to ask the consultant to recommend a preferred system, and to give reasons for the choice. This recommendation should be regarded as one more piece of information in the decision process, rather than a delegation of the decision to the consultant. It is essential that the people within the company who will be responsible for implementing the system make the final choice. If there is any feeling that the system has been imposed, or that if it fails then someone else is to blame, the willingness to make it work will be weakened. No system is ever a perfect fit, and it requires real commitment to overcome the shortfalls. People who knowingly accepted those shortfalls will work hard to get around them, and make the system work.

4

Implementation

Implementation the right way

Implementing MRPII is a daunting task for any company. It involves installing a company-wide integrated computer system while simultaneously adopting a completely new, planning-based approach to managing the business. The high risk and low success rate associated with MRPII have become notorious throughout manufacturing industry. It is hardly surprising that many managers prefer to seek lower-risk options for improving business performance.

Many surveys have been carried out to investigate the success rate of MRPII implementations. Some of these surveys support the belief that the great majority of implementations fail, but others point to the improved performance achieved by companies using MRPII. These apparently contradictory findings are, in fact, quite consistent. Relatively few companies seem fully to adopt the MRPII philosophy, and so achieve the benefits they had expected. Nevertheless, most companies that implement at least the MRP module of an IBS do seem to register some improvement in operational performance.

This is a fairly promising start. Undoubtedly there are companies that have tried MRP and abandoned it, but those that stay the course can expect at least some benefit. Implementation failures, it seems, may still be successful in absolute terms, even if they do not achieve the project objectives. This is not a reason to set easier targets, but it may encourage managers who have previously been unwilling to commit to anything as apparently risky as MRPII to reconsider.

Some MRPII implementations do succeed in achieving fully the business objectives that were set for them. Indeed, sufficient implementations have been successfully completed to permit a fairly clear picture to emerge of how it should be done. Companies following the guidelines set out in this chapter should be able to avoid most of the pitfalls that await them. Ultimately, though, each company has to design its own implementation project. There is no system of 'MRPII by numbers' that can be followed mechanically and result in assured success. There are really just two ingredients for success: full understanding of the MRPII concept, and commitment to it. Both must originate from the chief executive and the top management team.

Project management structure

Responsibility for leading the implementation rests with the core project team established at the beginning of the system selection process. This core team should contain specialists from materials management, production, sales and marketing, product development, production engineering, quality, personnel, and finance. If the company already has an IT department, then this should also provide a member of the core team. Each team member should have a reasonable level of authority, but need not be the departmental head. Drive and enthusiasm are much more important than rank.

The team leader should be chosen from a user department, rather than from IT. The role of the IT department is to provide technical support, not to be seen as the 'experts' who are going to impose and implement a computer system. In practice, project leaders are most commonly from materials management or production backgrounds. Personal qualities, however, are as important as background. The project leader must command widespread respect throughout the company, must have good communication skills, and must see the role as an exciting career development opportunity. Project management skills are also important, but these can be learnt.

The project manager must become the champion who drives the implementation through against all the obstacles. No matter how great the commitment of top managers, their focus cannot remain on the project continually. The project manager's can, and must. It is the project manager's responsibility to keep the momentum going, overcome as many of the inevitable problems as possible, and report to top management those that require their attention. Inevitably the project manager becomes identified with the project and is seen as its prime owner, no matter how great the overall corporate commitment. The success of the project stands or falls on the ability of the project manager to fulfil this demanding role.

It is quite impossible for a project manager to perform the task properly without being assigned to the project on a full-time basis. Other members of the core team could be part-time or full-time, depending upon their roles within the team and upon the size of the company. Most companies find that at least one full-time assistant to the project manager is required. This can be a valuable development role for a young graduate. Part-time members should be released from sufficient of their routine duties to devote the necessary time to the project. Ghost members, who are always absent or are usually represented by a subordinate, are not acceptable. It must be recognized that an implementation project typically takes between twelve months and two years, so secondment to the core team must not be undertaken lightly.

The project team should meet frequently. At particularly intensive periods a brief daily update will be necessary. At quieter times meetings should be held at least twice weekly.

Overall direction of the project is provided by an executive steering committee. All functional heads must be members of this committee, which should be chaired by the chief executive. The project manager must also be a member of the committee, to ensure a close liaison between the two groups. The steering committee should normally meet at fortnightly intervals; more frequently if any aspect of the project is causing concern.

One member of the executive steering committee must have the special responsibility of project guardian. This person has to ensure that the interests of the project are always considered when top managers are dealing with other matters of business policy. The role of guardian also includes protecting the project manager from untoward pressure at difficult times, whilst being alert for signs that the incumbent is falling short of the challenge. The person nominated as guardian requires above all a strong nerve and an ability to remain detached from day-to-day crises.

The third leg of the project management structure is a changing mix of task forces set up to address specific issues. Each task force must be allowed to co-opt whoever is needed for the task in hand. Task forces should always have pre-determined end dates; they must not be permitted to evolve into permanent committees. Each task force should be led by a member of the core team, who reports progress at core team meetings.

Effective teamworking

Both the core project team and the various task forces need to function effectively as teams. For this to happen it is essential that they have clear goals to achieve. The goals of the core team are set by the steering committee; those of the task forces are determined in turn by the core team. The leader of each team must ensure that its goals are clear, unambiguous and feasible.

Team members are not delegates, representing the interests of a particular department. While they are working on the project they are members of a team who happen to have important expertise in specific areas. This is often a difficult transition for an individual to make. It becomes an impossible one if the departmental heads to whom the team members report are not sympathetic with the wider needs of the business.

Freeing the time of busy people to join a team is always difficult. One useful technique is to require team members to draw up a plan for releasing themselves from some of their routine work. This plan must be agreed with each individual's line manager before the team begins its work. In this way the extent of each individual's involvement in the team is agreed, and proper arrangements are made to cover absence from routine work. The possibility of conflicting priorities arising later is significantly reduced.

Sometimes teams run into problems which they are unable to resolve. An escalation procedure is needed to deal with these problems. Task forces must be able to refer problems to the core team, and the project manager must be able to refer issues that the core team cannot resolve to the steering committee. These referrals, when they occur, should be seen as the proper functioning of the project management structure, not as a failure by the referring group. It must be possible to invoke the escalation procedure at short notice, rather than wait for the next scheduled meeting, in cases where the problem could delay the project.

Project planning

An early task of the core team is to expand the outline project plan that was drawn up during the feasibility study into a more detailed document. The project plan sets milestones, determines resource requirements and encapsulates commitments made by outside suppliers. Progress must be continually monitored against the plan, and any slippage, or potential slippage, highlighted for corrective action. The overall timescale should be short enough to provide a challenge, but not so tight that any unforeseen difficulty inevitably results in the whole plan slipping. The aim should be to keep the end date as firm as possible, whilst allowing for some rescheduling within that time to cope with changing circumstances.

The plan establishes the sequence in which the elements of MRPII are implemented. There is not very much choice in this, since the basic building blocks such as the bills of material and inventory control need to be in place before MRP or costing can be carried out. The main discretionary area is the extent to which activities can be undertaken simultaneously. For example, it may be possible to implement financial ledgers in parallel with manufacturing activities, and activate the links between them at a later time.

Firstly, an overall implementation timetable must be prepared, showing broad project milestones. This timetable should be agreed by both the project team and the executive steering committee. The project plan explodes these activities into a much greater degree of detail, assigning resources and specifying accountability for every action. This amount of detail cannot all be included at the start, since much of the work is many months into the future and therefore uncertain in nature. Detail must be added progressively, as time moves on and greater understanding of the work to be done is gained. Even so, broad assessments of overall resource requirements must be made at the start, and strategies for providing these resources agreed. Any significant variation from these resource requirements that appear as later sections of the plan are firmed up must be dealt with promptly. Sound project planning may not always be able to prevent bad news arising during implementation, but it should certainly aim to highlight problems in time for corrective action to be taken.

The plan, and the demands on resources it imposes, must be approved by the steering committee. Departmental managers must be consulted, so that arrangements can be made for releasing people from their everyday work. Time will be needed for training courses, secondment to task forces, and creation of data. It is no use expecting people simply to absorb the extra work. Either additional temporary resource must be made available, or other work must be set aside.

Many companies find it helpful to use computer-based project management systems to construct their implementation plans. The value of these systems is not so much in creating the initial plan, but in keeping it up to date. The plan must be continually developed, monitored and adjusted throughout the eighteen months or so of the implementation. A computer-based plan that can be brought up to date in a few minutes is much more likely to be maintained in times of heavy workload than is a manually-prepared document. Spending time updating the plan can seem a very low priority in times of crisis, but overall project control easily slips away if the direction imposed by the plan is lost.

Education and training

Education and training are two quite distinct processes. Education, in the context of an MRPII implementation, is concerned with communicating overall MRPII principles. It has nothing to do with the software package that is to be used, or with specific implementation tasks that are to be carried out. The aim of the education process is to create understanding at all levels in the organization that the company is to change. Planning will be done differently, new methods of reporting will be introduced, different performance criteria will be applied, and higher expectations of achievement will be established. Old, ingrained methods and beliefs about the way the business works must be discarded. All this will happen only if a thorough educational process is extended throughout the organization.

The education programme must recognize the varying learning needs at different levels in the organization. Middle managers, for example, need more information than production operators, and a different educational style. The message must be consistent at all levels, however. It must also be timed in such a way that the changes it foreshadows follow soon afterwards. The desired behavioural modifications will only happen if the theory is followed up very quickly by practical experience.

Training is an entirely different process. The objective of training is to ensure that each individual is taught how to carry out the changed tasks for which he or she will be responsible. Much of the emphasis in training is related to the use of computer-based systems, but not all of it. For example, different methods of handling and storing materials may be needed to ensure that stock records can be maintained accurately. Storekeepers need thorough training in how these new methods will work.

Education and training are of vital importance in implementing MRPII successfully. If corners are cut in this area, there is a real risk that the implementation programme will fail to achieve its objectives. Early MRPII implementations often severely underestimated the extent of education and training needed. More recently there has been a greater willingness to invest in training, but the educational process is still largely ignored. The result of underresourcing education is that the IBS is implemented, but the company joins the ranks of those that have failed to understand, and achieve, real MRPII.

Business process design

MRPII means changing the way the business operates. The vision statement, which was discussed in Chapter 3, provides the overall direction. It sets goals and it identifies policy issues which the top management team must address. Preparing the vision statement is the initial stage of business redesign.

As the project moves into the implementation phase, the second stage of business redesign must be carried out. The purpose of this stage, business process design, is to interpret and develop the vision statement, and to determine its impact upon the key business processes of the company.

These key business processes, and some of the activities they embrace, are:

- **Demand management.**
  - sales forecasting
  - sales order entry and delivery promising
  - master production scheduling.
- **Production scheduling.**
  - inventory policy
  - shopfloor scheduling and control
  - shopfloor data capture.
- **Material supplies.**
  - supplier relationships
  - contractual and scheduling arrangements
  - incoming goods inspection policy.
- **New product introduction and engineering change.**
  - design approval and authority to change
  - timing of change and use of superseded stock.
- **Financial management.**
  - inventory valuation
  - calculation of cost of sales
  - cash flow projections.

These key business processes must change as the company moves into MRPII. Many of the issues involved have already been discussed; others are covered later. All the issues must be thoroughly reviewed and resolved before the company can move any further into implementation.

A task force must be created to tackle each of these business processes. The task forces should include senior managers from all areas of the company that are involved in the business process concerned. One or more members of the core team must also be included. The work of these task forces is partly learning and partly decision making. It is essential that the impact of MRPII on the business process is fully understood, and that all the relevant techniques are considered, before any decisions are made. The necessary MRPII expertise must therefore be imported into the task force, probably by using external advisers.

The combination of education and decision making that characterizes these task forces is a very effective way of learning. Motivation to learn is much greater when there is a real problem to be solved, and mature managers learn better through discussion than in the classroom.

The output of the business process task forces is a set of business process definitions. These written statements set out the objectives of the business process in question, and describe how these objectives will be satisfied as the company adopts MRPII. The business process definitions must be formally accepted by the executive steering committee.

System configuration

Once the business process definitions have been approved, the third stage of business redesign, system configuration, can be carried out. This is the task of setting up the system parameters, default values, item master codes and other data that together determine how the IBS will function. Configuration utilizes the considerable flexibility available in package software to customize the system to the (new) working practices that the company intends to adopt.

Sometimes the software is installed and accepted before this stage of business redesign has been reached. There is then great pressure to start entering data and begin operator training immediately. This desire must be resisted until the company is able to make the correct configuration decisions. It is essential that the system is properly configured to operate in the way the company requires.

System configuration is carried out in a similar way to business process design. Task forces are again established, this time containing more operational staff and fewer managers. Education is provided, together with some specific training in how to configure the IBS. The task forces develop the business process definitions into specific configuration decisions. These decisions include the use of safety stocks and lot sizing rules, whether regenerative or net change MRP will be used, how materials will be issued to works orders, what forms of cost roll-ups are required, whether purchased goods should be booked into goods inwards inspection or straight into stock, and so on. The issues to be considered in making many of these decisions were discussed in Chapter 2.

The reasoning involved in all the configuration decisions taken should be recorded, so that any future changes are not made in ignorance of the wider implications on the way the system operates. These records also provide valuable input to the preparation of procedure manuals for operating staff, a topic discussed later, under *Data maintenance procedures*.

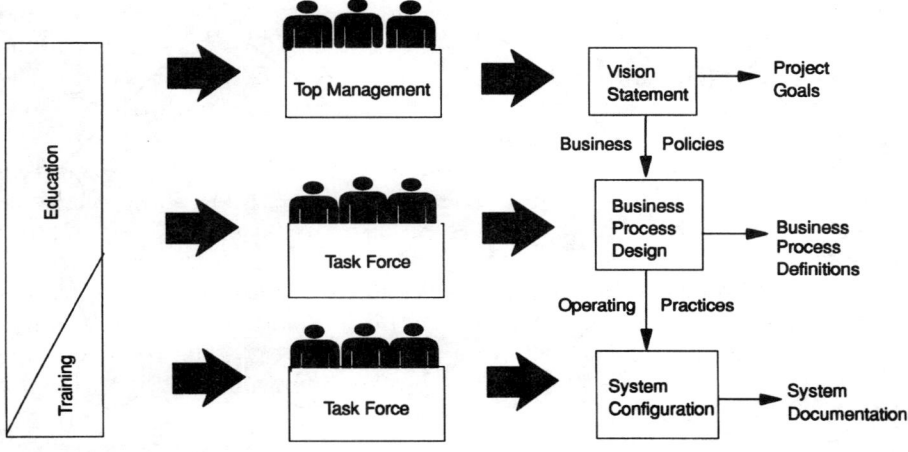

Figure 4.1 Business redesign

The three stages of business redesign: vision statement, business process design and system configuration, are illustrated in Figure 4.1.

Data integrity

MRPII demands very accurate data if it is to produce usable information. This can be an extremely difficult message to convey in companies where crisis management is a way of life, and it is immaterial whether the crisis is caused by erroneous data or some other factor.

The integrated nature of MRPII makes the impact of data errors particularly significant. This effect is illustrated in the following example. Figure 4.2 shows a bill of material structure for three products, P1, P2 and P3. Each of these products is assembled from different combinations of five manufactured components, C1 to C5. The components are produced from four types of raw material, M1 to M4. Inventory is controlled by a re-order point system, and there are errors in the stock records of P3 and C2. Two stock errors in twelve stock items is 83% stock accuracy, which the stock controller would probably regard as reasonable. The 17% of orders that are incorrectly issued are hardly likely to be noticed amongst all the other problems that the use of a re-order point system entails.

If this situation is transposed to an MRPII environment, the position is now as shown in Figure 4.3. MRP has exploded the items with stock errors down to the lower levels in the bill of material. As a result, gross requirements have been generated incorrectly for all lower level items. Stock accuracy is still 83%, but requirements accuracy is only 25%. At the bottom level (purchased items), none of the requirements generated by MRP is accurate. If there were errors in the bill of material as well, the situation would be even worse.

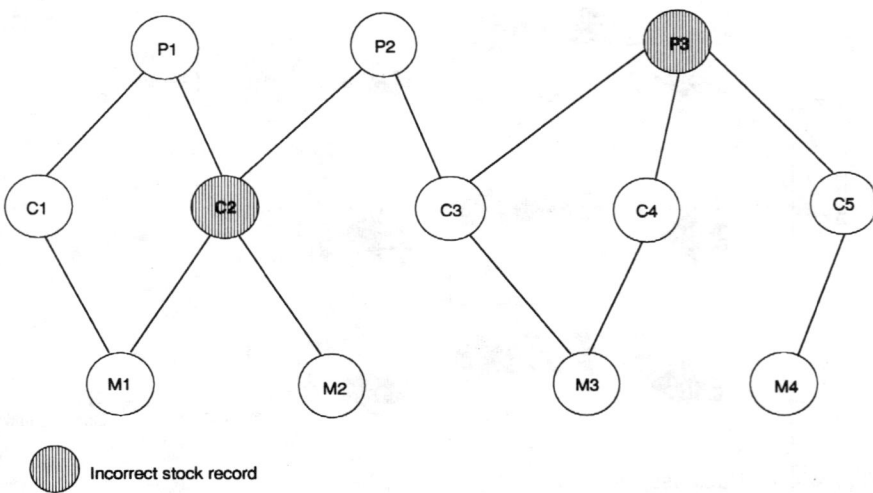

Figure 4.2   Re-order point system: 83% requirements accuracy

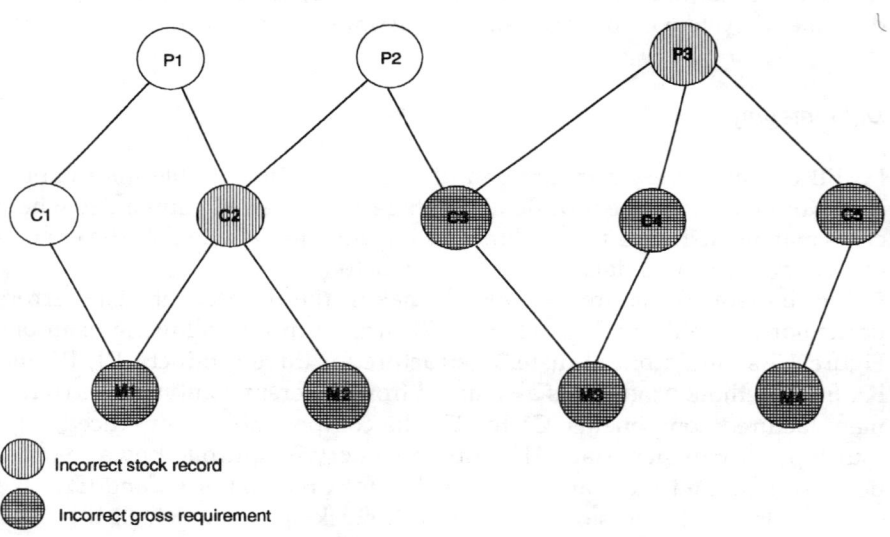

Figure 4.3   MRP: 25% requirements accuracy

Similar situations can arise elsewhere. Inaccurate routing records do not simply mean that works orders will be incorrect; capacity planning, scheduling and costing are also wrong. Unless very high standards of data accuracy are achieved throughout the system, right from the start, an MRPII implementation will not leave the starting blocks.

As a general rule, all data held in the system should be at least 95% accurate before a company can even consider using MRP, CRP or costing. Even then the results will not be satisfactory (although they will be an improvement on the previous system). The medium term aim must be 98% or higher, and the ultimate goal can be no less than total accuracy.

Of course there is some data in the system which does not have an absolutely correct value. Operation times, lead times, safety stocks and so on are all the result of estimates or averages. For this kind of data, accuracy means that a value is present, and it is reasonable.

Sometimes the desire to improve data accuracy is one of the main reasons a company decides to implement MRPII. This is a perfectly valid objective, since a competent IBS provides a structured database within which data can be managed accurately. The data entry routines used to update the database usually contain a range of validity checks on the data being entered. These checks warn the operator of possible error conditions, and prevent the entry of transactions that do not conform to pre-determined ranges of values. Furthermore, access to the data entry routines can be restricted through the use of password control, so unauthorized changes to the data can be prevented.

These features ensure that MRPII provides a disciplined approach to data integrity. Unfortunately, this concept of MRPII's inherent disciplines can lead managers to believe that merely installing an IBS will somehow make their **people** and their **procedures** disciplined too. MRPII is not a shortcut to overcoming existing inadequacies; successful MRPII is dependent upon well trained people using carefully thought out operating procedures.

Achievement of total data accuracy is a management task. It is not simply a question of demanding more care from subordinates; data integrity is a task that requires the direct involvement of all managers. The following sections explain the steps involved in achieving data integrity.

Data maintenance procedures
Operating procedures are needed that describe the way in which any change to the data used within an IBS must be made. These procedures must be carefully thought through and documented. The system supplier's user documentation is not adequate for this purpose; customized manuals are needed that cover all actions involved in changing data, not just the keyboard activities. These manuals should specify, for every type of data update that can arise within the company, the following:

- when data is to be changed
- how the change should be authorized
- who is responsible for making the change
- what system transaction must be used
- whether and how the change should be checked and verified
- what audit trails are available to trace transaction history.

This process can be illustrated by a simple example: the return to stores of surplus material from production. In this case, timing of the update would normally be the point when the material is received and located in the stockroom. Authorization might be a return to stores note, signed by the production supervisor, confirming that the material is surplus to immediate production requirements. Responsibility for making the change might rest with the storekeeper who receives and locates the material.

The specification of which system transaction to use is often one of the most critical elements of the procedure manual. In the case of a return to stores, the software might offer the following options:

- unplanned (miscellaneous) receipt
- return from works order
- reversal of issue transaction
- stock adjustment
- no stock transaction.

Each option could be valid in certain circumstances. The unplanned receipt might be appropriate if the material is surplus floor stock, or if the source of the material is unknown. Return from works order would apply if the material had been overissued to the order (perhaps a complete coil of strip steel had been issued and the balance is now being returned), or if the order was closed before completing the full quantity. Reversal of issue transaction could be used if the material had been issued in error. Stock adjustment (following a stock count), or no transaction at all might be appropriate if it is believed possible, or known, that the material was not properly booked out in the first place.

The choice of transaction should not be left to the discretion of the storekeeper. The manual must specify which transaction to use in every conceivable situation. The manual must also be cross-referred with other relevant procedures. For example, if the stores manual states that the return to stores note will specify the reason for the return, and the source of the material, then the production supervisor's manual must require that this information is provided. The return to stores note should be designed such that it contains prompts for this information.

Having established how the transaction should be selected, the stores manual next addresses the question of checking and verifying the change. Part of this process is to specify the way in which the quantity returned must be checked (by counting, weighing etc) and the action to be taken if the outcome is different from the quantity advised. Then the manual must specify whether there is a need to check the accuracy of the system transaction. In our example of a material movement, where very large numbers of transactions may be raised every day, it would be unusual for every one to be checked. Nevertheless, the less common transactions, and perhaps all transactions entered by trainee storekeepers, may need to be confirmed by the stores supervisor.

Finally the manual must describe the audit trails available in the system. In this example there should be a variety of printed reports and screen enquiries that show details of all stock transactions by item, within date order. The manual should describe how these may be used to establish information such as the time of the transaction, the identity of the operator, and/or of the VDU at which the change was made, the reference number of the return to stores note, and the quantity transacted.

This example has focused upon a particular type of stock transaction. Unless the procedure is fully thought through and documented, errors could arise in inventory, in works order costs, in work in progress records, and in aggregated issues-to-date figures. All other types of stock movement must receive the same attention.

Procedures must also be written and implemented that will ensure the accuracy of all other data held in the system. In the case of changes to bills of material and routings, the integrity of the company's central product and process database is at issue. The manual covering these changes must focus particularly upon the timing of the change, authority to change, and verification of changes made. These issues can only be determined within the context of a complete engineering change control procedure for the company.

Without proper written procedures, there is no chance of data integrity being maintained. Simply issuing copies of manuals to all concerned, however, will achieve little. The main purpose of the manuals is to provide material upon which to base operator training. The manuals must be made available to operators for reference, but if the training has been carried out thoroughly they should rarely be needed.

Secure stores

Inventory accuracy is a matter of particular concern because of the enormous number of transactions that are processed in the average manufacturing company. Achieving an acceptable level of stock accuracy demands considerable care, thorough training and carefully documented procedures. It is generally accepted that the best results are obtained when stores staff are given responsibility for their own stock recording. Any theoretical advantage from using clerical staff with superior keyboard skills tends to be outweighed by the benefit arising from storekeepers accepting ownership of the stock records. Entering data at source, in the stockroom, also eliminates delays in updating the system and reduces the risk of paperwork going astray.

Ownership of stock records can only be achieved if storekeepers have full responsibility for receiving, locating and issuing the items concerned. If production operators have access to the stockroom, and are able to help themselves to stock items, then they will. Unauthorized withdrawals from stores are often done with the best of motives. Perhaps there was an urgent job to be finished and the storekeeper was not available, or it was the night shift and the stockroom was not manned. The intention at the time was to report the withdrawal, but somehow that never happened. Less worthy reasons for unauthorized withdrawal include surreptitious replacement of items that have been scrapped, and pilferage.

The only answer is to control access to the stockroom. Partition walls must be built, and doors must be locked when the store is unattended. Storekeepers then know that they are totally responsible, and accountable, for the accuracy of the stock in their care. To some managers the cost of imposing this type of security seems excessive, but storekeepers are unlikely to accept ownership if there is any possibility of interference with the stock under their control. The fact that the company is prepared to spend money protecting its investment in inventory can only reinforce the message that accurate control of stock is a priority.

Error-proofing
Every effort should be made to reduce the opportunity for stock errors by using error-proofing techniques. There are many initiatives that could be taken including, for example:

- using standard containers that hold a pre-determined quantity of items, possibly with a sample item attached to the outside of the container as a visual check on the contents
- using bar coding to avoid the need to enter part numbers into the system manually. Bar coding need not be restricted to the shopfloor; product catalogues that incorporate bar codes can be used to assist sales order entry, for example
- moulding or stamping part numbers into components during the manufacturing process, to aid identification
- direct linking of electronic counters that are built into production machines or weigh-counting scales to the data entry system
- enforcement of high standards of stores housekeeping, so that everything is where it should be, is accessible, and is identified.

Error-proofing is rarely given adequate attention, presumably on the grounds that if people were careful they would not make mistakes. Yet the application of a little thought to situations where errors are likely to occur is well worthwhile. Often simple, low cost ideas can be generated which significantly reduce the possibility of errors being made.

Data audits
No matter how much care and attention goes into data maintenance, errors will creep in from time to time. A programme of routine audits must be performed to keep these errors under control. The objectives of data auditing are:

- to establish the current level of data accuracy, and identify trends
- to determine the causes of errors, and so initiate actions to eliminate these causes
- to enable the frequency and extent of future audits to be assessed
- to correct the errors found during the audit.

Perhaps the most familiar example of data auditing is the use of cycle counting to verify stock records. Cycle counting is a continuous process of stock checking in which a small number of items is counted every day. Items are selected for counting at varying frequencies, so that high value items, and those which are transacted most frequently, are checked most often. The number of items checked each day needs to be high to begin with but can be reduced when an acceptable level of inventory accuracy has been achieved.

The number of daily counts might have to be increased again if accuracy deteriorates in the future.

A useful technique to use if an initially low stock accuracy fails to improve is to select a small sample of stock items and count them every week, or even every day. It is easy to trace every stock movement that has occurred in such a short period of time, and so uncover any persistent errors in the way the transactions are being performed. Once these errors have been dealt with (perhaps by training, correcting the software, or buying a new set of weigh-counting scales), a more conventional form of cycle counting can be adopted.

Keeping stock records accurate requires continuous attention, because the volume of stock transactions is so high. Other key data in the system such as bills of material, routings, work centre data, supplier details and so on also need to be audited from time to time. Because this kind of data is relatively static, continuous checking is not necessary. It is sufficient to check a few items at random, at monthly intervals. If any discrepancies are found, more checks may be needed so that any new source of error that has arisen may be identified and eliminated.

One of the best ways of auditing the accuracy of the data in the system is by using it. One of the characteristics of integrated systems is that because the same information is used in so many different ways, errors do not stay hidden for long. If data accuracy is low this characteristic renders the system unusable, but once the minimum level of accuracy is reached it is a great strength. A virtuous circle can be achieved in which the more the system is relied upon to provide management information, the more accurate the data contained within the system becomes.

For example, an obscure error on a routing may not be evident to production engineering. To the cost department, however, it becomes obvious when the rolled-up cost for the item in question turns out to be very different from that of a similar item. Similarly, it may be all too easy for stores to book a delivery of materials against a purchase order due next week, instead of this week's order. When the earlier order goes into arrears however, the purchasing department will soon realize what has happened.

The aim is to create a culture within the organization that enables errors discovered in this way to be reported and corrected. It is no use people simply grumbling about the inadequacies of other departments, and not reporting the error that they have found. Nor should someone who is told of an error take offence, and respond by suggesting that other departments should mind their own business. Managers should not assume that these reactions could not occur; they do. Departmental conflicts and rivalries are too well established in most companies to disappear simply because a new system has been installed. If a company is to achieve real business integration its managers must create a new working culture based upon mutual trust, co-operation and support. Shared data means shared responsibility for that data, regardless of who enters it into the system.

Cutover

There are two ways of cutting over to live running, depending upon the position from which the company is starting. If the company has little or nothing in the way of existing computer systems, cutover should be a gradual, staged process. At each stage some of the existing methods of working are replaced and discontinued. The new techniques should be thoroughly bedded in before work starts on the next stage. There should be no pressure to make progress any faster than can comfortably be handled. Companies adopting this approach can gradually move towards using MRPII concepts to manage the business as the software falls into place to support them.

Increasingly it is the case that companies implementing MRPII already have an older-generation, computer-based system, even though they have never adopted closed loop planning methodologies. For these companies, implementing a new system is more difficult. Staged cutover means parallel running the old and the new systems, since the old system cannot be discontinued until most, or all, of the new system is in place. For example, stock recording is always one of the first aspects of a new system to be implemented, and MRP one of the last. Yet until MRP is operational, the old methods of inventory control need to be maintained in parallel with the new system.

Parallel running is to be avoided as much as possible. In the past it has sometimes been advocated as a means of removing the risk from implementing a new system, but the reality is rather different. Parallel running is unsatisfactory because:

- duplicating transactions in two systems doubles the workload for the people involved, and increases the risk of error
- the two systems inevitably operate in different ways, so the data contained within them is never directly comparable. Any discrepancies can therefore be difficult to reconcile
- if problems arise with the new system, the tendency is to fall back on the old system to get the job done, rather than to resolve the problem. The new system is not improved, and merely loses credibility.

When moving from one computer-based system to another, the best approach is to convert as quickly as possible. The 'big bang' approach, where all data is converted electronically at the same time, is not always possible, but the objective should be to minimize the time period during which both systems are live. The outcome of this process is not the overnight creation of an MRPII company. MRPII will only follow when the company starts using the system to support a different way of managing the business. The immediate benefit obtained from the cutover may therefore not be that great. Managers must resist the temptation to relax their efforts just because the software is in place. The hard work is yet to start.

A big bang cutover, or one that approximates to big bang by minimizing the period of parallel running, depends upon a high degree of confidence that all will be well. If there is any doubt that the system is working properly, that the people using it are fully trained in the tasks they need to perform, and that all contingencies have been foreseen and accounted for, the cutover will be a leap into the unknown. The way to avoid uncertainty is through piloting.

There are two stages of piloting. The first is the conference room pilot, which is a simulation exercise rather than live running. The second stage is the live pilot, in which a small, representative part of the business is used to test the company's state of readiness.

The idea of the conference room pilot is to set up a number of VDUs in a single area (typically, of course, the company's conference room), so that representatives of the various functional areas can together work through a predetermined sequence of events. Customer orders are entered, stock allocated, MPSs created and MRP runs performed. The process continues through the release of orders, stock issuing and receiving, invoicing, and accounting. Difficulties are resolved as they arise, across the table, and any further training needs are identified.

A training database, separate from the live company data, is set up for this purpose. The training system is used during training sessions and pilots, and is available for practice at other times. The data used should be extracted from the company's own product data, with which staff are familiar. The use of unfamiliar test data provided by the supplier should be avoided.

The training database should be retained after implementation has been completed. It can be used for refresher sessions, for training new members of staff, and for testing different techniques. Unfortunately the training data is usually the first thing to go when the computer starts to get overloaded. A wise precaution is to check that the supplier has made provision for this data when sizing the hardware requirements.

Conference room pilots need to be carefully prepared in advance. Initial data must be set up so that the outcomes of the actions taken are meaningful. The participants must stay close to a predetermined script which is designed to simulate as many real life situations as possible. The conference room pilot provides the final opportunity before live running to test the operating procedures, audit the training, and try out the supporting paperwork systems. Once the conference room pilot has been successfully completed, a process that can take several weeks, the next step is the live pilot.

The live pilot should ideally be based upon a small, self contained part of the business that incorporates all the main business processes. A minor product range which does not share common components with other products is the ideal, but is not always available. The chosen pilot area should contain sufficient complexity to make it a real challenge; successful operation of a simple pilot may not be a reliable indicator of the chances of company-wide success. On the other hand, pilots that contain a form of complexity not found elsewhere in the business should be avoided. This local complexity could divert attention from issues that are more likely to be important elsewhere.

Cutover is the most critical period of the implementation, and the importance of thorough planning cannot be overstated. A cutover that fails, leading to the re-introduction of previous systems, can damage the business in the short term and can undermine confidence in the new system throughout the company. A second attempt at cutover is much more difficult, and a third may not be possible.

Gaining commitment

If the people within the business are committed to MRPII, there is little doubt that the inevitable problems arising during implementation can be overcome. Gaining this degree of commitment is a task for the top managers. If the top management team is convinced of the benefits of MRPII (and they should not be proceeding if they are not), it should not be difficult to demonstrate this conviction to the remainder of the company. Commitment from the top is contagious; when it is clearly visible few people at lower levels in the organization remain immune.

Time and effort are needed to convince people that top management's commitment is real and lasting. Old hands will remember numerous past instances of management initiatives which turned out to be no more than a passing phase. Why should they believe it is any different this time? Will the professed commitment to MRPII take the form of proactive support for the implementation, or is it just words, easily said, soon forgotten?

Having demonstrated their own active commitment, top managers must next persuade their employees that the change will benefit each of them personally, or at least not disadvantage them. Change is always a little threatening, and the status quo usually seems a more attractive option than the unknown. Effort is needed to help people see the project in a positive way, and to remove as many of the doubts and worries as possible.

There are several actions that can be taken to put these conditions for commitment into place.

Leading from the front

Perhaps the best indication that top managers can give of their commitment to MRPII is to demonstrate that they are willing to change their own behaviour. If the people at the top are seen to change, then MRPII really must be important.

Communication

Top managers must convey their vision of the future for the organization as an MRPII company. Plans for implementation, updated by progress reports, should be communicated regularly to all employees. Implications of the project on employment levels and working practices need to be brought into the open at the earliest possible stage, or concerns will fester in the background. These issues need to be addressed at some point, and there is nothing to be gained by delaying.

Resources

There is nothing more likely to persuade people that managers are not serious about the project than failure to provide the resources needed. Temporary staff may be required to replace people seconded to the project team, to cover for staff who are being trained, or to help with the initial data entry activities. If existing staff are expected to absorb all this work without assistance, they could be forgiven a lack of enthusiasm for the project.

Education

A key objective of the education programme is to make people aware of the benefits of MRPII. It is not only the company that benefits; people within the company do as well. A good MRPII implementation reduces hassle and builds more co-operative ways of working, leading to a more pleasant working environment for everyone.

Of course, there are always the expeditors and fire-fighters whose job knowledge, contacts and determination have kept the business going until now. They feel threatened by MRPII, since it seems their role and status will disappear. In practice, the knowledge and skills that made them valuable to the company in the past are unlikely to be made obsolete by MRPII. The talents of the people in the business are an essential element of MRPII. What must change is the way these talents are applied.

Training

Once people are convinced that change is inevitable, and that they will not be disadvantaged by it, their next concern is that they will be given adequate training. Particularly for those using a VDU for the first time, but for others as well, there will be secret doubts about their ability to cope. Once they see that adequate provision has been made for training, and they gain confidence in the trainers, these doubts are soon overcome. Managers must seek to reassure their people at an early stage that the need for thorough training has been recognized, and will be addressed.

In the early stages of implementation it may be worth setting up a hotline which anyone within the company can call if they are in difficulty. Staff servicing the hotline would either give an immediate solution to the problem or find the answer and call back. The existence of a hotline is a very visible way of demonstrating to staff that they will be fully supported while they are learning how to use the new system.

Listening

One of the difficulties in introducing MRPII is that its highly structured and integrated approach can make it appear very inflexible compared with previous ways of doing things. Whereas manual systems can be personalized with individual touches and idiosyncrasies, MRPII has to be operated by the book. Failure to stick to the rules can have unforeseen implications for other users of the system. It is therefore all too easy for MRPII to be seen as a straightjacket, imposed by senior management, with no opportunity for junior staff to contribute.

If this perception is to be overcome it is important to give people an opportunity to influence the system they will be operating. This consultation process must be carried out at an early stage, before system selection and configuration decisions have been taken. Although at this point most people within the company will have an incomplete picture of the MRPII concept, it is still well worth listening to their views and ideas on their own areas of specialism. They, after all, are the company experts in what they do.

Later, when system training is carried out, staff should be given feedback on how their ideas have helped to shape the system. This may include explaining why it has not been possible to act on some of the ideas that were put forward. Even a rejection of one's ideas, as long as the reasons are explained in a positive manner, is more acceptable than never having been asked.

Mediation
It is quite likely that, at some point in the project, conflict will occur. No matter how committed individual managers are to the MRPII concept, differences of opinion will arise in the application of those concepts. Senior managers must be quick to spot these conflicts and must be ready to step in to mediate before any real damage is done. Since the area of contention is usually very specific and technical, it is quite likely that no-one within the company has the knowledge to make a final decision on who is right. Even if there is someone with sufficient technical knowledge, company politics and the need to maintain good working relationships may make it impossible for that knowledge to be acted upon.

In these situations the chief executive may decide to apply the wisdom of Solomon and adopt a compromise solution that pleases no-one. A preferable approach is to refer the issue to an independent adviser who has both expertise in MRPII and a knowledge of the company concerned. The role of external advisers is considered more fully later in this chapter.

A touch of theatre
If proper attention is given to the actions described above, most people in the company will be willing to give the project their support and commitment. Sometimes top management like to take the process further, and obtain some tangible evidence of this commitment, particularly from their middle managers. Often it is the middle managers who are the hardest to convince. They, after all, are the people who always have to turn the flood of policies and directives generated by top management into practice, whilst simultaneously keeping the day-to-day operations of the business running. The initial reaction to any new initiative is often to keep one's head down and see if it goes away.

A touch of theatre may help to convince the doubters. A formal written statement of the objectives of the project is drawn up, and all the managers are asked to sign the statement to demonstrate their commitment. The impact is reinforced if a signing ceremony is arranged at which everyone signs in turn, starting with the chief executive. The statement can be framed and displayed in a prominent position, as a reminder to the signatories of their commitment and a visible sign to the rest of the company that management are taking MRPII seriously.

This approach may not suit all companies, but it should not be dismissed out of hand. After all, even if no-one takes it very seriously, the novelty value of the exercise should at least bring the project to people's attention. The more publicity the project receives, the more people will accept that it really is going to happen. Most people would prefer to be part of a successful implementation than a lone voice of resistance.

Measuring progress

A good implementation programme includes a great deal of measurement. We have already seen how data accuracy needs to be measured continuously, as part of the auditing process. Project control is also dependent upon measurement; in this case the metric is progress against the plan. The third dimension of measurement is regular monitoring of key performance criteria within the business so that improvements resulting from the implementation can be assessed. These performance criteria will include, but not be restricted to, the areas of benefit established by the feasibility study.

By monitoring business performance criteria in this way, the natural tendency for planned benefits to evaporate is countered. Inventory does not fall just because there is a better system for controlling it; positive action is needed to remove the buffers. Staff who find their workloads being reduced do not usually ask to be redeployed, they find other things to fill the time. Production will not suddenly begin to work to due date, just because those dates have been calculated by MRP, no matter how thorough the education process they have been through. Measurement reveals these areas of inertia, and allows managers to take the necessary actions to overcome them.

As measurement begins to show up the successes that the project is achieving, the communication process needs to be brought into play to let everyone know that the implementation is making progress. A bit of positive feedback imparts an air of success, and helps maintain the momentum.

Persistent implementation errors

Where MRPII implementations fail to meet expectations, the primary cause is usually one or more errors from a fairly short list of failings that recur time after time. These failings all result from insufficient attention being paid to the implementation guidelines already described. They are not the only things that can go wrong in a badly managed implementation, but they are all show-stoppers. Any one of these failings is enough to prevent the implementation from succeeding.

The IT project approach

One of the most common errors results from a belief that MRPII is just an integrated computer system. Implementation is seen merely as an IT project, and the IT department is given the role of leading it.

Since no-one in the organization understands the need to adopt new methods of working, the suitability of the system is assessed by how closely it mirrors current procedures. User managers insist that every last detail of the existing system is duplicated in the software before they will have anything to do with it. The IT department has to comply, in order that implementation can proceed; large-scale modification of the system follows. The resulting heavy workload in the IT department leads to a belief that it is under-resourced, so more staff are recruited.

The delay involved in carrying out the modifications causes target dates to be missed, and the implementation slowly grinds to a halt. No performance improvements have been achieved, and the modifications carried out have destroyed much of the integrity of the system, making it impossible to implement the later modules. User managers in areas where the system has been implemented are still not happy, in spite of the modifications, and are now insisting upon a second round of changes. The system supplier long since withdrew support, and the IT department, although doubled in size, is snowed under with work.

This picture may seem extremely bleak, but it is not exaggerated. Companies that are particularly vulnerable to this situation tend to be larger organizations which have a history of major business system implementations. Smaller companies which take an IT project view of MRPII are usually protected from carrying out excessive system modifications by a lack of resource to do the work. Implementation is no more successful, however, because user managers feel no ownership of the system and do not see why they should have to change to suit it. Some of the simpler modules may be implemented, but then the project is aborted.

The missing factor in these failed implementations is senior management education. The top management team probably believe that they understand MRPII, and that they are committed to it. In fact they do not understand enough for that commitment to be translated into a viable implementation programme. For the lack of a few hours' education, vast amounts of company resources can so easily be wasted, and potential benefits not achieved.

Unrealistic MPS

In this instance a more realistic approach is taken to the project, and progress is made. Implementation reaches the point where the company is ready to start building an MPS and running MRP. The most difficult aspect of MRPII has now been reached; unfortunately many companies fail to meet the challenge.

There are two failure modes at this point. The first occurs when the sales department start to get cold feet about MRPII. Until this point in the project, the sales people may not have taken too much notice of what has been happening. Their view tends to be outward-looking, and the details of how the orders they win are converted into delivered goods are not generally of much concern. When the company begins to create a structured method of building and maintaining the MPS, the realization strikes them that they are very much involved.

Suddenly the sales people find that they are being asked to provide regular sales forecasts. Worse, these forecasts are being used to determine which products will be available to sell. Whereas production would once slip urgent, short-lead-time orders into the programme and hope for the best, now they are responding by providing choices; if this new order goes in, they say, something else must go back.

The sales people suspect that the old enemy, production, has outflanked them. All this talk about better delivery performance, fewer shortages and shorter lead times, which persuaded sales to support MRPII, turns out to have been a cover. What production have really been doing is implementing a system that will improve production efficiency by reducing flexibility to meet customer requirements. At this point sales withdraw their support from the project. Without the involvement of sales there is no possibility of building an agreed, realistic MPS, so the old ways of chopping and changing the production programme continue.

Sometimes companies manage to get beyond this hurdle, but still fall prey to the second MPS failure mode. Here a structured method of master production scheduling has been put in place, and the MPS is signed off by all concerned. Then a major customer telephones the chief executive, complaining that sales will not promise the short delivery date needed on an important new order. This has never happened in the past, the customer continues, but now they must consider taking all their business elsewhere. The chief executive responds by promising the customer the date required, and then tells the manufacturing manager to get on with it.

The order is pushed in, and the MPS becomes overloaded. Arrears build up in production and other orders go late. Due dates become unattainable, capacity plans show large workloads still outstanding in past periods. Fire-fighting and expediting take over from planning, and everything returns to the state that existed before the MRPII project began. The overall effect is that closed loop MRP fails.

It is in these situations that the commitment of senior managers to MRPII is most severely tested. How can the need for ever greater flexibility in meeting customer requirements be reconciled with the apparent straitjacket imposed by structured master production scheduling? Is MRPII really just a mechanism for making companies more production-led, when the commercial imperative is to become customer-focused?

The answer to these questions is as follows. To give all customers the best possible service all the time, much better planning and control is required than has previously been possible. There was never any difficulty in rushing one urgent job through production to satisfy a particularly demanding customer. The price was in the poor delivery performance, inability to forecast despatch dates, high production and inventory costs, and long lead times that were accepted as the norm for the bulk of customer orders.

Commitment implies an act of faith by top managers that by working hard to change into an MRPII company, all customers will benefit in the long run. Commitment also means facing up to some very difficult choices. Certainly urgent orders can be added to the MPS, but only if other orders are moved back to make room for them. Up to now it has been all too easy to tell production to squeeze in an urgent job, without asking what else will suffer. Even if this question had been asked, it could not have been answered. Queue jumping all the parts needed for the new order through many production resources has a completely unpredictable effect on the orders that are pushed aside. Anyway, it was much easier not to know, but instead to pretend that somehow production would cope without anything else being delayed. This was management by fantasy.

These difficult choices now have to be tackled. Few companies can respond to all possible urgent demands on them, all the time, no matter how hard they try. The best course of action, therefore, is to inform all customers about the move to MRPII, the restrictions it imposes, and the opportunities it offers for much greater delivery reliability. If customers are drawn into the MRPII education process, so that they can understand what the company is trying to achieve, they may be willing to modify their ordering policies accordingly. Perhaps their delivery requirements have always had some padding in them, to allow for unreliable delivery. Most customers, in all walks of life, prefer reliable delivery dates to worthless promises of early despatch. Even the most demanding customers will probably respond well to being treated with greater honesty.

In a more enlightened world, marketing departments would be desperate to tell their customers of their new commitment to MRPII, seeing it as a marketing coup. Customers would react by gaining confidence in their supplier, recognizing its ability to offer much higher standards of service. If BS5750/ISO9000 accreditation is becoming a condition of doing business in some industries, why should not MRPII be regarded as equally desirable?

Poor data accuracy

The need to achieve at least minimum standards of data accuracy has already been discussed. The topic is repeated here because failure to follow this advice is still one of the main implementation errors.

Achieving accurate data can be a time-consuming and expensive task. It can also seem rather trivial; something that managers should not really have to involve themselves in too deeply. In practice, though, it is attention to detail that brings benefits. Exhortations from above, poster campaigns or threats of disciplinary action achieve little. Most people believe they work reasonably accurately already, so assume the message is directed at others.

Managers have to do two things. Firstly they have to educate people in the need for higher standards than have previously been acceptable. The 'good enough, everyone makes mistakes' standards of accuracy are not acceptable for nurses and airline pilots, and neither are they acceptable any longer in business. Secondly managers have to remove as many as possible of the factors that can lead to errors. Training programmes that are backed up both by thoroughly prepared procedure manuals and by the introduction of secure stores are essential. It is also important, if people are to process data accurately, to stop poor quality information reaching them in the first place.

For example, orders received by fax that are not fully legible should be checked with the customer, rather than being interpreted by guesswork. Stores requisitions in bad handwriting should be queried, and those not quoting a part number rejected. People must be persuaded that they are not helping the company by making judgements on what the information really means. Anything that is not completely clear must be verified with the originator. This may not be a popular message. Some people take pride in using their experience to resolve problems themselves; the less assertive may feel uncomfortable confronting others with their errors, particularly if the response is unhelpful. These obstacles will be overcome only if managers tackle them head-on. The conclusion is inescapable; data integrity is a management responsibility.

Overcomplex bills of material

An overcomplex bill is one which has more levels than is absolutely necessary. They make the task of implementing MRPII much more difficult than it need be. In Chapter 2 we saw how introducing an additional level of sub-assembly into a product's bill of material increases the number of material movements that need to be performed. Every level in the bill requires a works order (except the lowest one, which requires a purchase order), and every works order creates additional stock transactions.

Whenever a works order is completed, one of two things happens to the items that have been made. Either they are passed into a controlled stores or they remain on the shopfloor, as floor stock. Passing the items into stores provides an assurance that stock transactions will be properly processed and quantities accurately counted. On the other hand this approach results in materials movements and handling costs that add no value to the product. Floor stocks do not undergo physical movement, but require computer stock transactions to be made just as if they had been moved into a stockroom. Floor stocks are extremely difficult to keep accurate, and are not easy to cycle count.

The flatter the bill, the fewer the works orders that are planned. This in turn means fewer stock transactions and stocking points, and less scope for error. Flattening bills means more than simply eliminating any levels that are clearly unnecessary. All manufacturing processes must be examined, and any consecutive stages of production which do not need to be controlled by separate works orders should be combined under a single part number. A company making sound mixing equipment for recording studios and theatres found that by taking this approach it was possible to remove three levels from the bill of material. As a result the flow of materials was greatly simplified and lead times were significantly reduced. Furthermore, an MRPII implementation which had stalled picked up momentum again and reached a successful conclusion.

There are other examples. A munitions factory had been struggling unsuccessfully for many years to implement MRPII. A tank round (high explosive shell) that it manufactured had seven active levels plus three phantom levels in its bill of material. As a result, many works orders were needed to manufacture a single batch of shells. The tank that fired the round was manufactured by a successful MRPII company. The bill of material for the tank, a vastly more complex product than the shell, contained only eight levels. There was a programme under way to reduce this number further. The tank manufacturer's success with MRPII was not unconnected with its bill of material policy.

The moral of this story is that there is no absolute number of bill of material levels that is always too great. Complex products inevitably require more levels than simple ones. The problem arises when the bill of material structure creates work that is clearly unnecessary and disrupts natural material flows.

Loss of momentum

A well-managed MRPII implementation typically takes around 18 months; many take much longer. It is extremely difficult to keep the momentum going over this period of time. All kinds of unforeseen events can arise, such as take-over bids, changes of senior managers, unforeseen competitor activity, recessions and lay-offs, and legislative changes. These and other occurrences can all throw an implementation off course.

Faced with events such as these, companies often allow implementation projects to run down. Perhaps most of the system modules have already been installed, and some benefits achieved. A decision is taken to disband the implementation team temporarily, so that its members can return to their normal duties until things settle down again. Of course the danger is that the team is never re-formed. The company gradually settles for a partial implementation, and the project is abandoned.

Unfortunately, partially implemented MRPII is not a stable state; without attention it decays. Audits are not performed, so data accuracy declines. Informal manual systems supplement, and gradually take over from, the formal system. Dissatisfaction with the formal system grows to such an extent that all but the most basic elements are abandoned. The result is not what the company originally intended, and is certainly not MRPII.

It is difficult to protect an implementation against unforeseen changes in the business. Two points are worth bearing in mind, however. Firstly, the greater the commitment to the project throughout the management team, the less reliant is the project on the continued presence of any one individual. Secondly, the faster the project can be completed, the less it is exposed to risk. A thorough education process in the early stages of the project, followed up by a challenging implementation plan, is the best way to keep the momentum going.

Software problems

Problems with software are rarely the primary cause of a failed implementation. Nevertheless problems do sometimes arise, and these can impact on an MRPII implementation in three ways.

It does not work

Instances of package software failing to operate properly are relatively rare, but problems can sometimes be experienced. It may be that the system is newly-written and still contains software bugs. As long as these bugs are speedily dealt with by the supplier this should not be a serious problem, although it can delay implementation. Unfortunately some suppliers take rather longer than they should in dealing with the bugs that are reported to them.

A second way in which the system may fail to work is if the hardware that has been provided turns out to be inadequate for the job. This may result in unacceptably long response times, and may even prevent some of the software modules being implemented until the hardware is upgraded.

The possibility of either of these situations arising can be minimized by following the system selection process described in Chapter 3. In particular, it is wise to choose a proven system, and to visit existing user sites before making a final decision.

It is a poor fit

Software is sometimes acquired which is found subsequently to be unsuitable for the company concerned. This suggests that system specification has been very badly performed. Sometimes companies have little choice in the matter; the system might have been imposed by the parent company, in a misguided attempt to standardize software across all group companies.

In some cases, the failure of an MRPII implementation is blamed unfairly on the software. No system is ever a perfect fit, and when an implementation is running into difficulties it is very easy to blame the software for not meeting every last requirement. More than one company has fallen out with its system supplier because the software did not seem to be delivering the expected facilities. In the majority of cases the true reason for the implementation failing lies elsewhere.

Excessive customization

The most common software-related cause of failure is excessive customization. Once a company starts on this slippery slope, the chances of a successful implementation are dramatically reduced, while implementation costs are likely to spiral. So many successful implementations have been achieved using standard software packages that the need for extensive customization in any circumstances must be in doubt. If a system cannot be found that is a reasonable match with the company's requirements, then specialist advice should be sought.

One of two circumstances generally applies. The first is that the company has some unusual characteristics that mainstream software packages cannot satisfy. An experienced consultant would be able to identify any relevant specialist software. Alternatively, the company has misunderstood MRPII, and is attempting to reproduce its existing system rather than change the way it operates. In this case the consultant would be able to provide the education needed by managers involved in the selection process.

Re-implementation

The assumption has been made in this chapter that companies implementing MRPII are either starting from manual systems or are replacing outdated computer systems. In both cases, the focus of the implementation project is the introduction of a new IBS. There is a further, large category of companies which have a different starting point. These are businesses which already have a perfectly adequate IBS, but which have failed to bring about the changes necessary to create an MRPII environment. The task that faces these companies when making a belated attempt to introduce MRPII concepts is sometimes described as re-implementation.

Re-implementation brings rather different problems than those described so far in this chapter. First-time implementations, involving new software, can readily be projected within the company as exciting, challenging, forward-looking and of benefit to all. High expectations can be aroused, and much enthusiasm generated. This goodwill can overcome many of the problems that arise during the implementation process.

When undertaking a re-implementation, this enthusiasm and momentum is not easy to stimulate. People are much more sceptical the second time around, having experienced the problems of implementation and suffered the disappointments of (at least relative) failure. Re-implementations require even more careful planning and project management than first-time implementations, if such a thing is possible. After all, if a re-implementation project goes wrong there is unlikely to be the opportunity of a third attempt.

Obstacles to success

There are three main obstacles to the success of a re-implementation project that add to the first-time implementation issues already discussed. These obstacles are described below.

Credibility of the software
Since the existing software is associated with the lack of success of the original implementation, it will be widely regarded within the company as wholly or partially to blame for that failure. This makes it difficult for people to see how a re-implementation project, based upon the same software, could possibly succeed.

Furthermore, people are by now very familiar with the day-to-day operation of the system, or at least those parts of it that are in use. Aspects of the system that work well tend to be taken for granted, but any that do not are continuing irritants. The prospect of having to continue living with these irritants will not be well received.

Credibility of senior managers' commitment
Managers need to work hard to convince people of their total commitment to the project, when their previous commitment clearly failed to push the initial project through to success. Why should it be different this time? Perhaps this is merely a last-ditch attempt to get something working before admitting defeat and going back to the old ways.

Very strong leadership is required to persuade the sceptics. Senior managers must keep repeating the message at every opportunity, and make themselves highly visible during the re-implementation process. If they fail in this task, their commitment will be written off as a nine-days' wonder.

Resistance to education and training
The objective of a re-implementation programme is to make substantially better use of the same software. Making better use of a system means using it differently, so it is inevitable that users will need to unlearn many established practices and procedures.

Re-implementation education and training programmes must therefore be able to capture the attention of people who already feel that they know all they need to about the system. In some instances the way the system is being used may be perfectly valid, and will remain unchanged. Other procedures, however, must change, often for reasons that are not obvious to the users concerned.

In an earlier example we saw that there may be many different ways of returning surplus production materials to stores. In a poorly executed implementation it is usually the case that procedures have not been properly thought through and documented. As a result the system users, the storekeepers in this example, cannot have been trained adequately in how to use the various transactions that are available. Being resourceful in-dividuals, the storekeepers would soon hit upon an approach that appeared to keep the stock records reasonably accurate. There seems little doubt that, having gone through this process, the storekeepers would be highly resistant to a subsequent training programme that required them to use a different approach.

It is particularly important in this situation to explain why the present approach is wrong (perhaps because it is leading to inaccurate work in progress records), rather than simply issuing new instructions without explanation. Even then, frequent audits of the way in which the system is being used should be carried out for the first few months. The danger of people sliding back into the previous ways of doing things should not be underestimated.

Planning a re-implementation

The starting point for a re-implementation project is for the top management team to agree anew its commitment to MRPII. This can only be done if the managers concerned share a full understanding of the MRPII concept. Once this commitment has been given, the project must proceed through three main stages.

By following these three stages, and bearing in mind the need to overcome the obstacles already described, a successful re-implementation can be achieved.

Identify reasons for past failure

If the reasons for the previous failure to achieve MRPII are not fully understood, the company cannot be sure of avoiding them the second time around. A thorough, dispassionate review of the previous attempt must therefore be undertaken. This review must avoid allocating blame, since the objective is to learn from previous mistakes, not demotivate people who may well have important roles to play in the re-implementation.

In practice, responsibility for the mistakes made during the original implementation project can always be traced back ultimately to top management. If there was inadequate education, it was because top management did not make the resources available. If the project was badly managed, top management appointed the project manager. If master production scheduling failed to bridge the gulf between production and sales, top management failed to show the necessary leadership and understanding of MRPII concepts. It is therefore up to top managers to take a lead in abandoning defensive positions and to make a frank assessment of the reasons for failure.

The outcome of this review may simply be a determination to approach the implementation differently this time. In other cases there will need to be some more concrete preparatory work. Perhaps there are real drawbacks with the software that need to be corrected, or perhaps an organizational change is called for. It may even be that the organization is so lacking in discipline, and so resistant to any form of change, that any attempt at re-implementation is unlikely to succeed. Under these circumstances, senior managers may consider initiating a formal process of cultural change, typically through a total quality management (TQM) programme, before moving on to re-implementation.

If the review reveals a major inadequacy in the software, a strategy for overcoming this inadequacy is needed. The strategy may involve limited modification of the software, although this is never a desirable route. In an extreme case the decision may be reached that the IBS being used is simply not suitable for the company, and must be replaced. Given the high degree of commonality between all reputable IBS packages, such a situation is quite unusual. What is not unusual is to find companies blaming the system when the real cause of implementation error lies elsewhere.

Restore relationships with the system supplier
It is frequently the case that relationships with the system supplier break down during or after an unsuccessful implementation. Sometimes there is a dramatic split, accompanied by non-payment of invoices and legal action, because the company blames the supplier for the failure. In other cases there is a gradual parting of ways, as the company settles for a partial implementation and requires no further assistance or new system releases from the supplier. In either case, an early task during re-implementation is to restore relationships, if at all possible.

There are several ways in which the supplier can contribute to the project. For example, there will be a need for much user training, to which the supplier should be able to contribute. Also it is possible that new software releases are now available which supply functionality that the company needs. Even if this is not the case, the supplier may be willing to carry out any essential customizing, and be willing to support these modifications through future software releases.

Manage the re-implementation project
The issues to be addressed in managing a re-implementation project are essentially the same as those arising in a first-time implementation. A suitable project management structure must be established, a project plan prepared, education and training programmes drawn up, and so on. The need for education is even greater than in a first-time implementation, because it is so much more difficult to convince people that real improvement is possible.

It is always helpful if the project plan can be structured in such a way that early success is achieved. This is particularly true in the case of a re-implementation, where anything that helps to create an aura of success will contribute to the momentum of the project.

As long as the company follows the guidelines given at the beginning of this chapter in *Implementation the right way,* there is every chance that the re-implementation will succeed where the original attempt did not. The fact that the software is already installed must not be allowed to detract from the need to apply sufficient resources to the project. The task is very large and the stakes are very high. It is up to top management to make sure that this time the project is successful.

Advisers and mentors

Responsibility for implementing MRPII cannot be contracted out. MRPII requires the active involvement of people at all levels in the company, and this will only be achieved if the there is local ownership of the implementation project. Claims from external specialists that they are able to implement MRPII on behalf of a company should be treated with scepticism.

This does not mean that there is no place in an MRPII implementation (or re-implementation) project for external advisers. Indeed there is little merit in companies struggling along unaided when they could call upon help from MRPII specialists. The main sources of help are:

- **System suppliers.** Many of the more established system suppliers have moved beyond merely selling and supporting software, and now actively market implementation assistance as well. This development is partly due to a realization that companies need this kind of support if the sale is to evolve into a good reference site. It also, of course, represents an additional source of revenue for the supplier. Many suppliers, however, lack staff with the broad experience of MRPII needed to undertake this kind of work satisfactorily.
- **Sister companies.** Companies which form part of a group may have a sister company which has already implemented MRPII. Key people from that company who have learnt from experience how to go about a successful implementation could contribute a great deal, and efforts should be made to secure one or more temporary secondments to the new implementation.
- **Independent consultants.** Many consultancy companies and academic institutions offer MRPII expertise of varying degrees. Companies seeking assistance from this quarter should check the track record of the consultancy, and of the consultant assigned to the project, very carefully. If an adviser retained during system selection provided valuable assistance, it would make sense to continue the relationship throughout implementation. The adviser has already acquired a good understanding of the company, has gained the confidence of the people, and understands its vision of the future.

There are three areas of assistance that can be provided by external advisers.

Education programmes

Education programmes are almost always better carried out by specialist consultants. Even when there is expertise within the company it is better for the educational process to be led by outsiders. The purpose of education is to change existing perceptions about how the company should plan and control its operations. This is only likely to be achieved if the message is communicated by someone who is visibly outside the company's hierarchy and internal politics.

Some consultancies which specialize in MRPII education run regular public courses and produce highly professional educational material. They may also market videos and books that can supplement face-to-face education. The alternative is to use consultants who may be more willing to tailor their approach to the particular needs of the company concerned. The result may not be as glossy, but it might be more relevant to a particular business.

Technical expertise

From time to time during an implementation, technical issues arise which the company may not have the expertise to resolve. Even worse, the company may not recognize that there is an issue to be addressed. If the company has an external adviser who makes regular visits to carry out implementation health checks, these issues can be easily identified and resolved.

These issues may sometimes relate to difficulties with the software, or to the desirability of acquiring additional modules. In these circumstances the company may feel that an independent consultant could offer more impartial advice than an employee of the system supplier.

Project management

An MRPII implementation may be the largest project ever undertaken by the company. This means that members of the project team have to learn project management skills at the same time as they are struggling to understand the demands of MRPII. A consultant who has previous experience of large projects can assist with the preparation and maintenance of the project plan, removing some of the burden from the project manager.

Even when a sound plan is in place, and regular review meetings arranged, the consultant still has a role to play. Review meetings can be greatly sharpened by the attendance of someone who is able to highlight areas of slippage, and who is not influenced by internal collusion, possibly unspoken, to accept the delay as inevitable.

No company likes paying consultancy fees, but the cost of not doing so can be very much higher. With such a wealth of information available about the high rate of failure in MRPII projects, it seems more than a little presumptuous for a company to assume it can succeed without professional help.

Summary

The aim of this chapter has been to explain the essential tasks that must be addressed in an MRPII implementation, and to highlight some common pitfalls. No attempt has been made to propose a universal MRPII implementation plan, since no two companies approach MRPII from the same start point or with identical business objectives. Each company must create its own implementation plan, based upon its particular needs and resources.

Nevertheless, it is worth summarizing here some of the key issues discussed in this chapter. Any implementation plan that fails to address these issues starts out with a major handicap. Critical tasks are to:

- select the right people for the core project team, especially the project manager, and give them the time and resources to do the job properly
- prepare a realistic project plan, and stick to it
- educate everyone in the company, to the appropriate level
- use the business redesign methodology (Figure 4.1) to initiate specific implementation tasks. Never forget that MRPII means fundamental changes to the business
- train thoroughly
- manage data integrity
- measure progress and take corrective action when necessary
- take advice from someone who has done it before.

Implementing MRPII can appear to be a daunting task, but with a sound, adequately resourced plan and top management support there is no reason why a company should fail to meet its objectives. In this competitive world, it may well be that a greater business risk than implementing MRPII is deciding **not** to implement MRPII.

— 5 —

Limitations of MRPII

MRPII: a universal solution?

The MRPII concept is not industry-specific. Companies with manufacturing processes ranging from bulk chemical manufacture to craft working successfully adopt MRPII. Products ranging from fast moving consumer goods to large, one-off engineering projects are planned and controlled by closed loop MRP. Is it true, then, that MRPII is a universal solution, equally applicable to all forms of manufacturing?

The answer is a qualified yes. There is no form of manufacturing where MRPII is inapplicable. On the other hand there are situations where it is particularly difficult to achieve success with MRPII, and where success brings fewer benefits. Even in these situations companies persevere with MRPII, largely because of the lack of a satisfactory alternative. If a company wants systems integration, together with a structured approach to short, medium and long term planning, it has no option but MRPII.

MRPII is based upon a model of how manufacturing companies operate. The model is quite flexible, enabling it to be adapted to a wide range of circumstances, but it is not an exact representation of any one business. The limitations within the model are more significant in some types of business environment than others. Before embarking upon an MRPII implementation it is prudent to be prepared for those limitations that may make the journey more difficult than expected.

This chapter examines some of the potential drawbacks of MRPII, and relates them to the business situations in which they are likely to be significant.

Industry differences

The term 'manufacturing' covers such an enormous range of activities that some forms of manufacture must prove more amenable to the MRPII concept than others. There are various ways of categorizing industry types, but in the context of MRPII the most useful categorization of industries is as follows:

- flow-based
- batch
- jobbing
- specialist.

The general applicability of MRPII to each of these industry categories is discussed below.

Flow-based industries

Chapter 3 explained why flow-based manufacture does not fit well with some conventional MRPII techniques. Flow-based manufacture was defined as embracing continuous process, repetitive, and levelled schedule manufacture. The essential characteristic of all these forms of manufacture is that works orders are not a suitable mechanism for planning and controlling production activities. Software featuring rate scheduling, as an alternative to works orders, overcomes this difficulty.

Companies in flow-based industries that attempted to implement MRPII before the availability of suitable software found the task extremely difficult. These industries are now well catered for by software suppliers, however, and there is no reason why MRPII should not be successfully implemented by companies in those industries.

Some process plants are built to manufacture a single product, or a set of co-products, and operate in a steady-state mode. Since MRPII is primarily concerned with planning material and capacity requirements in circumstances of varying product mix and volumes, its benefits in this environment are fairly limited. Other flow-based industries present more complex planning and scheduling issues, and derive greater benefit from MRPII.

In the latter category are an increasing number of companies that would once have regarded themselves as batch manufacturers. The introduction of cellular manufacture, flow-based factory layouts and level scheduling has moved them into the category of flow-based manufacturing. These companies can derive great benefit from MRPII, but they may need different shopfloor scheduling and control systems than they would have used as batch manufacturers. Production scheduling issues are discussed in Chapter 6.

The general trend in process industries is that product variety is increasing, changeovers are becoming more frequent, and customers are demanding faster and more reliable service. For companies experiencing these changes, MRPII is the obvious means of managing the greater complexity and providing faster response.

Batch manufacturing industries

Batch manufacturing is the environment most commonly associated with MRPII. Typically batch manufacturing includes the manufacture of component parts, fabrication and sub-assembly (sometimes through several production stages), and final assembly of a range of finished products. All the characteristics of complexity that MRPII was designed to deal with are present: variable product mix, multiple bill of material levels, a large variety of shared manufacturing processes, and manufacture in discrete batches.

Within batch manufacturing there are four different ways of responding to customer demand: make for stock, make to forecast (which is really a variation on make for stock), make to order (standard products), and engineer to order (including bespoke design or customization). It is probably true that most batch manufacturing companies combine a mixture of these approaches, although they may be biased towards one of them. All four methods of operation are consistent with MRPII principles, although some IBS products are aimed specifically at one or other of these environments.

Batch manufacturing in general is the form of manufacture for which the MRPII concept was developed, so there are no special implementation difficulties in companies of this type. Considerable benefits are obtained by batch manufacturers who carry out well managed MRPII implementations.

The greatest benefits go to those companies with the most complex products and manufacturing processes. This does not mean that a complex MRPII implementation is a good implementation; on the contrary, every effort should be made to simplify shopfloor activities. It is simply that where the environment is unavoidably complex, MRPII is markedly superior to any alternative form of planning and control.

Jobbing shops

Jobbing shops generally operate as sub-contractors to other manufacturing companies. They manufacture either individual components or simple sub-assemblies, rather than complete commercial goods. Quantities are often small, although some contracts may involve quite large batches. Sometimes the skills of jobbing shops lie in fairly narrow areas: computer numerical control (CNC) machining, plating or printing, for example. Other jobbing shops possess a variety of general-purpose machinery and will turn their hands to a range of different products.

Some jobbing shops, such as toolmakers, provide a design service, while others simply produce to their customers' drawings or specifications. Although there may be some repeat business, much of the work is one-off contracts. This characteristic can cause a significant cost penalty in the use of MRPII.

MRPII needs a great deal of information before it can make any contribution to the planning process. Data such as item master details (part numbers, lead times, lot sizing rules etc), bills of material and routings must all be created for every new product. Where there is little repeat business, the not insignificant cost involved in setting up this data must be justified by the benefits obtained in the planning and control of a single contract.

Two of the great strengths of MRPII are the medium to long term planning of materials and capacity, and the short term co-ordination of components required for assembly. It is to these strengths that jobbing shops must look to provide the benefits that can justify the use of MRPII. Unfortunately, in a jobbing shop environment neither of these strengths is as significant as it is for batch manufacturers.

Firstly, attempts at medium to long term planning are hampered by forecasting difficulties. Demand forecasting is difficult enough for batch manufacturers, but they at least know what products they will be offering for sale; only the quantities are at issue. A jobbing shop frequently has little idea of even the kind of products its customers will require.

Secondly, in the case of the co-ordination of components required for assembly, MRPII certainly can contribute. The benefits, however, may not be very great. Jobbing shop products often contain relatively few components, and sometimes only a single item, so the task of planning assembly is fairly straightforward even without MRPII.

This analysis should not be taken as evidence that MRPII is unsuitable for jobbing shops. Many companies in this sector do make complex products that need the co-ordination MRPII can provide. Others have sufficient repeat business to justify setting up product data in an IBS, and to enable forecasting of demand to be carried out. Furthermore, some IBS products provide valuable help in creating quotations for new contracts, enabling estimates to be combined with historical data to build up a tender price. If the contract is won, further detail can be added to the original estimate to create full process plans.

Nevertheless, if jobbing shops that have a high rate of new product introduction are to benefit from MRPII they must minimize the cost of entering product information into the IBS. One way this can be achieved is by linking any computer aided design (CAD) system that is used in product design with the database of the IBS. Certain item details and basic bill of material data can be transferred in this way without the need to re-key the data. Some IBS suppliers offer support for links of this kind, which can be very valuable to jobbing companies in particular. Without standard software facilities, the differences in data structures and data handling can make it quite difficult to transfer product details between CAD systems and an IBS.

A technique for speeding up data entry that can be used where the new product is similar to a previous one is to copy the existing data. Complete bills of material and routings can be copied from the earlier product to the new one, and any differences corrected by exception. Companies that may find this technique of value should make certain when selecting an IBS that it does in fact provide the necessary facilities.

In some ways the argument about the cost of data entry is fallacious. If the product is to be made, then information must be generated somewhere to specify materials, processes, lot sizes and so on. Entering this data into an IBS only results in extra cost if it has already been created elsewhere. The objective must be to ensure that data is only created once, and is automatically made available to any other business application that needs it.

This means, for example, stopping planning engineers from writing out operation details onto process lay-outs for subsequent keying into the system by clerks. The IBS must be the primary repository for data, not a back-up. Planning engineers must, like everyone else, enter their own data directly into the system. The principle of data entry at source applies to engineers and other technical and professional staff, just as it does to storekeepers and order processing clerks.

Specialist industries

Most MRP-based software has been developed using the concepts and terminology of engineering manufacture. Engineering-based systems can be quite unacceptable in other industries, either because the terminology is totally foreign or because functions important in those industries are lacking. Several major system suppliers now offer process industry versions of their IBS products but few have ventured into other, more specialist, industry sectors.

An example of an industry where engineering-based software is generally unsuitable is garment manufacture. Garments tend to be supplied in a range of sizes and colours. A ladies' blouse available in four sizes and three colours would require twelve separate item records in an engineering-based system. Each size and colour variation would be regarded as a separate product. Yet to the garment industry all variants are part of a single product, or 'style'. A retailer might place an order for, say, 100 dozen blouses, without specifying the mix of sizes and colours; these would be called off later.

Specialist garment industry systems are available that can deal with this situation with ease. Other specialist software is available for industries such as food, textiles (knitting, weaving and spinning), printing, plastic injection moulding, and foundries. Much of this software has been developed by small companies whose main area of expertise lies in the industry in which they operate. As a result, these systems sometimes lack sophistication in their approach to MRPII concepts. Companies selecting specialist industry software should take particular care not to take for granted the presence of core MRPII features in these systems.

Often the availability of sophisticated MRPII facilities such as RCCP or ATP is less important than the particular industry features that are offered. In these cases the manufacturer would be perfectly correct to select the specialist software. Nevertheless, the assumption should not be made that just because the system contains an MRP module, the full range of MPS, MRP and CRP features will automatically be present.

MRP and CRP: oversimplified techniques?

MRP was developed as a means by which the processing power of computers could be applied to the most complex production planning problems. It can produce a twelve-month manufacturing schedule for a wide range of products, each containing thousands of components, through an enormous variety of manufacturing resources, all within the space of a few hours' processing time. This problem would be hugely complex even without the considerable scope that exists for unpredictable events and random statistical fluctuations. It is wholly unreasonable to expect that MRP, or indeed any other process, could produce an optimal schedule so far ahead, in so little time.

MRP's approach is to make several simplifying assumptions, which reduce the problem to one that can be solved by simple arithmetic. Within this arithmetical procedure there is no comparison of alternative solutions, no in-built criteria for success or failure, and no use of knowledge-based techniques for making judgements and decisions. MRP is a purely mechanical process that converts the MPS into a set of detailed actions. The outcome is only as good as the MPS; its feasibility can only be established through the use of CRP.

The main simplifying assumptions made by MRP and CRP are:

- fixed lead times
- infinite capacity
- queuing time
- fixed batch quantities.

The effects of these assumptions are discussed in the following sections.

Fixed lead times

In carrying out lead time off-setting, MRP makes use of the planning lead time contained in the item master record of the part number being processed. Lead times, like lot sizing rules and safety stocks, must be meaningful if MRP is to produce useful information. Lead times are considered to be fixed, because they are not changed by the MRP process itself. Furthermore, it is not realistic to expect the planner to adjust large numbers of lead times before each MRP run, to take account of any temporary bottlenecks in production.

Lead times therefore need to represent a typical throughput time for the item in question. It would be wrong to inflate lead times to cover every possible eventuality, since this would cause the cumulative lead times for finished products to be overstated. Excessive product lead times result in higher inventory than necessary, forecasting difficulties, and reduced customer service. Clearly it is important to keep the lead times of individual items as low as possible.

Unfortunately there is no method of calculating optimal lead times. Lead times comprise a number of elements, not all of which can be measured accurately. The processing time at each operation can usually be established with reasonable accuracy by measurement or through the use of estimating techniques. The run time to process a complete batch of items will, of course, depend upon the number of items to be processed, and this may vary from order to order.

Other elements of lead time do not vary with batch quantity. Machine set-up times can be determined in a similar way to processing times, although they may vary depending upon the tooling already on the machine when the set-up starts. Transit times between operations may be relatively constant if, for example, some form of powered conveyor is used. If the batch has to wait for the availability of a fork lift truck the transit time could be much less predictable.

In practice, all these elements of lead time are usually completely overshadowed by queuing time. It is quite common to find queuing times of between ten and one hundred times the run time for the batch. In consequence, planning lead times are usually set without reference to the individual elements of run time, set-up time, transit time and queue time, and are based purely upon experience and judgement. Chapter 7 examines how lead times fixed in this way can be verified and, where possible, reduced.

No matter how carefully planning lead times are set, the fact remains that the actual lead time for a particular batch is dependent upon a combination of events that are unique to that batch. These events determine the length of the queue at each work centre when the batch arrives for processing, the sequence in which those queues are processed, the availability of operators at the time required, and so on. Lead times are inevitably subject to variation from batch to batch, and the assumption made by MRP that lead times are fixed is an approximation.

All managers have experienced the urgent job that was completed within a fraction of the normal lead time. MRP, however, cannot plan for this type of lead time compression. The best that can be done is to master schedule an urgent job at the date it is required, and accept that lower level items will be planned by MRP with due dates that in some cases have already passed. These dates must be manually overridden with realistic dates based upon the shorter lead times that will apply for this batch. These dates can be protected from being rescheduled by subsequent MRP runs by changing the status of the orders to firm planned (see Chapter 2).

Although the planning lead times used by MRP are generally set without reference to the individual lead time elements, these elements are needed to enable operation start dates and due dates to be calculated. When MRP plans an order, it only determines the date the entire order must start and finish. It is not concerned with the dates of the various operations that make up the routing of the order. Operation dates are needed, however, for two reasons. The first reason, discussed below, is to enable capacity requirements to be time-phased. The second, discussed in Chapter 6, is to permit queues to be sequenced.

Operation dates are calculated individually for each works order, using information on the lead time elements for every operation to be performed. This information (set-up time, processing time, transit time and queuing time) is held in the relevant routing and work centre records. Collecting and maintaining this data is a major undertaking for companies where it is not available prior to MRPII implementation. There may be thousands of manufactured items to be analyzed, and each item may have several operations. The task can only be performed properly by experienced production engineers, and these are a scarce resource in most companies. The time and cost involved in carrying out this work must be considered at an early stage of planning an MRPII implementation.

Operation dates are calculated either by working forward from the order start date, or, more usually, by backward scheduling from the order due date. Since this calculation is quite independent of the planning lead times used by MRP, there is no guarantee that the overall order lead time calculated will be the same. If backward scheduling is used, for example, the calculated start date for the first operation may not coincide with the order start date generated by MRP.

Some systems permit the two lead times to be reconciled by providing the option of using the calculated lead time to update the MRP lead time. This approach has an initial appearance of precision, since a calculated lead time, based upon the normal lot size, must surely be better than an estimate of the overall lead time for the item. In fact, of course, the calculated lead time is based predominantly upon separate estimates of the queuing time at each work centre the item passes through. An overall estimate of total lead time may actually be more accurate than an accumulation of many separate estimates of queue time.

Infinite capacity

Capacity requirements planning uses calculated operation dates to assign the load imposed by both planned and released orders to the time buckets defined for that CRP run. These time buckets are normally a week, or longer. There is no point in using shorter periods for CRP because the operation dates are not sufficiently accurate. Actual queue times at each operation may vary quite considerably from the standard queue times used in calculating the operation dates. As a result, a CRP report based upon very short time buckets (say one day) would assign much of the work to the wrong bucket.

There is a second reason why CRP time buckets need to cover at least a week. The workload on each work centre in a particular time bucket is calculated by aggregating the loads imposed by all the orders which are planned to use that work centre. If the total load in a period exceeds the available capacity of the work centre, CRP merely reports the overload. CRP does not contain any mechanism for restricting further orders from being planned during that time bucket, nor does it attempt to smooth the load. A CRP report based on daily time buckets could therefore show wild swings from one bucket to the next, with heavy overloads on some days being balanced by underloads on others. Such a report would be of little use to the planner or to production.

Using a time bucket of at least a week enables the worst of the random fluctuations in load to be smoothed out, so that a more realistic picture of overall work centre loading is obtained. Even then, there may be temporary overloads affecting certain work centres which make achievement of the MPS impossible. The planner must decide if the situation requires an amendment to the MPS, followed by a revised MRP run. In practice this rarely happens in most companies, and instead some contingency action is taken to deal with the overload. Various methods are available including using alternative machines, working overtime, sub-contracting and splitting batches.

The inability of MRP and CRP to work within finite capacity limitations can be seen as an oversimplification. On the other hand the RCCP activity, if properly performed, should ensure that any overloads are temporary and manageable. Furthermore, since there is usually a variety of ways in which capacity may be increased temporarily, perhaps MRP is right to assume that capacity is elastic. Choosing between the alternative ways of expanding capacity is a task that would be difficult to automate on a routine basis. Merely highlighting the overload for the attention of the planner, as CRP does, is arguably the most practical approach.

Queuing time

The real oversimplification in MRPII's use of planning lead times and its method of calculating operation dates is queuing time. The queuing time element is by far the greatest part of overall lead time. Why is this so? Could not queuing time be excluded from lead times altogether? Would this not result in batches passing from operation to operation without being delayed in queues at each work centre? Sadly this is not the case.

Imagine what would happen if all queuing time were eliminated from lead times, and then CRP was run using daily time buckets. Workloads would fluctuate from day to day and, on some days, would exceed capacity. Some operations could not, therefore, be completed on the day planned, and would become overdue. The only way this lost time could be retrieved would be by speeding up subsequent operations, and this may not be possible. Without queuing time, there is no slack within the lead time to absorb the lateness.

The problem is that there is nothing in the logic of MRP and CRP that prevents contention between two or more jobs requiring the same resource at the same time. Over a longer period, say a week or more, capacity may be adequate. That is no help if two eight-hour jobs are needed from a single machine on a Monday, and there is no spare capacity until the following Friday; by then one of the jobs will be late. Queuing time is used to overcome this problem. Including queuing time in manufacturing lead times creates slack to absorb delays caused by temporary queues.

Unfortunately, by including queuing time in planning lead times MRP is not just recognizing that queues will sometimes form, it is creating them.

The longer the queuing time that is allowed, the earlier orders need to be issued to production if they are to be finished on time. The number of jobs in work in progress increases, and as a result the queues become longer. It is a fine balancing act to establish queue times that are long enough to prevent arrears being inevitable, without incurring excessive work in progress levels.

MRP is not really to blame for this situation. Queuing time was an element of lead times before MRP came upon the scene. The criticism is that MRP fails to address the problem, and therefore perpetuates long lead times. Other, more recent scheduling techniques are sometimes considered to be superior to MRP because they aim to minimize queuing time. The claims of these techniques are examined in Chapter 6.

Fixed batch quantities

The last of the major simplifications made by MRP and CRP is the assumption of fixed batch quantities. Whenever MRP plans a new order it applies the specified lot sizing rule to determine the quantity to order. The assumption is then made that this batch will pass from operation to operation as a single entity.

There are two problems here. The first is that there is no recognition of capacity availability in calculating the batch quantity. What seems a sensible lot sizing rule in normal circumstances may not be if one of the work centres through which the job passes is presently overloaded. The second problem is that in practice a batch is not a single entity, but a collection of individual items. There is no reason why the entire batch must be processed before it can move to the next operation.

In practice batches are often split after an initial quantity has been produced, so that the subsequent operation may be started. If the machines are close together, and the processing times are similar, items may pass individually from the first machine to the second. In the case of a severe bottleneck arising, a batch may be split so that only the quantity needed immediately is processed. The balance is held back until the overload has cleared. This makes nonsense of the original use of the lot sizing rule, which was presumably intended to achieve efficiency in production.

Neither of these situations presents major difficulties to companies using MRPII, but they illustrate a lack of intelligence in the MRP process. They provide a further reason why the operation start dates and due dates calculated for the order are at best only approximate indications of when the work will actually be performed.

The impact of simplification

The simplifications described here impact on all MRPII users to a greater or lesser extent. The assumptions of fixed lead times and batch quantities impact most severely upon companies which have complex flow paths through their production facilities. The more operations there are to be performed, and the further apart the work centres are located, the greater the scheduling problem. Many companies now recognize that MRPII alone cannot solve this scheduling problem and that a different approach is needed. The solution is to simplify the problem by improving physical material flows through the use of cellular and flow-based manufacture. MRP lead times can then be reduced to reflect the faster throughput that these improvements permit.

The infinite capacity assumption causes the greatest difficulty in companies where a significant number of work centres are working at, or near to, their capacities. Whereas RCCP can cope adequately with a small number of critical resources, it cannot handle large numbers of simultaneous constraints. In practice, relatively few factories are in the position of having multiple simultaneous constraints. This is a risky position for a company to find itself in, and an increase in resources is probably a greater priority than seeking a scheduling system that can deal with the problem.

All in all the drawbacks caused by the simplifications of MRPII are usually acceptable, subject to two provisos. Firstly, great care must be taken to ensure that MRP lead times are no longer than is absolutely necessary. Secondly, some means of scheduling production on a day-to-day basis is required to ensure that queues are processed in the right sequence. Short-term scheduling must reconcile real life constraints with the approximate plans generated by MRP and CRP. Both of these issues are considered in later chapters.

Although MRP and CRP make use of some fairly sweeping simplifications, the overall outcome can be acceptably close to reality. Without these simplifying assumptions it would not be possible to make the medium to long term projections needed to plan current and future purchasing and capacity requirements. There is simply no alternative to MRPII that combines this ability to create long term material and capacity plans with short term works order control.

MRP nervousness

Each new MRP run generates planned orders and reschedules existing orders as necessary to satisfy the situation with which it is faced. These recommendations are reported in exception reports, which must be actioned by the planner. The number of exceptions reported by each MRP run depends primarily upon the extent of change to the MPS since the last run. A single change to the MPS can cascade down through the bill of material of the product concerned, causing a large number of MRP exceptions. Restraint in making MPS changes is needed if a reasonable degree of stability is to be achieved. Chapter 2 discussed the use of time fences to restrict the extent of change permitted in the early part of the planning horizon.

The tendency of MRP to recommend many actions in response to a small number of changes is one dimension of a phenomenon described as 'MRP nervousness'. The second dimension of nervousness is MRP's tendency to make large adjustments in order quantities and time-phasing in response to small changes in demand. These two aspects of MRP nervousness are discussed below.

Schedule stability

The MRP process creates a rigid linkage between the MPS and the dependent demand items that are to be planned. There is no flexibility or elasticity in the calculation to damp out insignificant changes. If stock of an item is projected to fall to 999, when its safety stock level is 1000, then corrective action will be planned which will affect all the components of that item.

A human planner in the same situation would weigh up the situation before initiating any replanning. If the stock projection was based upon a forecast, which may well change in the future, or if (as in this case) the shortfall was very small in relationship to the safety stock level, or if a replenishment batch was due shortly anyway, it is unlikely that any action would be judged necessary. MRP is unable to apply such reasoning, and instead applies its remorseless logic to the situation.

If the volume of changes is to be restricted, every effort must be made to maintain a stable MPS. Accurate forecasting helps, but is never an easy option. The use of time fences to impose an artificial stability on the MPS also helps, although it can run counter to attempts to increase flexibility in response to customer demands.

Companies most affected by schedule instability are those which are subject to highly variable demand while also having long manufacturing lead times. Such companies have little choice but to work to reduce overall lead times. The alternative approach of buffering production from the vagaries of customer demand by the use of safety stocks does nothing to reduce nervousness, as we saw in Chapter 2. Safety stocks protect against uncertainty, not disruption.

The multiplier effect

The problem of nervousness is exacerbated by MRP's tendency to react to change by making mountains out of molehills. A multiplier effect comes into play which exaggerates small changes in circumstances that occur from one MRP run to the next. This multiplier can operate in several different ways to create rescheduling actions that are out of proportion to the change that initiated them. Two examples are given here.

The effect of lot sizing rules

A simple example of the lot sizing effect is the item that needs its stock level of 999 topped up to 1000. Lot sizing rules determine that if an order is required, then a batch of 500 must be manufactured. This batch places demands on lower level items, which in turn may fall below their safety stock levels.

Several large orders could be created through this process, consuming materials originally purchased for more urgent items, and absorbing limited manufacturing capacity.

Rescheduling released orders

Once a planned order has been approved by the planner and turned into a scheduled receipt, MRP has only two means of changing it. The order can be

PERIOD		1	2	3	4	5	6
GROSS REQUIREMENT		10	10	10	10	10	500
SCHEDULED RECEIPT		50					500
PROJECTED BALANCE	0	40	30	20	10	0	0
PLANNED ORDER							

MRP run number 1

PERIOD		1	2	3	4	5	6
GROSS REQUIREMENT		10	50	0	0	0	500
SCHEDULED RECEIPT		50	500				
PROJECTED BALANCE	0	40	490	490	490	490	40
PLANNED ORDER							50

MRP run number 2

Figure 5.1 Example of rescheduling a released order

recommended for re-dating (either expedite or delay) or it can be recommended for cancellation. Order quantities cannot be changed.

Figure 5.1 shows an example of re-dating at work. MRP, working on a minimum order quantity of 50, originally planned a batch of 50 in period 1 and a batch of 500 in period 6. A subsequent MRP run has generated some changes to the gross requirement line. An extra 40 items are needed in period 2, while demand totalling 30 has disappeared from periods 3 to 5.

MRP has reacted by expediting the batch of 500 by four periods and planning a new order in period 6. The effect of this rescheduling has been to create an unexpectedly large scheduled receipt in period 2, which is merely causing a high stock level during periods 2 to 5. Perhaps it would have made more sense to leave the batch of 500 in period 6, and plan the new order for 50 in period 2. If this approach had been taken there would have been far less disruption, and the stock in periods 2 to 5 would have been only 40 units.

The rules by which MRP operates do not permit this more sensible approach, however. These rules say that existing scheduled receipts must be expedited before new orders can be planned. In most circumstances this logic gives the best results, since it would usually be confusing and impractical for MRP to plan a new order earlier than an existing released order for the same item. Nevertheless, the result of this logic can be some unnecessarily severe reschedules.

Combating the multiplier effect

Although the multiplier effect is an enduring feature of MRP, there are techniques that can be used to minimize its effect. The following actions can all contribute to a reduction in the number and magnitude of spurious MRP exception messages.

Firstly, care should be taken in the use of lot sizing rules. The ideal is to use a lot for lot policy wherever possible, to eliminate the problem of a small requirement being rounded up to a minimum order quantity. Flattening the bill of material also helps. The fewer levels there are in the bill, the less opportunity there is for the multiplier effect to work. Converting planned orders into scheduled receipts as late as possible is good practice because it reduces the extent to which those orders may need subsequent rescheduling. Finally, planners should not be tempted to make frequent changes to MRP parameters in an attempt to fine-tune the system. Every time safety stocks or lot sizing rules are changed, MRP will generate many knock-on actions through the bill of material.

Filtering the messages

In many companies the regular MRP run sends huge stacks of computer paper full of recommended reschedules to the desks of the planners. Many of these recommendations will not be actioned, because they are too trivial to bother with, too late to process, or too numerous to scrutinize. Sometimes the mounds of paper are reduced in size by incorporating filters in the print programs that prevent minor changes being printed at all. The definition of a minor change is controlled by the planner through system parameters. For example, the planner may specify that no expedite action of less than five days, and no defer action of less than ten days should be printed.

Neither manual scrutiny nor predetermined filters are very efficient methods of deciding whether or not to action an MRP exception. Simply ignoring small changes can be disastrous if it results in a small but vital shortage on a major contract. Conversely, automatically accepting a change just because it is large could be inappropriate if the magnitude of the change results from the multiplier effect rather than a customer need. Knowledge-based systems have been used to add sophistication to the process of reducing the number of exception messages. These systems attempt to mimic the decision process that a human planner would follow, given sufficient time, in deciding whether or not to action a reschedule.

It is important to remember that any method of filtering out exception messages is only hiding them from view, it is not changing the logic applied by MRP. If no action is taken, and the situation that led to the reschedule message is unchanged, the same exception message is reported (or filtered out) by future MRP runs. Eventually the mismatch of supply and demand that caused the recommended reschedule passes into history, possibly at some cost in customer service.

When MRP recommends that an order should be rescheduled it does not amend the original order date; this must be done by the planner in approving the action. Exception messages are generated by MRP as it works, level by level, down through the bill of material. As part of this process, all works orders which have not yet been kitted must be exploded down to the next level. When an order has been recommended for rescheduling, a problem arises. At which date should the demand be exploded to its components; the existing start date of the order or the recommended reschedule date?

Clearly MRP must assume that its recommendations will be accepted by the planner, so demand for lower level items must be dated accordingly. As a result, a planner actioning some exception messages whilst ignoring others may find that those reschedules that have been accepted are rendered unachievable. Unless there is surplus inventory available, it is only possible to expedite a works order if the components and raw materials from which it is to be made are also expedited. The planner, in deciding that it is too late to expedite one order, may not realize that this means components not being available when needed for another order that has been expedited. The exception report makes no linkage between the two messages that would highlight this dependency.

The only sure way of handling exception messages is to action all of them. If there are too many, then action must be taken, as described earlier, to improve schedule stability and reduce the causes of the multiplier effect. Excessive exception messages are a sign of poor health in an MRPII implementation. The cure lies in treating the disease, not the symptoms.

Is nervousness a reason to be nervous?

The fact that nervousness is a characteristic of MRP is not a reason to lose faith in the MRPII concept. There is no planning methodology that can turn a volatile and poorly managed delivery schedule into a stable and efficient manufacturing plan. Nervousness merely happens to be the way in which MRP warns that liberties are being taken with the planning process.

The crucial task for managers in dealing with nervousness is to realize that it is happening. Planners may simply assume that the quantity of exception messages they have to deal with is normal. Whether they action all of the reschedules and cause disruption to production, or ignore many and jeopardize customer service, the origin of the problem can easily be missed. It is only when the true cause of the problem has been identified that the correct action can be taken to deal with it.

Perhaps the part of the company most heavily affected by nervousness is purchasing. Each time a rescheduling action is passed down to a lower level item, there is a further opportunity for the multiplier effect to operate. At the same time, lead time off-setting brings the action nearer to the current date. As the last link in the chain, purchasing always receives the least notice of the reschedule. The next section examines how well MRPII copes with this and other aspects of the purchasing task.

Purchasing in an MRPII environment

MRP plans orders for purchased items in exactly the same way that it does for manufactured items. These new orders must be reviewed and approved by the planner, at which point they become purchase requisitions. The next step is to convert the purchase requisitions into purchase orders, by sourcing them with a suitable supplier. Approval and sourcing can be carried out simultaneously, but in some companies approval is carried out by a materials or inventory control department whilst sourcing is the responsibility of buying.

Purchasing has changed dramatically since MRPII concepts were first developed. Competitive tendering and adversarial relationships have been widely replaced by long term supply arrangements and co-makership. At the same time, the trend for manufacturing companies to focus upon core skills while sub-contracting non-strategic items makes purchasing more important than ever. This changing role of purchasing places different demands upon MRPII. In principle, MRPII has much to offer this new world of co-operative supplier relationships. In practice, however, the software tools available often fall short of the need.

Discrete orders

To MRP, each time-phased requirement represents a single order, quite independent of any other order that may be outstanding for the same item. Each order can, if desired, be sourced with a different supplier. This approach is consistent with old-style purchasing, where the buyer would source every order individually, based on the lowest price negotiable at the time of placing the order. Using several suppliers simultaneously for the same item was regarded as good practice, to ensure continuity of supply. Lot sizing rules could be used to ensure that each discrete order was large enough to qualify for volume discounts. Because these large orders often represented several weeks' requirements, they appeared at infrequent and irregular intervals.

One problem with this approach is that the supplier does not know when to expect the next order, if ever, so is unable to plan for it. The supplier therefore requires long lead times to respond to the order when it does arrive. These lead times can be built into the MRP process without difficulty, but they inevitably have the effect of extending the cumulative lead time for the finished product. As a result, longer range forecasts are needed. Because these forecasts are inaccurate, the task of maintaining a stable schedule is made more difficult.

The result is that nervousness is endemic, and suppliers are swamped with reschedules. The arms' length relationship between buyer and supplier makes it difficult to avoid disputes arising over the extent of the rescheduling and the consequential poor delivery performance.

Purchase scheduling

Most companies are now seeking to improve supplier relationships, typically by:

● reducing the number of suppliers they use
● buying a wider range of items from the remaining suppliers
● entering long term single-sourcing agreements
● using purchase schedules, rather than discrete orders to schedule deliveries
● involving suppliers in new product development at an early stage
● forming partnerships with suppliers based upon shared benefits rather than zero-sum negotiations.

It is in the use of purchase schedules that the impact of these changes is felt most strongly by MRPII.

Types of purchase schedule

There are two main types of purchase scheduling, the blanket order and the rolling schedule. The blanket order can be regarded as a half-way house towards improved supplier relationships. Here the buyer shows a longer term commitment by placing a bulk order, typically for one year's material. This material can be called off as required, but the buyer is committed to take any outstanding balance at the end of the year. This type of scheduling involves a limited commitment towards the supplier, but demonstrates a complete lack of trust between the two parties. The blanket order is seen as necessary to prevent either of them from defaulting on the agreement.

The effect of blanket orders is that the buyer takes all the risk that demand for the goods made from the material in question may not reach expected levels; the supplier is protected from any reduction in demand for the material. The supplier's risk is that next year's blanket order may go to a competitor who has submitted a lower tender. This uncertain situation is not conducive to long-term investments in quality, product development or productivity by the supplier.

Rolling schedules require a much greater mutual trust. The assumption is that the arrangement is permanent, without the constant threat from the buyer that in a few months the work could be withdrawn. In return, the supplier acknowledges that its business is dependent upon the success of the buyer's products. Any variations in demand for these products will have an immediate impact upon demand for its own materials. The supplier is therefore provided with a strong motive to help in making its customer's products as competitive as possible.

The essential characteristic of both forms of scheduling is that they effectively eliminate purchasing lead time. Schedules provide the supplier with a view of demand as far into the future as possible. Suppliers use this information to reserve capacity and plan their own raw material purchases. Fluctuations in demand can be accommodated because the long-term nature of the relationship encourages the supplier to give the customer priority, and perhaps to hold some material in stock.

The administration of the blanket order method requires that an annual purchase order is raised which specifies the annual quantity but not the delivery schedule. Although this order is the primary contractual document, it must not be input to the purchasing system (unless the software specifically includes provision for blanket orders), since it would prevent MRP from scheduling individual call-offs. There is no such difficulty with the rolling schedule, where the schedule itself is the only contract.

Scheduling and MRP logic

One of the great strengths of MRPII is its ability to generate long-term plans. A schedule of purchased material requirements can be produced for the required number of weeks or months simply by providing the MPS with a sales forecast that extends far enough into the future. Lot sizing rules must be used that do not batch together requirements over a period greater than the delivery frequency. If weekly deliveries are required, then the lot sizing rule for the material must be one week's requirement.

The standard MRP approach is to regard requirements arising in different time buckets as discrete planned orders. This is rather different from a schedule, where the requirements are elements of a single supply contract. A technique that can be used to simulate a purchase schedule is to convert each planned order into a separate line on a single purchase order. Each line is for the same item, but all lines have different due dates.

There are two difficulties with this approach. One is that any slight over- or under-deliveries are left as exceptions against a particular order line, whereas ideally they should be rolled across to the next due date. The second difficulty is rather more serious. A subsequent MRP run making a modification to the schedule will do so by moving complete orders (i.e. purchase order lines) between periods, in a similar way to the example in Figure 5.1. A small change in demand in one period can cause large scale rescheduling of subsequent quantities. The result is a very lumpy demand for the supplier to satisfy, and one that does not reflect the actual requirement for the material.

An alternative approach is not to create released purchase orders at all, but to leave all requirements generated by MRP as planned orders. MRP is then free to change the quantities due in each time bucket in response to changing circumstances, rather than having to move inappropriate quantities between buckets. No purchase order is created, but the supplier is sent copies of each new planned order listing. This approach also has its drawbacks; in this case the failure to convert the planned orders into released orders causes distortions elsewhere in the system. For example, when the goods are delivered there is no scheduled receipt in the system against which the consignment can be checked and accepted into stock.

The above discussion is based upon the assumption that each material is scheduled from a single supplier. If requirements for a material are to be split between two or more suppliers, MRP has no means of apportioning total demand amongst them. Manual intervention is therefore needed to produce individual supplier schedules from the total demand reported by MRPII. This is an undesirable practice, and a further reason to consider single sourcing.

Purchase scheduling entails a further complexity. Negotiations with suppliers often result in a variety of different agreements for limiting schedule variability. Few suppliers can provide an open-ended commitment to absorb any fluctuation in demand from one issue of the schedule to the next. Some means is therefore required to prevent MRP from making any changes within a frozen period of the schedule specified for each item.

A true scheduling capability that would deal with all these complexities is lacking in MRPII. A frozen time period is inconsistent with MRP logic, which has as its objective the balancing of supply and demand at all times, irrespective of any supply constraints. Adjusting quantities in released orders, rather than dates, is also inconsistent with the way MRP operates. For the determined user there are ways around all of these difficulties. For example, firm planned orders could be used to provide stability in the frozen period, while non-released planned orders would permit total flexibility beyond that time. The result is, however, unlikely to be ideal.

As is always the case when making generalizations about MRPII limitations, some IBS suppliers have recognized the problems and attempted to develop solutions. Although these solutions may not deal comprehensively with all the difficulties described here, they can often satisfy the specific needs of particular companies. The fact remains, however, that in most IBS products the main thrust of purchasing support lies in the handling of discrete orders, rather than purchase schedules.

MRPII's ability to project material and capacity plans well into the future is, perhaps, its most important characteristic. It is ironic that its mechanism for turning those plans into workable purchase schedules remains somewhat underdeveloped.

Sub-contracting

MRP recognizes two basic categories of items; manufactured parts, which have lower level components in their bills of material, and purchased items, which do not. MRP plans works orders for the first category and purchase orders for the second.

Sub-contracting sits rather uncomfortably between these two categories. It may be defined, in the context of MRPII, as meaning a manufactured item that undergoes processing outside the company. Within that definition there are the following possibilities:

- Sub-contracting may be permanent, for example because a specialized process is required that is not available in-house, or temporary, to overcome a production bottleneck.
- All operations needed to manufacture an item may be sub-contracted, or merely a single operation.
- Material may be supplied to the sub-contractor on a free issue basis, or the subcontractor may provide and charge for the material.

Controlling sub-contracting requires special procedures in the use of both works orders and purchase orders.

Works order aspects
By definition, items that require sub-contracting either have additional in-house operations to be controlled, or they have materials to be planned, or both. These functions can only be performed if sub-contract items are categorized as manufactured, rather than purchased. This enables MRP to plan works orders in the normal way, although the subsequent handling of these works orders varies from normal practice. The particular approach taken to processing a sub-contract works order depends upon which of the circumstances listed above applies.

There are two techniques which are commonly applied when using works orders to control sub-contracting. The first of these techniques is to set up one or more work centre records for 'sub-contract work centres'. These work centres are treated in the same way as in-house work centres. They allow sub-contract operations to be included on the routing record, thus enabling a description of the operation to form part of the works order routing. Furthermore, the sub-contracting cost may be reported as operation costs, and reported against the sub-contract work centre.

The second technique is to amend the one-time routings and bills of materials contained in works order records, as described in Chapter 2. The use of this technique enables non-routine sub-contracting to be specified for an order without making a permanent change to the item details.

OPERATIONS TO BE SUB-CONTRACTED

			ONE OPERATION		ALL OPERATIONS
PERMANENT SUB-CONTRACT	FREE ISSUE MATERIAL	A	Routing record for item to show a permanent sub-contract operation.	B	Avoid if possible : convert to purchased item by requiring supplier to provide material.
NON-ROUTINE SUB-CONTRACT	FREE ISSUE MATERIAL	C	Raise works order. Amend the operation that is to be sub-contracted to a sub-contract work centre.	D	Raise works order. Delete all operations except for one 'sub-contract complete' operation.
	SUPPLIER'S MATERIAL	E	Only applies to first operation. Raise works order. Convert first operation to sub-contract work centre. Delete material requirements from the one-time bill.	F	Raise works order. Delete all operations except for one 'sub-contract complete' operation. Delete material requirements from the one-time bill.

Figure 5.2 Sub-contract works order techniques

Figure 5.2 shows the possible sub-contracting variations, and indicates how works orders should be handled in each case. The figure excludes permanent sub-contracting using the supplier's material, because that is straightforward purchasing (any subsequent in-house operations should be transferred to a separate part number). Variation B should be avoided, where possible, because purchasing a complete item is so much simpler than controlling sub-contracting.

Purchasing aspects

There is no indication from MRP of the need to raise a sub-contract purchase order. The buyer is generally notified by either planning or production when the job is ready to go. Any free issue material to be sent to the sub-contractor must first have been issued to the works order, and any in-house operations that precede sub-contracting completed.

At this point, the buyer raises a purchase order for the sub-contract work involved. This must not be a normal production order, or MRP will assume both the works order and the purchase order to be potential supply, and will attempt to cancel one of them. Some IBS products allow special sub-contract orders to be raised; if there is no such facility, the purchase order must be handled as an order for consumables or services, and should not use the item part number. In either case, MRP ignores the purchase order and the supply/demand balance is maintained.

A similar situation occurs when the goods are returned from the sub-contractor. A purchase order receipt must be processed to close the purchase order, but the materials must not be booked into stock. Instead the materials must be returned to the works order from which they were originally sent. Any remaining in-house operations may then be completed, after which the goods are received into stock from the works order.

Review of sub-contracting procedures

The techniques described above enable sub-contracting to be managed without upsetting MRP's balance of supply and demand, and without losing track of material movements. They also allow routing information to be produced which specifies the sub-contracting requirements, and they permit cost information to be collected. In so doing, these techniques introduce a few distortions into the information system.

For example, costs are collected against a work centre number, which may lead to sub-contracting costs becoming included in summaries of manufacturing costs. Also the purchase order is external to MRP, so it cannot be planned or rescheduled automatically. Sub-contract materials remain part of the works order; the only way to indicate that they have been moved off-site is to book the sub-contract operation on the works order as started. When the materials are returned, there is no automatic indication to production that they are available for the next operation.

All of these difficulties can be addressed, but to do so requires very good co-operation between production, stores, planning, costing and purchasing. As long as this co-operation exists, backed up by comprehensive training and procedure manuals, sub-contracting can be handled effectively.

The commercial factor

Buying, in contrast to delivery scheduling, is essentially a commercial activity. The trend towards long-term supplier relationships has changed the nature of this activity, but the buyer remains responsible for ensuring that the company's purchases are made on the most advantageous terms. Rolling schedules are not always the best means of fulfilling this responsibility. Some situations where commercial considerations lead to different purchasing policies are described below.

Commodity buying

Prices of commodities such as metals (e.g. copper, lead and zinc), petrochemical products, including plastic moulding materials, and foodstuffs such as coffee and wheat are established primarily by international markets. The formation of close supplier relationships will not prevent the buyer being faced with rapidly escalating prices in times of short supply. Buyers generally like to hedge against such events, and one way of doing this is by speculative buying.

If a buyer considers the price of a commodity is likely to rise, then it may be worth investing in increased inventory. This inventory is run down when the buyer judges that the price is at a peak.

There is no way that MRP can prompt these decisions, or even recognize why they have been taken. Repeated exception reports will therefore be produced, for as long as inventory levels continue to infringe normal safety stock rules. It is possible to amend the safety stock level to reflect the current situation, but this could trigger unnecessary replenishment orders when the stock is eventually allowed to run down. Some managers may consider that the constant warnings contained in the exception reports do no harm if they help prevent the buyer becoming too ambitious in this gamble against the market!

Consignment stocks

The ideal form of supply may be small batches delivered at frequent intervals, but not all materials lend themselves to this approach. Consignment stocks can be an effective alternative. Here the supplier delivers in bulk into a bonded stock held on the customer's premises. The customer draws from this consignment stock as required, only paying the supplier for the materials consumed. The customer benefits through having an assured supply, while paying in just-in-time mode. The supplier reaps the benefit of bulk deliveries, while effectively tying the customer into a long-term supply commitment.

Consignment stocks must be kept separate from working stocks of the material that have become the customer's property. Most IBS software can accommodate this by using different stock locations or a different warehouse identity. The consignment stock should be taken into account by MRP, so that (free of charge) purchase orders can be raised to top up the consignment stock. On the other hand, consignment stock should not be included in inventory valuations. Some means of tracking movements from the consignment stock to the working stock is required, so that usage can be monitored for payment purposes.

Safeguarding supplies

All buyers must be alert for the possibility of disruption to supplies. Possible industrial action at supplying companies, or within the transportation system, bad weather, international supply shortages, or a decline in delivered quality all pose risks to continuity of supply. A buyer anticipating problems will almost certainly wish to build up some extra stock, possibly off-site if space is lacking in the material stockroom.

Handling this situation involves:

- ordering materials in excess of MRP planned orders
- disregarding MRP exception messages
- maintaining separate stock records for any materials held off-site
- arranging for material transfer transactions to be processed when materials are brought onto site.

If the threat is expected to last for some time, safety stock levels should be amended to enable MRP to maintain stocks at the new, higher, level.

Purchasing: a neglected area

MRPII tends to take a rather simplistic approach to the purchasing function. For companies that plan discrete orders for all purchased materials, rarely sub-contract, and do not involve themselves in commercial speculation, this is not a problem. Companies with more complex purchasing practices will have to work rather harder to adapt MRPII logic to their situation. The right choice of software is important for these companies, but it is most unlikely that any system will solve all their problems.

Is this really a significant failing of MRPII? After all, the techniques described here resolve many of the difficulties that are likely to arise. The very nature of purchasing as a commercial function means that decisions will be taken that defy any predetermined system logic.

This is a valid argument, and the difficulties discussed here should certainly be kept in proportion. On the other hand, the ability to communicate speedily and accurately with suppliers is becoming ever more important. Many companies are adopting strategies of integrated logistics and supply chain management. These strategies emphasize the need for information to flow smoothly through the supply chain, so that the plans and activities of all the organizations contributing to the final product can be co-ordinated. The increasing use of EDI, in which computers in different companies are able to communicate directly with each other, is one aspect of this development.

Full integration of the supply chain, however, will require more than just EDI, important though this is as an enabling technology. Supply chain integration demands nothing less than the creation of supply chain MRPII. The integration of the material schedules of the final assembler with those of first and second tier suppliers can only be achieved through the use of MRPII's long-term planning capabilities. At present the rather simplistic approach of MRPII to purchasing is a constraint on achieving the necessary information flows. A more intelligent means of developing purchase schedules will be needed if MRPII is to evolve in this way.

Summary

In this chapter we have looked at some of the main limitations in the MRPII model. Many of these limitations are only of significance in particular business environments. Some can be overcome either by careful choice of software or by applying a few simple techniques that have been described here.

The objective of this discussion has not been to undermine the merits of MRPII; other methods of manufacturing planning and control have weaknesses that are at least equal to those of MRPII. Nevertheless it would be most unwise to embark upon an implementation without a clear understanding of what MRPII cannot do, as well as what it can. Being prepared for the problems is the first step to overcoming them. Pretending that MRPII will address every need is the most certain route to disappointment.

There is one further aspect of MRPII that is widely regarded as being naive and inadequate, and that is its approach to shopfloor scheduling and control. This is the subject of the next chapter.

6

Shopfloor scheduling and control

Working the plan

The main thrust of MRPII is to create a company-wide planning culture. In an MRPII company, long term business plans are progressively focused until they eventually evolve into detailed short term material and capacity plans. These material and capacity plans meet the short term market requirement, are feasible, and are consistent with the long term business objective. The planning process ensures that no works order is released for which there is insufficient material, so there is no possibility of delays through shortages. Furthermore, no works order is released for which production capacity will not be available at the time it is needed. There is therefore no reason for unplanned queues to form which might slow down the passage of orders through production.

In view of the hard work, co-operation, compromise and skill required to reach this point it seems only right to expect that the reward will be the problem-free execution of released orders, on time and within planned resource levels. Sadly this reward cannot be assumed. The shopfloor is a highly complex environment, full of competing pressures, random variability, unforeseen events, and distracting measurements and controls. If reasonable success is to be achieved in completing orders on time, suitable methods of shopfloor scheduling and control must be installed.

The term 'production activity control' (PAC) is sometimes used to describe this task. The use of yet another three-letter acronym seems inappropriate in this case, however. Whereas terms such as MRP, MPS and CRP have precisely defined meanings, PAC is simply a kitbag of tools that can be used to facilitate the execution of works orders within the factory. Many of these tools are competing alternatives, so PAC is not so much a solution as a set of choices. The expression 'shopfloor scheduling and control' is preferred here because it offers a clear picture of the task to be performed, and does not suggest that a standard solution is available.

In a world where MRPII concepts are available to all, and where increasing numbers of companies use IBS products that are essentially equivalent, achieving an edge in manufacturing performance is not easy. The area of shopfloor scheduling and control offers scope for differentiation, not to mention imagination and innovation, that can be exploited by managers who really understand the issues involved. Several different approaches to shopfloor scheduling and control are described in this chapter. All are concerned with improving the effective control of the production process. The remarkable thing about them is their diversity.

MRPII scheduling aids

The shopfloor scheduling and control techniques to examine first are the ones most commonly associated with MRPII, and particularly with MRP-based software systems. These techniques have their origins in the early days of MRPII, and remain closely linked with the MRPII concept. Subsequent sections examine techniques that have evolved separately from MRPII, but which can be embraced within its philosophy.

Input/output control

Input/output control makes use of information generated by CRP to determine the planned movement of work between work centres. Using the operation start dates calculated by CRP, the workload due to arrive at each work centre each period (usually one week) is aggregated and reported. Similarly, the planned output from each work centre is calculated from the operation finish dates. Actual input and output is derived from works order reporting, and is compared with the planned input and output.

Input/output analysis may reveal a variety of situations requiring management action, for example:

- A shortfall in the actual workload reaching a work centre, caused by delays upstream, may result in an overload when the planned work does eventually arrive.
- A shortfall in the work leaving a work centre suggests that a capacity constraint has arisen within that work centre.
- A planned or actual input rate that exceeds the capacity of a work centre suggests that a build-up in work in progress is likely to occur.

The usefulness of input/output information depends partly upon the way in which work centres are defined. There is no standard definition of a work centre, and the following approaches are all acceptable in the right circumstances:

- **Single machine type.** Each unique machine, or group of identical machines, constitutes a work centre. If there are two nominally identical machines, but one is newer and is used exclusively for higher tolerance jobs, each machine must have its own work centre number.

- **Machine group.** A group of machines all having broadly similar capabilities and under the control of a single supervisor form a work centre. Most jobs carried out within the work centre could be performed on more than one of the machines, but not necessarily on all of them.
- **Cell.** A machining cell containing a range of quite different machines that are used in the manufacture of a family of products forms a single work centre. Some additional means of local capacity planning and scheduling may be required to manage the workload within the cell. The team leader may be able to perform this task manually, or alternatively a computer-based scheduling system could be used.
- **Work group.** The work centre represents a group of production workers rather than machines. This definition applies particularly in an assembly environment where people, rather than assembly benches, constitute the capacity constraint. A similar situation can arise in machine-based work, if there are more machines available than people to operate them.

Input/output control can most usefully be used in one of two ways. The first is to control the level of work in progress within the work centre. If actual input exceeds actual output, the difference between them is an increase in work in progress at that work centre. A fundamental rule of effective shopfloor control is that work should not be released into a manufacturing facility faster than it can be processed. Excess work in progress clutters up the floor, increases the probability of out-of-sequence working, and becomes dirty and damaged.

Input/output monitoring only provides specific information for this form of work in progress control in cases where work centres represent groups of machines or workers. These work centres tend to be physical zones or departments with their own supervisor or manager. They may even be seen as a factory within a factory. Release of orders to these work centres can be regulated to match actual output very simply, by reference to the input/output report for that work centre.

The single machine work centre is quite different. A works order usually passes through many such work centres before the item is completed. Some of these work centres may be arranged close together, to facilitate material flow. There may be several such work centres in a single production department. It would not be realistic to withdraw work from this flow every time that input/output control indicated a temporary queue building up at the next machine.

The solution is to control groupings of work centres, typically based upon the production department, rather than individual work centres. The work arriving at all the work centres within the department can be aggregated and compared with the total work leaving the department. This calculation is much simpler if all the orders processed in the department pass through the same first and last operations. Where this applies, only these two work centres need to be monitored. Sometimes a particular work centre determines the throughput of the entire department. In these situations the work entering the department should be regulated to match the output from this bottleneck process. Any temporary build up of work after the bottleneck can be ignored since, by definition, there is surplus capacity at these operations.

Generally it is better if processes that are heavily loaded, and therefore potential bottlenecks, are treated as single machine type work centres. Additional control of these processes can then be achieved by using input/output control in a rather different manner. In this second application of input/output control the objective is to maintain high levels of utilization of these critical bottleneck processes. This objective is achieved firstly by ensuring that the planned output is close to machine capacity, and secondly by ensuring that actual input is sufficient to prevent the machine becoming starved of work. If either of these conditions is not met, management action is required.

There is no reason why different types of work centre should not coexist within the same factory; different manufacturing facilities may lend themselves to different forms of control. Deciding the best structure for work centres, and how they will be used in capacity planning and scheduling, is one of the key configuration tasks referred to in Chapter 2. The mistake that must be avoided when implementing MRPII is simply to convert an existing cost centre structure into work centres without considering the impact upon capacity planning and scheduling.

Sequencing

MRP makes the assumption that queues of work are both necessary and inevitable, permitting day-to-day and hour-by-hour smoothing of workloads. Input/output control can be used to keep those queues stable and of reasonable length, but does not seek to eliminate queues altogether. Like CRP, input/output control is only meaningful if applied to relatively coarse time buckets, typically of one week. Since the content of the queues will vary continuously during that time, a more responsive technique is required to sequence the jobs in the queues.

Job sequencing support is provided in the form of work-to lists, sometimes known as dispatch lists. Work-to lists are daily reports of the jobs at each work centre, printed in the order in which they should be carried out. Simple priority rules (also called dispatching rules) are used to determine the sequence. Rules that are often applied include earliest operation due date, earliest operation start date, and critical ratio. Critical ratio is calculated by dividing the time remaining in which to complete the operation by the processing time required. A critical ratio of less than one means that the job will inevitably complete the operation late.

The operation dates used in producing work-to lists are recalculated each time the report is produced, to ensure that they are based upon the latest works order dates. MRP exception reports result in many order due dates being rescheduled while the job is in progress, and the work-to list must reflect the latest position. The common practice of printing order dates on the shop documentation accompanying the order can cause confusion. It is better to leave dates off the shop documentation and to use work-to lists (either printed or on screen) as the sole source of priority information.

Work-to lists can either show only those orders that are currently queuing at the work centre or they can include orders that are due to arrive imminently. Ignoring future orders encourages queues to build up, since jobs cannot be sequenced until they actually arrive. On the other hand, if future orders are included and the first few jobs on the list have not yet arrived, confidence in the value of the list may be eroded. A compromise is to supply separate lists showing jobs currently queuing and jobs imminently due.

Perhaps the best approach is to use a combined list, and to encourage supervisors to communicate with upstream work centres to find out why the orders they need have not yet arrived. The reply may be that the order is ready and about to be delivered, in which case starting a less urgent job would be a mistake. Or it may be that a part of the batch has completed the previous operation and is waiting for the balance. In this case it would be sensible to make a start on the parts that are available and let the remainder of the batch catch up later.

Some companies take a strong line with supervisors on the use of work-to lists, insisting that jobs are done in the order shown, without exception. In other companies a more flexible approach is used, allowing the supervisor discretion to process orders out of sequence. For example, a decision may be taken to run together jobs with similar set-ups, even though this means pulling one forward. If discretion is allowed, it must be within strictly defined limits. Any experienced supervisor can find an almost unlimited number of convincing reasons for working out of sequence. Unfortunately the overall effect may be to optimize the efficiency of the work centre in question whilst destroying the effectiveness of the entire plant.

Finite capacity scheduling

Work-to lists merely provide the sequence in which queues should be processed; they do not specify when the jobs should be started, or when they will finish. Nor do they give advance warning of any jobs that might fall into arrears. Whilst many companies find that work-to lists provide sufficient control to ensure that order due dates are achieved, at least most of the time, others seek greater precision. Finite capacity scheduling systems aim to fit the planned workload into precise time slots within the limited capacity available, and therefore to specify accurate start and finish times for every operation to be performed. More than this, the precision of finite scheduling creates an expectation that actual performance will be improved.

Scheduling objectives

If finite scheduling offers the hope of a more efficient schedule, then we must define what is meant by schedule efficiency. The following scheduling objectives are possible:

- due date adherence
- minimum work in progress
- minimum lead times
- maximum machine or operator utilization

The broad objective of due date adherence has further sub-divisions. Measures used could include percentage of orders completed on time, number of late orders, or average lateness. Earliness may be regarded as 'on time' or it may be considered as undesirable as lateness.

The various measures of schedule efficiency are not necessarily inconsistent, and in some cases may be complementary (minimum work in progress and minimum lead time, for example). However it is difficult to reconcile the objective of maximizing resource utilization with the other targets.

In an MRPII environment there is little that a scheduling system can do to influence most of these targets. Levels of work in progress and average lead times are both largely predetermined by the planning lead time used by MRP. Planning lead time determines the date at which an order should be started, and MRP plans the component materials to be available on that date. Starting an order late or finishing it early may appear to have shortened the lead time, but in fact it has no effect on the overall time taken to make the product. Furthermore, idle materials waiting for the job to start and items made early, waiting to be kitted up for the next order, all form part of total inventory value. Work in progress levels may be lower, but stockroom inventory is correspondingly higher.

Machine utilization is also largely predetermined. RCCP, CRP, and input/output control have already attempted to maximize the use of scarce resources, and all that any work centre needs to do is to achieve the output planned for it. Higher utilization can only be achieved by bringing work forward, which is a pointless exercise, and an impossible one if the materials needed are not yet available. The aim of the scheduling system is not, therefore, to maximize utilization; it is to ensure that machines are supplied with the planned workloads. A scheduling system that leaves a heavily loaded machine idle for significant periods of time could find that it is impossible to make up the lost time later. A poor schedule could prevent required utilization levels being achieved, but a good schedule cannot improve on the plan.

The primary objective of a scheduling system, in an MRPII environment, is due date adherence. More specifically, it is to minimize the number of late orders. Any order that is not completed on time either delays the start of a succeeding order or results directly in a late customer delivery. Early completion, whilst not desirable, is much less harmful because it does not delay subsequent orders. As we have seen, an early delivery inflates stockroom inventory value, but in practice the value of the job in the stockroom is usually little different from its value when in work in progress.

Planning lead times play a major part in determining the competitiveness of a company's manufacturing performance. If lead times are excessive, a finite scheduling system cannot directly improve the situation. It may, however, indicate that planning lead times need to be changed. If orders are regularly finished early (or started late, but still finished on time) a reduction in planning lead times is called for. If the scheduling system is unable to achieve high due date adherence consistently then either it is the wrong system or planning lead times are too short.

Finite scheduling techniques

There are many finite scheduling systems available. The great majority work independently of the MRPII database, since they need access to far more extensive information about workloads, resources and capacities than is needed for MRP and CRP. Nevertheless they are generally designed to be interfaced with an IBS so that works orders planned by MRP can be downloaded to the scheduling system for finite scheduling.

The difficulty with finite scheduling is that to produce a realistic schedule it is necessary to mirror many of the real-life complexities of the shopfloor in the scheduling algorithm. This means that large amounts of data must be generated and kept accurate. Some examples of complicating factors are listed below:

- use of alternative machines or alternative routings
- varying shift patterns and holiday arrangements
- varying operator skills
- batch splitting and overlapping of operations under certain conditions
- clean-down cycles for colours and flavours
- planned maintenance schedules
- dwell times (e.g. after a heat treatment process)
- process constraints (e.g. ovens that need to be stacked with a certain product mix to permit even heating)
- variations in performance or tooling between nominally identical machines
- limited number of tool sets available
- limited availability of setters to carry out simultaneous set-ups.

Most people who have experience of the realities of shopfloor life could think of many more examples.

Factors such as these are very difficult to build into scheduling algorithms, quite apart from the problem of keeping the data accurate. Yet a naive schedule that ignores such complexity is unlikely to gain acceptance from those who are expected to work it.

A further problem is that works order status must be completely up to date before a scheduling run is performed. If the job scheduled to be started at 8.00am this morning was actually completed at 3.45pm yesterday, the schedule will not have much credibility. As we shall see later, collecting timely order status information is far from easy.

Finally, even if the schedule is realistic and up to date but an operator calls in sick, it will not be achieved. Once actual job timings start to deviate from the planned times, the schedule becomes no more than an expensive work-to list, providing no more usable information than a sequencing system would.

Finite scheduling, not surprisingly, has developed a reputation for being difficult to use successfully. Certainly there seems to be little future for all-embracing, company-wide systems. However it does seem that products are now becoming available that can be useful in the right circumstances, particularly where this involves making local scheduling decisions. Scheduling locally appears to more successful than centralized scheduling, probably for the following reasons:

- the information needed for scheduling is readily available
- the schedule can be re-run when necessary, rather than in accordance with a rigid cycle
- processing times are acceptably short, since only a sub-set of company data is analyzed
- the local work group has greater understanding of the scheduling process, and greater commitment to the schedule produced.

Local scheduling is highly compatible with the trend that has been seen in recent years towards semi-autonomous manufacturing cells. To the IBS, the cell may be a single work centre; to the local scheduling system the cell contains many possible paths through several different machine types. The role of the centralized system is to plan and release works orders to the work centre. The local scheduling system, under the control of the team leader, then takes over the detailed scheduling task.

There are many different approaches to finite scheduling. This diversity offers choice, but the complex nature of finite scheduling can make it difficult to draw meaningful comparisons between systems. The main categories of scheduling systems are described below, and some of the factors to take into account in selecting and applying them are discussed.

Heuristic scheduling systems
Heuristic scheduling systems use simple priority rules, or algorithms, which are similar to those used to sequence work-to lists. In this case, however, specific start and finish times are assigned to each operation. In contrast, work-to lists simply list jobs in priority order.

Heuristic systems operate by regenerating completely new schedules at regular intervals. Although it may be possible to superimpose a few new orders on existing schedules, priorities are soon lost if the full schedule is not regenerated regularly. The inevitable deviations from plan that occur on the shopfloor also create a need to update the schedule at frequent intervals. As a result, schedule regeneration often takes place daily and certainly no more than weekly. Since each regeneration starts from scratch, the schedule is highly volatile from one regeneration to the next. There is therefore little point in scheduling very far into the future, since everything beyond the regeneration interval may change.

There are two quite different heuristic scheduling techniques, as follows:

Operation scheduling In operation (or vertical) scheduling, each resource is considered in turn at a point in time. Any jobs queuing at the first idle resource are reviewed and the highest priority job selected. Priority is determined by use of a dispatching rule such as earliest due date, critical ratio or shortest processing time, or by a priority indicator set manually by a planner. The remaining work centres are processed in turn, in a similar manner. The system then increments forward in time and looks for resources that have become idle. For each idle resource, the highest priority job is selected from the queue, as before. This process is continued as far into the future as necessary.

Operation scheduling results in a closely-packed schedule, since as soon as a resource becomes available the system looks for the next job to load. This can be important on heavily used resources, where it is essential that the schedule does not leave too many idle periods. The disadvantage of operation scheduling is that orders tend to be pushed into work in progress at the earliest opportunity, without taking account of possible delays at later operations. Overall work in progress levels may therefore be higher than necessary.

Order scheduling In order (or horizontal) scheduling, each works order is scheduled completely before moving onto the next order. A priority rule is used to select the highest priority order, and this order is scheduled through all its operations. The next highest priority order is then processed, and so on.

Orders can be scheduled forwards in time or backwards. In forward scheduling the first operation is loaded as soon as the required resource becomes available, after which each subsequent operation is loaded in the same way. In backward scheduling the final operation on the order is the first to be scheduled. This operation is loaded immediately prior to the order due date. The next step is to schedule the preceding operation immediately before the final one. This process continues until all operations have been loaded. If resources are not available when required for an operation, an earlier date is chosen when capacity is available.

If the due date of the order is too close, backward scheduling may not be able to fit in all the operations on the order before the first day of the schedule. In this case either the priorities must be changed, to give the order earlier access to the resources, or the due date of the order must be deferred.

The outcome of order scheduling is that the highest priority orders, which are scheduled first, have unfettered access to the resources. This gives them a clear line of sight through the manufacturing unit, ensuring that they are processed with minimum delay between operations. As more orders are scheduled, blocks of capacity are used up and it becomes more difficult for the system to find the resources at the time they are needed. Later (lower priority) orders can therefore become strung out over a prolonged period of time, waiting for access to the resources they need.

Artificial intelligence-based systems

Heuristic systems follow a set procedure, or algorithm, in deciding which job to load next. They are not optimizing systems and they lack the ability a human scheduler would have to ask "is it sensible to apply this rule at this time?" and "does that schedule look right, or can I improve it further?" The merit of heuristic systems is one of speed. Finite scheduling is not a task that can be performed manually, and producing optimized schedules in a reasonable time by mathematical methods or by comparing all possible alternatives defies even the most powerful computers. Some system suppliers are now turning to artificial intelligence (AI) techniques to develop systems that can apply a certain amount of reasoning ability to the scheduling problem.

An AI-based system, like a heuristic scheduling system, may also make use of algorithms, but is likely to have a selection of alternative rules at its disposal. It should be capable of developing strategies for applying these rules in different ways, to satisfy specific circumstances. Furthermore it must be able to evaluate the outcome of different strategies, to determine which is the most effective.

It is too early to be certain of the eventual impact of AI-based systems, but they do appear to have considerable potential. A schedule must always appear realistic to the work group that is to execute it, or it will be rejected. Unfortunately, schedules produced by heuristic systems do not always pass the sanity test. If AI techniques can produce schedules that seem reasonably sensible for most of the time, they should win the battle for acceptability.

Leitstand systems

Whilst AI-based systems seek to improve on heuristic scheduling by making the system more intelligent, leitstand systems aim to make greater use of human intelligence. They are widely used in Germany, where the word means 'control post', or 'command centre'. The concept of local responsibility for scheduling is well established in Germany, and leitstands have been developed to support this role.

Leitstands produce a pictorial representation of the schedule, in the form of a Gantt (horizontal bar) chart on the computer screen. An initial schedule may be generated automatically, using priority rules. The main role of the system, however, is to respond to changes made to the schedule by a human scheduler. As operation dates are manually amended, or new orders added to the schedule, the leitstand automatically makes the necessary adjustments to other operations that will maintain the integrity of the schedule. In this way the operator can easily undertake any fine-tuning of the schedule that may be necessary.

Leitstands have been described as computerized planning boards, and indeed they are based on the planning boards that once lined the walls of every foreman's office. They offer similar advantages of accessibility, ownership and visibility, with the added benefit of requiring much less work to maintain than a manual system. They may provide more stable schedules than automatic schedule generators, since the human scheduler may choose to add new jobs manually, with minimum disruption, rather than initiate a complete schedule regeneration. On the other hand leitstands are certainly not optimizing systems. There is nothing about them that will force the operator to seek optimum due date adherence. Indeed the Gantt chart form of schedule representation tends to focus the operator's attention on resource utilization rather than achievement of due date.

A leitstand, therefore, is only as good as the way it is used. If the operator is clear about the scheduling objectives to be achieved, and works within clearly defined performance targets, the leitstand can be a valuable tool. If, on the other hand, the operator is allowed free rein to amend the schedule to suit local preferences, the leitstand could become no more than a computerized cherry-picker.

Process flow schedulers
Process industries, using flow-based manufacturing, have quite different scheduling needs than companies engaged upon batch or jobbing manufacture. Special process flow schedulers are available for these industries.

Process flow schedulers operate in situations where there are no discrete works orders, and production plans instead take the form of rate schedules, or daily output targets. The role of the process flow scheduler is to manage the flows between the various production stages that make up the process. Process flow schedulers recognize the point at which materials begin to flow from one stage and the delay before they arrive at the next. They need to take account of fixed process cycles, dwell times, vat capacities, sampling requirements and other factors that impact upon the flow of materials through a process plant. The objective of these systems is to ensure that output targets (rather than order due dates) are met, material flows controlled and intermediate inventories managed, and events such as plant clean-downs planned.

The key feature of process flow schedulers is an ability to model the process which is to be scheduled. Since flows are largely predetermined by the physical nature of the process, the questions of local priorities and sequencing are less significant than in a batch scheduling environment.

Summary of finite scheduling techniques
This has been a brief discussion of a very complex issue. Within the four categories of scheduling system that have been described there are systems available that contain many more features than have been described here. Furthermore, the four categories themselves are not a universal standard for classifying scheduling systems. Unfortunately no such standard exists, adding further difficulty to the task of comparing and assessing the various alternatives. It is beyond the scope of this book, however, to provide a comprehensive critique of finite scheduling systems. The reason for

discussing finite scheduling is to consider how this technique relates to MRPII.

Finite scheduling can be a valuable addition to the mechanisms of MRPII, so long as its role is clearly understood. The objective of finite scheduling is to assist in the achievement of due dates planned by MRPII. Seeking any other objective will prove fruitless, and indeed harmful if it results in a decline in on-time delivery.

Finite scheduling, in an MRPII environment, cannot directly reduce lead times and inventory. What it may do is to create faster throughput of work, as a by-product of achieving due date adherence, enabling planning lead times to be reduced. It is through this reduction in planning lead times that MRP will be able subsequently to reduce actual lead times, and so reduce work in progress.

Similarly finite scheduling, in an MRPII environment, cannot directly improve resource utilization. What it may do is to schedule heavily loaded resources more efficiently, again as a by-product of achieving due date adherence. This may allow RCCP to assume higher levels of capacity availability, enabling a greater workload to be included in future MPSs. Resource utilization will then increase in response to the increased workload that is planned.

The concept of local scheduling is an important one. Leitstands offer considerable potential to the growing number of companies adopting cellular manufacturing. They provide a tool to help the supervisor or team leader to manage what can be complex flows of work through a cell. This level of control cannot be provided by MRP, not just because it is too remote, but also because of its inability to resolve contention at shared resources. The role of MRP is to plan the works orders. Local scheduling is responsible for achieving the planned due dates.

AI-based systems will become increasingly important, particularly as an aid to automation. Increasing use of computer-controlled machinery will create a greater need for automatic scheduling systems. Flexible manufacturing cells, automated storage and retrieval systems, automated guided vehicles, robots and other forms of automation will increasingly need to be integrated and their activities co-ordinated. This task requires robust scheduling systems that can manage the flows of materials, tooling and information through the manufacturing unit. AI-based systems seem the most promising means for achieving the necessary co-ordination and flexibility.

The OPT option

Optimized production technology (OPT) resembles MRPII in that it is a strategy for manufacturing planning and control that is dependent upon a computer system. It differs from MRPII in that some of the key scheduling algorithms contained within the computer system have not been disclosed. The system therefore remains a proprietary 'black box' the rights to which are owned by Scheduling Technology Group Limited. Nevertheless the philosophy of OPT has been widely expounded, most notably by Goldratt and Cox (1984).

In spite of having aroused a great deal of interest, OPT has never begun to approach the popularity of MRPII. Although initially marketed as an alternative to MRPII, OPT has more recently been positioned as a high quality finite scheduling system that can co-exist with MRPII. This is a more realistic assessment of the OPT concept, but it leaves open the question of how to reconcile two philosophies that view manufacturing planning and control quite differently. If we are to combine OPT and MRPII, we must be able to amalgamate the two philosophies.

OPT concepts

The starting point of OPT is the belief that the goal of manufacturing is to make money now and in the future. This objective can only be achieved by maximizing throughput, while simultaneously minimizing inventory and operating expense. In other words the aim is to increase sales revenue, while reducing capital employed and cost of sales. Since achievement of this objective will result in higher profit, better return on assets and improved cash flow it is difficult to disagree with OPT's central premise.

In seeking to maximize throughput, OPT recognizes that the manufacturing process is subject to a wide range of potential constraints. No company could satisfy instantaneously every possible combination of customer demand for its products. Machine overloads, shortage of operators or setters, lack of materials or tooling, or some combination of these and other factors would always impose a limit on what could actually be produced and shipped. Constraints exist everywhere; if they did not, every company would ship all its orders on time, all the time. As this clearly does not happen, OPT must be right in regarding the management of constraints as being of critical importance.

Some confusion has been caused by describing OPT as bottleneck scheduling. This expression tends to give the impression that OPT is only applicable to companies where there is a key manufacturing process (or perhaps a small number of such processes) that impose a continuous restriction on output. This perception is incorrect. OPT is not concerned with bottlenecks but with capacity constraints and, as we have seen, these are universal.

The belief that maximizing throughput requires effective use of capacity constraints leads OPT to the following conclusions:

- Capacity constraint resources (CCR) must be identified and scheduled to finite capacity, to ensure their utilization is maximized.
- Processes that have been identified as CCRs must not be allowed to run out of work. Inventory buffers should therefore be positioned immediately upstream of CCRs.

The need to minimize inventory and operating expense leads OPT to deduce that:

- Processes that are not constraining production should only produce work that is needed to support the CCRs. High utilization should not be an objective for non-CCRs, since it can only result in unnecessary inventory.
- Production schedules for non-CCRs should be driven directly by the CCR schedules, in order to synchronize work flows.
- Materials should only be released into production at the rate they are being consumed by the CCRs.
- The role of production operators is to produce to the production schedules. Operator utilization is not an objective, and operators should not produce any work that is not currently required.
- The only points at which stock should be held are the buffers that protect the CCRs.

The assertion that utilization of operators and non-CCRs is unimportant has proved more than a little controversial. Traditional methods of management accounting place great emphasis upon the need for high utilization of resources, both to achieve 'efficient' operation and to enable overheads to be 'recovered'. OPT addresses these objections by postulating a different form of management accounting, called throughput accounting.

Although throughput accounting provides OPT with a financial measurement system that is sympathetic to the OPT philosophy, it does little to improve the acceptability of OPT in industrial companies. Managers are asked not only to adopt a completely new approach to manufacturing planning and control, but also to abandon long established accounting principles. Only the very bold are likely to venture down such a road.

Assuming that the philosophy of OPT is accepted, implementation is dependent upon a suitable scheduling system. This system must be able to generate a finite capacity schedule for the CCRs, and derive from this a synchronized schedule for the non-CCRs. Here we move from OPT the philosophy to OPT the black box scheduling system. Although the precise algorithms of OPT are unknown, the scheduling process operates broadly as follows:

- Sales orders are exploded through their bills of material in a similar way to MRP but without lead time off-setting. A network is constructed in which all lower level requirements are linked back to the sales order.
- Operation details for all manufactured items are added to the network, using information from the routing record.
- Infinite capacity planning is used to identify those resources that will constrain the achievement of sales order dates. Critical resources are confirmed as CCRs by the planner.
- All operations in the network are analyzed into those that involve the use of CCRs and those that do not.

- The CCR operations are forward scheduled to finite capacity by the OPT scheduler, in a sequence determined by sales order due dates and priority indicators.
- A secondary infinite scheduler (SERVE) schedules the non-CCR operations around the CCR schedule, by:
  - backward scheduling operations that precede the CCR
  - forward scheduling operations that follow the CCR.
- Purchased items are scheduled for delivery to suit the manufacturing schedule.
- Any orders not using a CCR are merely backward scheduled from the sales order due date.

This procedure results in a schedule which ensures maximum utilization of CCR operations whilst minimizing throughput time. Since no allowance is made for finite capacity on the non-CCR resources, SERVE may create temporary overloads.

The complexities that the OPT scheduler must cope with include orders that have operations on more than one CCR, or that revisit the same CCR, in addition to the more usual finite scheduling complications like dwell times, alternative machines and disassembly processes. The precise way in which the OPT scheduler handles these complexities has not been revealed. Companies purchasing the OPT software must take the effectiveness of the algorithms on trust.

Nevertheless, some insight into the way the OPT scheduler works is given by a final clutch of OPT rules which proclaim that:

- Operations may be overlapped, by transferring items to a subsequent operation before the entire batch has completed the preceding operation.
- Batch quantities should not be set by fixed lot sizing rules, nor need they remain constant at all operations.
- Lead times are not fixed, but are a consequence of the schedule.
- Schedules should be established by looking at all constraints in parallel.

It is these finite scheduling rules that mark the real difference between the OPT scheduler and MRP. Whereas OPT determines batch quantities to suit the schedule and does not use planning lead times, MRP is dependent upon fixed batch sizes and fixed planning lead times.

In view of these major differences, it is far from obvious how OPT could co-exist with MRPII. The following case study provides a view of how one company reconciled the two philosophies.

An OPT case study

Alcad Limited employs about 270 people in the design and manufacture of nickel cadmium batteries. These batteries are assembled to order from a large range of cells, each of which contains positive and negative plates suspended in an alkaline electrolyte. Alcad's manufacturing process starts with the manufacture of positive and negative 'mass', the active ingredient of the plates. Specialized strip filling machines feed the mass, in powder or tablet form, into perforated steel pockets. Several pockets are spot welded together and pressed to form a plate. Groups of positive and negative plates are assembled together and undergo an initial electrical charging process, after which they are fitted into plastic cell cases. The assembled cells are given a final electrical charge, before being passed into the warehouse. Final assembly involves connecting together blocks of cells to make up a battery to the customer's specification.

In summary, Alcad's manufacturing process involves the following types of production:

- continuous process (positive and negative mass)
- repetitive manufacture (perforation of coils of strip steel prior to platemaking)
- batch manufacture (platemaking)
- batch assembly (plate group assembly, fitting to cell cases)
- fixed cycle processes (electrical charging cycles)
- jobbing assembly (final assembly of batteries).

Chemicals, steel strip, plastic cases, steel and copper connectors, and a variety of cables and fittings are purchased from outside suppliers.

Alcad had employed MRP for many years, initially using systems that operated in batch mode and subsequently converting to an on-line IBS. Although these systems were considered to be successful, senior management had not fully embraced the disciplines involved in closed loop MRP. Sales forecasting and master production scheduling were largely left to the materials department, and commitment to the resulting plans was only lukewarm. Top management failed to create a culture in which due date adherence was the primary manufacturing objective. Output volume and direct labour efficiency were considered to be the main criteria for success.

As a result partly of focusing on the wrong measurements, and partly of the inability of MRP to schedule the various manufacturing processes effectively, shopfloor control was inadequate. Work in progress levels were too high, delivery performance was capable of improvement, and co-operation between manufacturing departments was lacking.

When Alcad was purchased by a French company, SAFT, the new management turned to OPT as a mechanism for improvement.

OPT implementation
The implementation of OPT was managed by a project team led by the logistics manager. Included in the team were specialists from planning and IT, together with an implementation consultant from the system supplier who worked full-time on the project. Alcad's representatives on the team undertook an initial two-week OPT course to prepare them for the task ahead.

Education in OPT concepts was carried out at all levels from managing director to chargehand. Members of the joint union negotiating committee were also involved in the project at an early stage. Much use was made of training games to illustrate the OPT concept, and these were well received by all who used them.

OPT was an addition to Alcad's existing IBS, rather than a replacement. OPT software does not include commercial modules such as order processing or purchasing, nor does it include financial ledgers. OPT did not even replace existing mechanisms for maintaining bills of material and routings, or for recording stock movements. An important implementation task was therefore to link this data with the OPT software. Alcad found that the high levels of accuracy already achieved in maintaining this data were of great importance in implementing OPT successfully. Furthermore existing data was well structured within a relational database, so accessing it for use by OPT was straightforward.

OPT required far more data than was available within Alcad's existing IBS. Information was needed on potential constraints that were ignored by MRP, such as relationships of operators and setters to machines, which tools go on which presses, and so on. A detailed model of the factory had to be constructed. Task forces which included people from all levels in the company were set up to collect the necessary data. This process engendered considerable involvement in the project, and identification with its objectives.

The commitment of top management was tested as implementation proceeded. There were, of course, the usual setbacks, demanding a strong nerve from all concerned. More than this, there was also the need for top management to adopt a completely different view of how to manage the factory. The unfavourable short-term profit impact of dramatic inventory reductions was accepted by the parent company, because the longer-term benefits were understood.

The outcome

OPT is an unquestionable success at Alcad. Customer arrears have been virtually eliminated and work in progress dramatically reduced. Supervisors have clear, feasible schedules and they understand the importance of working to them. Alcad also has a sophisticated model of the factory. If a machine breaks down or a supplier fails to deliver, the effects can be readily simulated and alternative courses of action modelled. Guesswork has been taken out of production planning and replaced by predictability.

Machines are no longer operated simply to keep people busy, nor are long production runs regarded as economical. Training has increased operator flexibility, so that people can move to where they are needed. The workforce has accepted dramatic changes in working practices, in particular the need for mobility. A single, company-wide productivity bonus has replaced individual incentive payments. After an initial trimming of the workforce, Alcad finds that significant levels of enforced operator idleness are not an inevitable consequence of OPT. Nevertheless, the availability of some slack time has made possible levels of operator training that would previously have been regarded as uneconomic.

The conventional management accounting procedures that Alcad used before implementing OPT have not been changed; they are simply less important. Production performance is measured by schedule adherence and delivery performance rather than by financial measures. The changing roles of accounting and manufacturing are illustrated by an organizational change that followed the OPT implementation. Responsibility for IT, and for the provision of all management information systems, was transferred from the accounts department to logistics.

Before implementing OPT, Alcad used to hold stocks of cells. Now stocks are held of plates and assembly components, enabling the company to respond flexibly to customers' requirements with much less inventory than previously. Demand forecasting remains a difficult area. Forecasts are treated as stock orders, enabling OPT schedules to be projected 16 weeks into the future. This enables purchase requirements to be generated, although these may change as the schedule is gradually firmed up. Much time has been spent explaining to suppliers the importance of delivering orders on time. Since Alcad works so closely to schedule, suppliers can be left in no doubt about the impact on Alcad's production of late delivery.

Use of OPT has not been extended to the final assembly process, where standard cells are configured into the battery specified by the customer. The role of OPT is to ensure cells are completed on time. Previous methods of scheduling final assembly have been retained.

OPT within MRPII

It is clear from Alcad's experience that implementing OPT has strong similarities to implementing MRPII. Both require a programme of education and involvement throughout the company. In each case success is dependent upon high standards of data accuracy and the use of suitable integrated computer systems. Much of what was said in Chapter 4 about implementing MRPII applies to the implementation of OPT. Indeed much of what has to be done is identical. Alcad found that it needed its IBS implementation as a foundation for OPT. If it had not already implemented an IBS, it would have needed to do so.

Some parts of Alcad's IBS are no longer used. MRP and CRP have been replaced by OPT. Purchase schedules are printed by the IBS, but from information generated by OPT. Production schedules are produced directly by OPT, in a form tailored to Alcad's requirements.

The system that Alcad is now operating is in many ways equivalent to MRPII with finite scheduling. Indeed Alcad could have decided to adopt MRPII principles and introduce a conventional finite scheduling system instead of implementing OPT. Whether this route would have been equally successful is impossible to say. Nevertheless there is a feeling at Alcad that the cultural change that has been achieved is probably the most important element of its success. If the company had decided to implement MRPII, rather than OPT, a similar effect might have been achieved.

If Alcad had chosen the MRPII route, it would have adopted the concept of closed loop MRP (Figure 1.2). The use of the closed loop cycle as a tool for senior managers to run the business is explored further in Chapter 7. Nevertheless we have already seen in Chapter 1 how the business planning process guides and structures the task of master production scheduling. At Alcad the links between strategic business planning and master production scheduling were missing. The MPS was produced independently by the materials department, without the involvement of sales and marketing and without the formal acceptance of top management. Master production scheduling was seen as a matter for the specialists, unrelated to the company's business plans. In contrast, the aim of the closed loop MRP cycle is to integrate planning throughout the business.

Implementing OPT at Alcad has secured a commitment to the plan that was previously lacking, but it has done so without substantially changing the way the MPS is produced. Control of the process remains the responsibility of the materials department. An OPT routine is used containing an algorithm that attempts to optimize achievement of customers' required despatch dates. Management can influence the process by allocating priorities to particular orders. There is also an option to use the algorithm to maximize throughput, rather than achievement of required despatch dates. Once these parameters are set, however, the generation of planned due dates for sales orders and stock orders (i.e. the creation of the MPS) is totally automatic. Sales and marketing are no more involved in the process than they were before. Production departments and top managers have sufficient confidence in the OPT process to accept the outcome without a formal approval procedure.

Has OPT really automated the process of generating the MPS, or could some benefit be obtained from superimposing elements of the MRPII philosophy? In some ways the OPT approach to master production scheduling is somewhat naive. The assumption is made that all manufacture is to customer order; even demand forecasts are treated as if they were discrete orders. OPT does not use concepts such as planning bills, features and options, or ATP (see Chapter 2) to manage demand and control uncertainty.

Perhaps OPT could best be used within the closed loop MRP concept, replacing RCCP, MRP and CRP, but working within a structure of business planning and master production scheduling. It may even be desirable in some circumstances to retain MRP to generate long-term purchase schedules, using OPT only for shorter-term production schedules.

Would such a system still be MRPII? Yes, of course. Manufacturing resource planning is not dependent upon MRP and CRP. It merely requires the use of procedures for planning materials and capacity that are under the control of top management through a structured, closed loop methodology.

Summary of OPT

The following conclusions may be drawn about OPT:

- OPT is more than a finite scheduling system that merely schedules orders planned by MRP.
- OPT can be incorporated into the MRPII planning methodology.
- The task of implementing OPT is the equivalent of implementing conventional MRPII and finite scheduling simultaneously. It may be better to implement conventional MRPII first, and then move to OPT.
- OPT is not only applicable to factories with obvious and permanent bottlenecks.
- Successful implementation of OPT at Alcad was associated with:
  - simple material flows in a highly coherent plant
  - sub-contracting of all but core components
  - batch assembly of a standard range of products.
  The suitability of OPT in companies with complex material flows and multiple levels of bill of material, or in process industries or jobbing shops should not be taken for granted. Case studies do exist, however, which suggest that OPT is applicable in different environments.
- Use of conventional management accounting methods is not a barrier to successful OPT, so long as management concentrate upon the correct (non-financial) performance measures.
- As a centralized scheduling system, OPT does not comply with ideas expressed earlier about local scheduling. It may be more difficult to achieve shopfloor acceptance of imposed OPT schedules in companies that are larger than Alcad, where the impact of a single production department on the company as a whole is less visible. Alcad places great emphasis on involving management and the shopfloor through regular schedule adherence meetings which analyze performance, identify reasons for failure, and implement corrective action. Supervisors are actively encouraged to accept ownership of their schedules.

OPT is more than a finite scheduling technique, but less than MRPII. It is an important concept, and one that deserves wider use than has so far been the case. A clearer understanding of the role of OPT within an MRPII strategy should assist greater acceptance.

The Japanese revolution

The Japanese approach to production management, focusing upon simplification, avoidance of waste and continuous improvement, has become well established in the West. In particular the idea that inventory is wasteful, hides problems that should be revealed and solved, and adds unnecessary complexity has created very great interest in JIT manufacture. Although the Japanese revolution was initially seen as a rejection of Western dependence upon computer systems, information processing and mathematical modelling, it is in fact largely complementary to them.

It is true that JIT manufacture emphasizes the use of manual procedures for scheduling production, but this does not necessarily exclude the use of computer systems. The original and most complete realization of JIT is the Toyota production system (TPS). To quote the originator of this system, Taiichi Ohno (1988), "At Toyota, we do not reject the computer, because it is essential in planning production levelling procedures and calculating the number of parts needed daily." Clearly a form of master production scheduling and material requirements planning is an indispensable feature of the TPS.

Pull scheduling concepts

One of the essential characteristics of JIT is the use of pull scheduling to control daily production activity. Pull scheduling techniques use demand from downstream processes to determine the output required from earlier stages of production. This is in contrast to push scheduling, in which all production activities follow a predetermined plan. MRP, finite scheduling and OPT all fall into the category of push scheduling. Pull scheduling therefore offers a completely different approach to shopfloor scheduling and control.

Pull scheduling was developed at Toyota, where the use of kanbans to activate production processes forms a central part of the TPS. There are three forms of pull scheduling in common use, all of which are variations on the kanban theme:

- kanban cards
- kanban containers
- kanban squares.

In each case the idea is to use the depletion of inventory at one stage in the manufacturing process to trigger an upstream process to manufacture a replacement batch. Only the specified quantity may be produced, representing a few hours' usage, and if there is no demand to be satisfied the upstream process must remain idle. This simple technique ensures that all upstream manufacture is synchronized with the needs of final assembly.

Kanban cards control this process by acting as a requisition, specifying the part number and quantity of the item required. Dual-card kanban systems use both a conveyance kanban and a production kanban. The conveyance kanban authorizes the movement of a container of parts from an interprocess storage point to the next operation. Depletion of interprocess stock causes a production kanban to be sent to the upstream work centre as an instruction to replace the stock. In a single card system, the kanban passes directly from the work centre that uses the part to the one that produces it, requesting a replacement batch.

In both cases the kanbans travel with special containers designed to hold the exact quantity of items that constitutes the standard batch size. The number of cards in the system determines the level of work in progress.

Starting with a comfortable quantity of cards, the number can be progressively reduced until problems start to appear. In a cycle of continuous improvement, these problems are resolved and further inventory reductions made.

In a simple environment, where the identity of the items required and the work centre in which they are made is self-evident, the kanban card may be dispensed with altogether. Re-supply is triggered by the arrival at the preceding work centre of an empty container. This is the kanban container system. Adjusting work in progress levels is more difficult than when using cards, since it is necessary to remove or add the required number of containers. When kanban cards are used, the removal of a card is sufficient to render a container dormant.

Kanban squares are areas marked out on the shopfloor in an area adjacent to the user work centre. Each square is capable of holding a predetermined number of containers of a particular item. The feeder work centre is required to keep the kanban square topped up with parts, but must not permit them to overflow the prescribed area. Kanban squares are useful for bulky items, where several containers are needed to satisfy a typical day's requirements. They can also be used to control the level of work in progress between workstations in a flow line.

Within these various types of kanban system there are two alternative concepts at work. The first is pure pull scheduling, where the only information that a work centre receives about the demand it is to satisfy comes from downstream work centres. The second, and probably more common approach is pull replenishment. Here the feeder work centre works to a daily production schedule supplied by a centralized planning function. The receipt of a kanban merely authorizes the movement of parts to the user work centre.

Dual kanban systems are generally the pure pull scheduling kind; both approaches are possible with the other forms of kanban. The advantage of pure pull scheduling is simplicity. There is no need for a centralized scheduling function co-ordinating the activities of the various work centres. Pure pull scheduling may, however, require larger interprocess inventories to protect upstream work centres from unpredictable demand.

Pull replenishment recognizes that upstream work centres are subject to dependent demand, so are capable of being supplied with advance warning of the demands to be placed upon them. We have seen how MRP plans the works orders needed to satisfy projected demand for dependent demand items. Kanbans can be more effective than works orders, however, in quick-response, JIT manufacture. Using works orders for batches representing only a few hours' usage of each item would result in enormous numbers of transactions and huge volumes of paperwork. The solution is for MRP to produce daily schedules for each work centre, to keep the centralized paperwork to a minimum, while using kanbans to control specific material movements. This approach retains the planning abilities of MRPII whilst adding the benefits of visible control, simplicity, and local influence upon scheduling.

Systems support for pull scheduling

If kanban control is to be incorporated into MRPII, then the software used must provide some additional features to support it. One example of JIT support is the use of rate scheduling in place of discrete works orders, which was described in Chapter 3. This technique is intended for flow-based production; in a JIT context it is particularly applicable to level scheduling, where demand for finished products is smoothed into constant daily quantities.

A second form of support for JIT manufacture is backflushing, which was described in Chapter 2. In a situation where works orders are replaced by daily schedules there is no kitting of the materials needed to manufacture a batch of items, and no material issue from stores transaction. Instead materials are held on the shopfloor and consumed as required. Backflushing (sometimes called 'post deduct') enables usage of materials to be deduced from reported completion of finished items. Although backflushing supports the JIT ideals of simplicity, shopfloor control and minimum paperwork, it lacks the rigorous disciplines of secure stores and positive tracking of material movements associated with MRPII.

Backflushing is best used in true JIT environments, where the amount of inventory on the shopfloor at any one time is very low. Any stock recording discrepancies will then be easily visible. Simply throwing open the doors of the material stores and abandoning kitting in favour of backflushing is a certain route to loss of control.

Some IBS suppliers offer further features that are claimed to provide support for JIT manufacture. It is doubtful whether many of these features are of much practical use. Few companies, for example, are likely to want their IBS to print kanban cards, when the whole point of kanbans is to delegate responsibility for scheduling to the shopfloor. Furthermore, unlike works order documentation, new kanbans are not required for each batch; instead they rotate continuously between user and supplier. Yet some suppliers promote the 'JIT friendliness' of their products by offering automatic printing of kanbans.

Of greater interest to most companies moving into JIT is how to draw back the centralized control of MRPII in areas of the factory where kanban is more appropriate, without undermining the integrity of their business systems. If certain processes are to be controlled by a pure pull scheduling technique, with no works orders or rate schedules, how will MRP and other aspects of MRPII respond to this void? An essential feature of MRPII is that it provides integration and consistency. It does not respond favourably to incomplete data.

One approach would be to remove completely the items involved from the bill of material, leaving any lower level items that are still to be scheduled by MRP linked directly to the higher level items still managed by the system. Kanban control may then be applied to the missing intermediate items. Because MRPII has no knowledge of the kanban items, there will be no distortion in the information generated. Most companies, however, would prefer to retain centralized information on all items, their routings, costs and other data, even if production is to be controlled by manual means.

The solution is to turn the items in question into phantoms (see Chapter 2). MRP blows through phantom parts without planning works orders, passing the demand down to lower level items where works or purchase orders are required. Intermediate phantom parts are free to be controlled by kanban methods.

In this way MRP provisions stocks of the lower level materials that are consumed by the kanban controlled part of the system. These materials are then processed, in accordance with kanban instructions, producing items used in subsequent stages of production. Once the kanban system has completed its task, production of the finished item is declared to the inventory system, and so becomes visible to MRPII. Declared production is backflushed, to downdate material stocks. Backflushing, like MRP, ignores phantoms, so it is stocks of the original materials that are downdated, not stocks of the intermediate kanban items (which are always zero).

Using phantoms in this way enables pockets of kanban control to exist within an MRPII environment. These pockets can be as limited or as extensive as required. Of course by using kanban control many MRPII features are relinquished. One example is the exclusion of kanban work centres from capacity plans. Other features that are foregone are the ability to track movement of materials through the manufacturing process, and the collection of actual costs and variances. These losses are all part of the choice between simplified shopfloor control and comprehensive computer-based systems that is implicit in any move towards JIT. MRPII is capable of providing extensive planning, reporting and decision support facilities, if required. There is no compulsion to use all these facilities in all circumstances.

From Class A to JIT – a case study

Although kanban control can operate within an MRPII environment, this does not mean that implementing JIT is a natural extension of the MRPII concept. The progression of Reckitt Pharmaceuticals firstly to Class A MRPII and subsequently to JIT illustrates the difficulties that can arise.

A Class A implementation
Reckitt Pharmaceuticals, a company within the Reckitt and Colman group, suffered from many of the problems that beset companies which do not use structured planning and control methodologies. In particular, inaccurate inventory records were causing large discrepancies between the management and financial accounts, responsibilities and accountabilities were blurred, and there were low expectations of what improvements could be achieved. The operations director decided that MRPII was the answer.

A project manager was appointed and his first task was to sell the MRPII concept to the senior management team, a process he describes as conditioning the company for MRPII. This task took several months of informal meetings and discussions with individual managers. Only when the climate was right (senior managers were asking when he was going to get on with it) did the project manager submit a firm project proposal. This proposal included a cost justification and outline project timetable.

The company was already using an MRP-based system which had been heavily modified. The system was operated primarily in batch mode. Not only were inventory records inaccurate, but there were alternative versions of the bills of material, and multiple sales forecasts. It was soon realized that although the system was not ideal, it was not the major problem. Implementing MRPII was understood to be a matter of changing the company culture, not the software. Nevertheless the modifications that had been made to the system were a hindrance to progress. It was not possible to reverse these modifications so the company had to buy a new version of the software. Operations were gradually transferred to the pure version, in a process described as 'virginizing the system'.

A project team of five or six people was formed; all were assigned full-time to the project. This was a major commitment for a company employing about 1,000 people in its manufacturing and commercial functions (plus a large research and development activity which was not involved in the project). Nevertheless this commitment is regarded as having been crucial to the eventual success of the implementation.

The project team was responsible for driving the project, using task forces to implement their decisions. The project manager reported to the sponsor of the project, the operations director, who acted as project guardian.

Implementation conformed to a fairly conventional, but well-thought-out and thorough approach, as follows:

- A small number of key people, including departmental heads, were sent on external courses.
- A poster campaign was used to arouse the interest and awareness of the workforce.
- Voluntary lunchtime training sessions were organized, led by departmental managers, at which training videos were shown. Some 90 to 95% of the people on the site attended these sessions.
- Programmes to improve inventory and bill of material accuracy were launched.
- Business planning and master production scheduling procedures were examined by top managers. Inconsistent policies were exposed and eliminated, key product families identified, and spreadsheet-based master production scheduling techniques introduced.
- A series of conference room pilots was arranged. Groups of about 14 people met for half a day each week for eight weeks, gradually working through the new procedures. To emphasize the fact that MRPII was not seen primarily as a computer implementation, there were no VDUs in the

conference room. Instead the emphasis was on talking through the issues, understanding the principles involved, and becoming familiar with the paperwork to be used. Attendees were expected to work through the computer transactions in their own time, between meetings.
- A live pilot was run after the conference room pilot, and live running commenced immediately after that.

In spite of all the preparatory work that had been done, the first six weeks of live running was a demanding time. The change to managing by due date rather than by volume of product was a traumatic experience. Nevertheless the preparation paid off and the performance of the company improved dramatically. The company was proud to receive the Class A award as a mark of its achievement.

The next step - JIT
Following this success both the operations director and the project manager who had jointly led the implementation moved on to other parts of the Reckitt and Colman Group. Nevertheless Reckitt Pharmaceuticals did not rest on its laurels. The company found that one result of implementing MRPII was a growth of confidence throughout the organization. This belief that more could be done was one of the factors that led the company into following its success with MRPII by launching a JIT implementation.

JIT meant that many things that had been set in place to support MRPII needed to be changed. Some of these changes were very far-reaching. For example:

- After much painstaking effort to convince storekeepers to accept responsibility for inventory accuracy, the stockroom doors were effectively thrown open again. JIT required that materials were to be kept at the point of use and consumed as required to satisfy demand from downstream work centres.
- The concept of working to a predetermined schedule, to satisfy volume targets within specified time slots, was replaced by a reactive culture in which production was required to respond to actual demand.
- Performance measures that had been introduced to support the concept of schedule adherence as the most important metric of production performance were no longer appropriate. Flexibility was now the criterion of success. New performance measures were required.

Reckitt Pharmaceuticals found that introducing these changes had the effect of undermining the MRPII implementation. As new concepts and new performance measures were introduced, the hard-won successes of MRPII were eroded. This erosion was not an inevitable watering down of MRPII disciplines in favour of JIT processes. On the contrary, the JIT implementation failed to achieve its objectives. The company was left with weakened management control, with little in the way of performance improvement to compensate.

The lessons from Reckitt Pharmaceuticals

Lack of commitment and preparation were not the reasons Reckitt Pharmaceuticals' JIT project failed to meet its objectives. The success of the earlier MRPII project is ample evidence of the company's ability to carry through a major project. Furthermore, the achievements of that project had created confidence and a willingness to change throughout the organization. The disappointing outcome of the JIT project, against this background, was a surprise.

Perhaps the very success of the MRPII implementation led the company to believe that JIT could be bolted onto the structures that had already been put into place. But JIT is not a natural continuation of MRPII. In particular the concept of pull scheduling is quite foreign to MRPII, and great care is needed if the two approaches are to coexist. In Reckitt Pharmaceuticals' case, the problem of achieving this union was compounded by a misunderstanding of the true nature of pull scheduling.

In general the use of pull scheduling is only possible if the items to be controlled are subject to steady demand. For some products, where volumes are high and variety limited, this situation occurs naturally. In such cases repetitive manufacture is the norm, and pull scheduling is a feasible option. For other products, where there is greater variability in demand, it may be possible to simulate repetitive manufacture by introducing level scheduling. This is not an easy thing to do, since it requires the elimination of batch production in favour of mixed model production.

Mixed model production means making all products simultaneously and continuously. If Product A is subject to a demand of 2,000 a month and product B is sold at a rate of 100 a month, then the daily schedule is for 100 of product A and five of product B. Since the requirement is constant, pull scheduling imposes essentially the same demand upon feeder departments each day. Fluctuations only arise in response to the minor day-to-day deviations that inevitably occur. Under these circumstances, individual work centres can be set predetermined output targets, and schedule adherence remains a key performance measure. If Reckitt Pharmaceuticals had introduced levelled schedules it would not have experienced the need to change controls that had been introduced during the MRPII implementation.

Introducing kanban systems before levelling the demand places an enormous burden upon production to respond to any possible variation in demand. To quote again from Taiichi Ohno (1988), "Toyota's final assembly line never assembles the same automobile model in a batch. Production is levelled by making first one model, then another model, then yet another." Reckitt and Colman has learnt this lesson well. A policy of level scheduling has now been introduced at its factories throughout Europe.

Even if Reckitt Pharmaceuticals had recognized the need for levelled schedules, it is probable that difficulties would still have arisen with its JIT implementation. The differences between the push scheduling approach of MRPII and the pull scheduling of JIT are always likely to cause conflict in the management of inventory. MRPII demands very strict and formal controls over inventory transactions and data accuracy, since inventory is the basis from which plans are derived. In contrast, JIT assumes that amounts of inventory will be small, visible, and subject to shopfloor control.

A very small number of companies may be able to use pull scheduling to control all their manufacturing activities. For the remainder, there will be a point at which push and pull scheduling meet. Education and training programmes need to address this area with great care and sensitivity. For Reckitt Pharmaceuticals the timing was wrong. In launching a JIT project soon after the conclusion of the MRPII implementation the probability of confusion and demotivation was too great. MRPII concepts had been explained in black and white terms, and JIT introduced shades of grey. Implementing elements of JIT as part of the original MRPII project might have permitted the issues to be put across in a less simplistic manner. Alternatively if MRPII had been in place longer before the JIT project was launched, its lasting values might have been better understood.

For MRPII does introduce values that are relevant to JIT manufacture, and without which JIT is not feasible. Reckitt Pharmaceuticals' experiences with MRPII taught the company that chaos and confusion are not inevitable characteristics of manufacturing. Responsibilities can be clear-cut, and managers can work together rather than in isolation. Planning, and the subsequent execution of those plans, is more effective than fire-fighting. Education is necessary, and people need to be informed of their place in the company's strategic direction. Implementing MRPII removed the fog and introduced clarity to the business. Whatever future direction the company takes, the fog will not be permitted to descend again.

The broader aspects of JIT

This discussion of JIT manufacture has concentrated primarily upon pull scheduling, for the simple reason that this aspect of JIT is the one most relevant to the subject of this chapter, shopfloor scheduling and control. We have seen that combining pull scheduling with MRPII is not straightforward. The problem does not lie in the computer systems, since there are ways to support pockets of kanban within a wider company system. The difficulty is in the educational process, since the concept of incorporating kanban into MRPII is much more difficult to communicate than the relatively straightforward message of unadulterated MRPII.

The differences between push and pull scheduling tend to diminish somewhat when pull scheduling is fully understood. Kanban is not a system for making instantly to order, no matter how great the variability in customer requirements. On the contrary, it is an attempt to introduce stability and repetitiveness into the manufacturing process. Far from being a system able to respond to random demand, kanban is only feasible when operated within levelled schedules.

There are strong parallels between the significance of level scheduling in

JIT and the pivotal role played by master production scheduling in MRPII. In both cases it is the clear responsibility of management to control the business by managing customer demand. The idea that managers can permit chaos to reign in their factories in a misguided attempt to please the customer is eschewed equally by MRPII and JIT. Being customer oriented does not mean abandoning control in favour of knee-jerk management. All customers benefit from a factory that is managed effectively in satisfying the demands that are placed upon it.

Pull scheduling is only one element of JIT manufacture. Implementing JIT requires the simultaneous introduction of many different initiatives including, but not limited to:

- set-up time reduction, to permit smaller batches
- operator responsibility for achieving right first time quality
- fast feedback of any quality problems identified downstream to the upstream processes that caused them
- close linking of manufacturing processes, particularly in U-shaped cells, to improve material flows and operator mobility
- team working and delegation of responsibility for problem solving to shopfloor groups
- visible shopfloor reporting of performance against targets
- display of work instructions and process plans at the workstation
- preventive maintenance techniques to improve machine up-time
- broadening of operator skills to improve flexibility
- consultation with and respect for all employees
- andon lights on machines, to indicate production problems
- operator authority to stop the line rather than risk producing defective goods.

None of these JIT techniques is in conflict with MRPII concepts. In fact much of JIT is concerned with issues that MRPII simply does not begin to address. MRPII overlays planning and control methodologies upon the existing physical and human resources, without addressing the need to improve those resources. JIT is a shopfloor-based, people-oriented approach which has the improvement of physical processes and the development of people as its focus.

Most companies would benefit from introducing at least some of the techniques that are associated with JIT, with or without pull scheduling. Whether or not the result is JIT is hardly relevant. Applying these techniques provides a further dimension to MRPII. Without them, MRPII offers no mechanism for continuous improvement. Class A is the ultimate achievement; beyond that MRPII has nothing to offer. JIT techniques have no end point; there is always more that can be achieved.

On the other hand, JIT is not a substitute for MRPII. JIT cannot assist in medium and long term planning, nor does it provided integrated systems for sales order processing, purchasing, costing and financial control; JIT is an execution system not a planning system. The potential for JIT and MRPII to work together is undoubtedly substantial.

Shopfloor data management

Although JIT is concerned primarily with manual control systems, the other approaches to shopfloor scheduling and control discussed in this chapter are all dependent upon computer systems. These systems require data; in the case of finite scheduling and OPT, far more detailed data than is contained in a typical IBS. As a result, secondary computer systems are needed to manage this additional data, and to provide the additional scheduling and control logic.

Many companies decide, at least initially, to make do with the scheduling aids contained within their IBS. Even so, the problem of entering large numbers of operation status or work booking transactions in a timely and accurate manner must be considered. A separate shopfloor data capture (SFDC) system may be needed for this purpose.

Introducing any form of data collection on the shopfloor can be an expensive and time consuming task. Many companies set off down this path with no clear idea of what they are trying to achieve, or even of the necessity of undertaking the journey. Sometimes introducing SFDC is seen as the panacea for an unsuccessful MRPII implementation, as if access to more data more quickly will somehow overcome the errors made during implementation.

Valid reasons for tracking works order activity are one or more of the following:

- to monitor order status, so that work-to lists can be produced which take account of completed operations
- to enable material yield or scrap to be closely monitored and controlled
- to improve the accuracy of capacity planning, by keeping an up to date picture of work completed and work still outstanding
- to provide data for a local scheduling system

Other, more questionable reasons that are frequently encountered include the following:

- to collect data that will allow the calculation of actual labour costs (the actual labour cost of a works order is generally only of interest in a jobbing/contracting environment)
- to provide input to operator incentive schemes (will the investment in shopfloor devices really be justified by improved productivity?)
- to provide a record of order status that will enable customer delivery enquiries to be answered (if the factory is working to schedule, the customer's order will be finished on time. If it is not, then knowing where the order is today will provide little indication of when it will be finished).

Tracking works order activity involves cost and complexity. Before embarking upon this route it is a good idea to reflect upon the JIT alternative, which is:

- to reduce the need for imposed production schedules by introducing pull scheduling systems
- to minimize quality problems and maximize material utilization through operator responsibility and workplace improvement teams, rather than through management control
- to reduce lead times and work in progress to such an extent that visual methods of monitoring capacity are adequate.

JIT may not be applicable in every case, but where it is the benefits are considerable. It would be unwise to invest heavily in works order tracking without first examining very carefully the JIT option.

For those companies that have been through this analysis but find they cannot eliminate the need to track shopfloor activities, there are some important issues to be considered.

Work status recording

Most, if not all, IBS products permit work completed at each operation to be recorded. Work bookings are often processed by specialist VDU operators, for two reasons. The first is that the data entry routines incorporated in the software tend not to be suitable for use by production operators. The second reason is that standard VDUs are not sufficiently robust for the shopfloor. Paperwork systems are therefore needed so that work bookings can be recorded at the point the work is done. These bookings are accumulated and passed to the VDU operator for entry. Such paperwork systems are labour intensive, inaccurate, slow and, where also used for payment purposes, liable to be abused.

Specialized data capture terminals, using bar coded input and providing prompts to assist operators, can overcome the need to generate paperwork bookings on the shopfloor. These terminals may be linked directly to the IBS, updating its database in real time, or they may be connected to a separate SFDC system. Advantages of a separate system include the following:

- Suitable systems are available off the shelf.
- A dedicated system can remain available during multi-shift operation, whereas the IBS may be closed down at night or dedicated to off-line batch processing.
- Specialized SFDC systems may offer additional features not available in the main system.
- Data can be uploaded from the SFDC system to the IBS at intervals, in batch mode. This can significantly reduce the decline in system response times to other users that might otherwise occur when large volumes of on-line transactions are processed.

The introduction of work status reporting must be carefully planned. The input of actual shopfloor events is where the planning system meets real life. Planning systems can make assumptions, simplifications and approximations; reporting systems must reflect all circumstances that can actually arise. If the system fails to respond in the way it should to a genuine booking, shopfloor confidence will soon be lost and data could become corrupt.

Some examples of the questions to be considered in planning a reporting system are as follows:

- Should every operation be booked, or only the important ones?
- If only some operations are to be booked, should the system automatically close all unbooked preceding operations?
- Can operations be performed out of sequence? If so, will the system automatically close earlier operations that have not yet been completed?
- Should supervisors have the authority to use an alternative machine or work centre? If so, how will the routing data be amended on the works order?
- How accurately can work be counted between operations? For example, how should the system react if, for a works order of 1,000 items, the first operation is closed at 980 and then 1,010 are booked at the second operation?
- Are end-of-shift bookings required for all part completed operations, to bring order information completely up to date?

Only when all such questions have been fully considered, current shopfloor practice checked (and double checked), system functionality tested, and procedures written can a company begin to plan operator training and system implementation.

Linking shopfloor systems to the IBS

Where shopfloor systems are used, whether simple SFDC systems or sophisticated finite schedulers, some means of linking them with the IBS is required. The shopfloor system needs information from the IBS, particularly works order details, in order to carry out its functions. The IBS in turn needs status information collected and processed by the shopfloor system. Usually it is sufficient to transmit data between the two systems in batch mode, although some SFDC systems can achieve near-instantaneous transmission of work bookings to the IBS.

Shopfloor systems often need more detailed process information than is contained in the IBS including, perhaps, jig and tooling details, machine capabilities and operator skill levels. This additional information is generally held within the shopfloor system. It is less obvious where to locate information that is needed by both the shopfloor system and the IBS.

One option is to duplicate the common data. This is the simplest approach, enabling the two systems to operate independently for most of the time. The disadvantage is that there is a risk of the two sets of data becoming inconsistent. This possibility can be minimized if system users are responsible for maintaining only one of the systems. This master data is then used to update the secondary system, through periodic batch updates. Even so, temporary inconsistencies could still arise in the data between updates.

A second option is for the IBS and the shopfloor system to share the same data, so ensuring consistency at all times. This approach tends to be complicated by incompatibilities between the different systems involved. These arise firstly at the level of hardware and operating system and secondly at the level of application software.

The increasing use of open systems is gradually reducing the first problem, ensuring compatibility between equipment supplied by different computer manufacturers. The second problem still remains. There is a lack of common standards for formatting product and process data in manufacturing systems, so system developers all adopt their own conventions. When systems from different suppliers are interfaced, some bespoke programming is always needed. This has led to some software suppliers occupying a market niche as specialist systems integrators.

Where only a very small number of shopfloor devices are to be linked to the IBS, one-to-one interfacing is a viable option. However there are growing numbers of computers in use on the shopfloor and it is becoming increasingly important to integrate them with the company's main planning and control systems. Linking many devices individually with the IBS is unrealistic, not only on cost grounds, but also because the result would be inflexible, difficult to maintain and of limited functionality. True integration means making data readily available to all existing and future applications through a common communications network. Managers who foresee a continuing need to link shopfloor (and other) systems with their IBS in order to achieve full business integration must develop suitable networking and data management strategies.

Computer integrated manufacturing (CIM) is the name given to this vision of business integration. The role of MRPII within CIM is discussed further in Chapter 8.

Horses for courses

This chapter has examined a wide range of techniques for shopfloor scheduling and control. These techniques each start from a different set of assumptions about the nature of the scheduling and control problem, and the extent to which human intervention is required.

Work-to lists use simple prioritizing methods, leaving detailed allocation of resources to the supervisor. Finite scheduling techniques range from computerized planning boards which are dependent upon the human operator to AI-based systems that attempt to mimic human thought processes. OPT constructs a whole theory of manufacturing around the concept of capacity constraints. Finally kanban systems aim to subvert the use of computer systems wherever possible, through applying human skills not to constructing schedules but to creating an environment in which the scheduling problem becomes trivial.

The existence of such different views of shopfloor scheduling and control is evidence of the complexity of the problem. There is no solution that is always right; the difficulty lies in selecting the best approach for a given situation. Examining the various options from an MRPII viewpoint, as we have done in this chapter, provides a framework within which their relative merits may be compared. In this context, the issue is deciding which approach will combine with MRPII to provide the necessary control over shopfloor scheduling and control. This is a much simpler question than trying to decide which of a selection of quite dissimilar techniques is 'best'.

The fundamental choices are between human decision making or automatic scheduling, simplification or data collection and processing, and local or central control. The decision will depend upon the nature of the business, the management style within the company, and the planning tools available. It is an important decision because each company is unique in the equipment that it uses, the capabilities and attitudes of its workforce, and the outlook and beliefs of its managers. An approach that succeeds in one company may not be appropriate in another, even if it is a direct competitor. The rewards for the company that makes the right choice can be considerable.

—— 7 ——

Managing through MRPII

A framework for planning and control

MRPII was described in Chapter 1 as a structured approach to manufacturing management. The framework upon which MRPII is based can be represented by the diagram shown in Figure 7.1. This shows a methodology for business management through progressive levels of planning.

The starting point of this methodology is the preparation of the strategic business plan, a process that maps out the direction of the company for at least the next two years, and possibly for the next five. This vision of the organization's future is converted into more concrete capital investment and human resource plans in the manufacturing and logistics plan. A rather shorter timescale is usual here, probably no more than two years ahead.

Demand management and master production scheduling are concerned with the conversion of sales forecasts and actual customer orders into a feasible manufacturing plan. The timescale for this activity is typically up to one year. The next planning stage develops the MPS into detailed material and capacity plans through the use of tools such as MRP and CRP. These mechanistic tools are controlled by planners who are responsible for approving and releasing purchase schedules and works orders. The final planning stage is the short term scheduling and control of shopfloor activities.

This structure has two essential features. The first is a focusing process, in which more detail is added at each stage as the horizon is shortened. The second feature is that each stage takes account of existing realities, through feedback loops from the lower level planning activities and ultimately from the execution of the plan. These two characteristics ensure that there is consistency at all stages in the planning process, and therefore that all levels of manager, from chief executive to shopfloor team leader, are working towards common goals.

Figure 7.1 represents the way MRPII companies work. Without this planning-based, structured methodology for managing the business, a company cannot claim to operate MRPII successfully. MRPII is a manage-

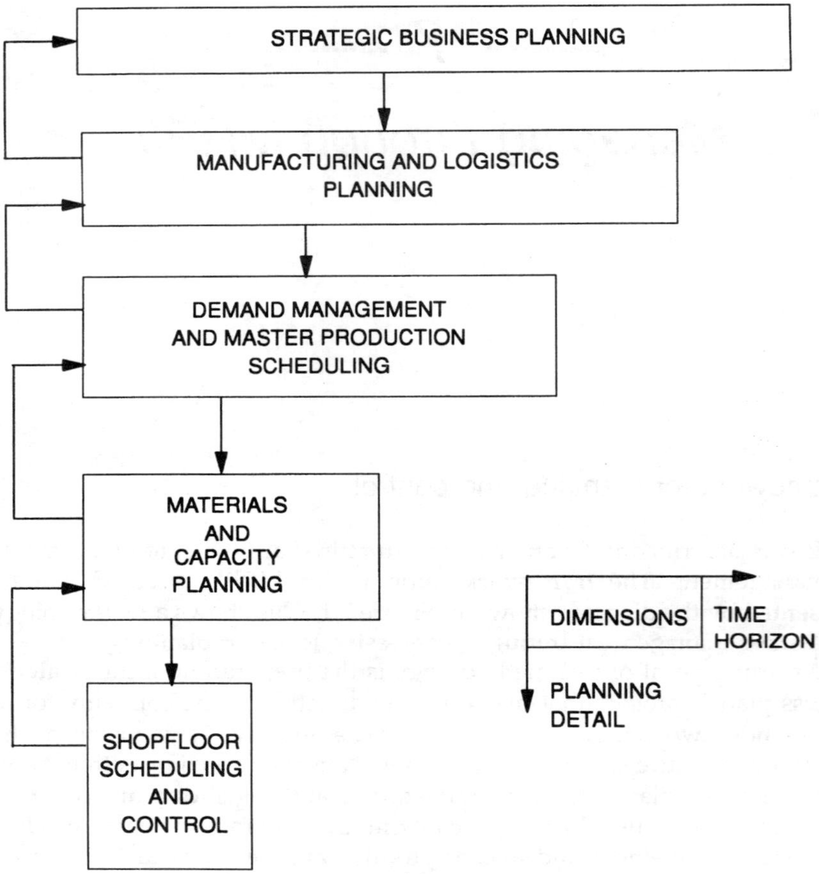

Figure 7.1   MRPII as a structured approach to manufacturing management

ment methodology upon which senior managers depend to order their actions, or it is nothing. Successful MRPII is often said to be dependent upon the commitment of senior managers, but the extent of this commitment is rarely defined. In fact nothing less than a total determination to manage through the structure shown in Figure 7.1 will do.

Managing through MRPII is not achieved by vague statements of support from the chief executive. Nor does it imply high computing costs or lack of responsiveness to customer needs. It simply means that no decision is made, at any level in the organization, without first examining all the implications and then revising existing plans such that the decision may be implemented smoothly and with confidence.

In the remainder of this chapter some of the specific actions required from managers in MRPII companies, particularly those managers near the top of the organization, are described.

MRPII implementation

The implementation of MRPII has been described in Chapter 4. Senior managers have a role to play that is of vital importance to the success of the venture. The delegation of project management to a full-time project manager does not exonerate senior managers from their ultimate responsibility for the project. Indeed it is quite impossible for a project manager, operating at a level below that of the top management team, to impose MRPII upon that team without their willing participation. One of the advantages of using an external consultant is to warn top managers when their own actions (or lack of action) are prejudicing the implementation. This task is usually impossible for an insider to perform.

Top managers must recognize that the business has to change if MRPII is to succeed, and that their role within the business will also change. They must throw themselves whole-heartedly into the project, attending education and training sessions, taking every opportunity to explain and support the project in dealings with their subordinates, spotting and defusing conflicts at an early stage, and dealing sympathetically with the inevitable worries and concerns that the project will engender.

This final point is an issue that cannot be avoided. If MRPII, and the systems integration which it brings, is successful, fewer people will be needed, and many of them will be doing different jobs. Foreseeing and explaining these changes at an early stage gives people time to adjust. They may decide that the time has come to seek other employment, or to take early retirement; alternatively they may see advantages in staying and learning new skills. Every opportunity should be provided to support these wishes, through severance packages, early retirement schemes, training programmes and internal transfer options. If an open approach is taken to the problem it may largely solve itself. Simply pretending that it does not exist will cause the worries to fester, breeding opposition and resistance to the implementation.

The role of senior managers in implementing MRPII may be summarized as follows. Their task is to:

- **commit** themselves to the MRPII concept
- **communicate** that commitment to all employees
- **appoint and empower** the project team
- **resource** the project
- **change** planning and control procedures, and performance measures, to suit MRPII methods
- **monitor** the progress of the project and the benefits achieved
- **sustain** a high level of project visibility and momentum by removing roadblocks and suppressing distractions.

Top managers in companies where MRPII has been less than totally successful should perhaps examine their consciences. It is possible they may find that the cause of the failure lies rather closer to home than they previously imagined.

Business planning

The first two stages of the MRPII methodology shown in Figure 7.1, strategic business planning and manufacturing and logistics planning, represent the business planning process that most companies carry out in one form or another. It is not the purpose of this book to discuss business planning in detail. Nevertheless there are issues of importance to MRPII that should be considered whenever business plans are being prepared.

Objectives of business planning

In the context of Figure 7.1, strategic business planning and manufacturing and logistics planning have three main roles:

- to ensure that the company adopts marketing and product strategies that will provide a continuing inflow of customer orders
- to plan the manufacturing resources needed to satisfy those orders
- to establish policies and targets to be used in demand management and master production scheduling.

Of these three roles, it is the final one that is of particular interest here. It is important to ensure that when the MPS is constructed, it takes into account the medium to long term targets established for the company. The long term is, after all, merely a sequence of short terms. If the short term plans do not constantly refer back to the long term plan, there is little likelihood of the company's long term objectives being achieved. Of course circumstances change, and the long term plans must be kept under constant review. The annual budget approach, in which a set of figures is generated from forecasts and assumptions that are not re-examined until the following year, is not good enough.

The main outputs required from the two stages of business planning, and the way they are used to constrain demand management and master production scheduling were discussed in Chapter 1. The methods by which these outputs are determined, the factors that are taken into account, and the judgements that are made will differ from company to company. The important technical issue is to ensure that the strategies and plans produced through this process are consistent with each other, accurate, and feasible. Unfortunately the planning tools used by many companies (which are typically spreadsheets of unknown integrity, using summarized data and approximate relationships) are rarely able to guarantee either consistency or accuracy.

MRP as a business planning tool

MRP is a planning system that converts a production plan (the MPS) into detailed purchasing and manufacturing plans. These plans can be further developed; manufacturing requirements can be converted through CRP into work centre loadings; purchase requirements can be expressed as cash flow commitments; stock movements can be evaluated and summarized by inventory category. In other words, MRP and its associated modules provide a very detailed planning model of the company.

This model can be applied to business planning as well as to operations planning. Clearly the live operational database cannot be used for this purpose, but a copy of it may be set up. Amendments can then be made as necessary. For example, new work centres could be added to reflect planned acquisition of new machines. Skeletons of proposed new products could be created in the bill of material and routing records. Different demand patterns could be analyzed by a sequence of MRP runs. Since the model is based upon a database used for operational purposes, there can be no doubt that plans created and tested in this way mirror reality.

Demand management and master production scheduling

In Chapter 4 it was stated that an unrealistic MPS is a common reason for MRPII implementations failing. Managing the MPS is one of the most important tasks for senior managers. It is also one of the most difficult, combining complex technical issues, conflicting departmental objectives, crystal ball gazing, and compromises. In companies where senior managers operate as a team, working together to achieve the best results for the company, the MPS is the glue that binds them.

In other companies, however, senior managers operate competitively rather than co-operatively. This may be through the deliberate policy of the chief executive, based upon a belief that competition keeps everyone on their toes, or it may be a historical phenomenon. In either case, this style of management is quite incompatible with effective master production scheduling, and therefore with MRPII. Chief executives of such companies are faced with a clear choice. They must decide either to change the culture from competitiveness to co-operation, or to abandon thoughts of introducing MRPII.

Constructing the MPS

There are many different objectives to be taken into account when constructing an MPS. In particular the MPS aims to:

- satisfy customer delivery requirements for current orders
- provision the raw materials and manufactured parts needed to satisfy forecasted future orders
- make effective use of company resources, particularly those which constrain overall factory output
- ensure a satisfactory net cash flow into the business

- permit sales volume and margin targets to be achieved
- maintain finished goods inventory at planned levels.

Even with the assistance of master production scheduling and RCCP systems, creating the MPS is a difficult task. The resources which are available and the targets that are to be achieved are determined by the business planning process. The task of the planner is to work within these constraints to produce the best possible plan; this is not a job for a committee. Balancing the many factors is a complex intellectual process best undertaken by a full time master scheduler.

It is not the role of senior managers to involve themselves in the creation of the MPS. The master scheduler already has more than enough objectives to satisfy without having to take into account a further set of instructions and suggestions, particularly when these may be based upon an incomplete view of the total scheduling problem. On the other hand, the MPS must have the agreement of senior managers before it is issued. The MPS is, after all, the principal decision-making instrument of the company.

Approval of the MPS is best achieved through an MPS review meeting. This meeting should be attended by the chief executive and the heads of production, sales, finance, materials and engineering. The master scheduler presents the proposed MPS, highlighting any compromises that it contains and explaining the conflicts that caused them. The meeting then has the choice of either accepting the proposed MPS or requesting changes. Assuming that the master scheduler has done a reasonable job in the first place, the only way the review meeting could improve the MPS is by amending the scheduling constraints. Therefore if the meeting decides to request changes to the MPS, it must also specify the new constraints within which the master scheduler must work.

In assessing a new plan, the MPS review meeting may not need to examine all the detail contained in the MPS. Often it is acceptable to work with summary information that has been aggregated from the detailed MPS. For example, it may be sufficient to consider cumulative demand and inventory data for product families rather than addressing individual products. Indeed this is usually true, except in those cases where the number of finished products manufactured by the company is relatively small, or where there are no discernible families. A review meeting that is presented with too much detail is likely to concentrate on discussing the detail, rather than the broad picture. In some companies, however, senior managers need to know how specific contracts have been scheduled into the MPS before they can sign it off.

The frequency of the MPS review meeting varies according to the timescales within which the company and its customers operate, but is typically monthly. Generally it coincides with the reconstructing of the MPS to incorporate the latest sales forecast. Between these major revisions of the MPS, the master scheduler must carry out continuous fine-tuning, to take account of incoming customer orders and actual production performance. These amendments must be made within the overall intention of the agreed plan. Where circumstances require that more substantial changes are needed, the MPS review meeting must be re-convened to approve them. Clear rules should be drawn up to specify the extent of change which the master scheduler is authorized to make without referring back to the review body. For example, product substitutions may be permitted within product families (without changing overall volume), but substitutions across product families would not be allowed.

Demand forecasting

As we have seen, one reason for a complete review of the MPS at regular intervals is to take account of the new sales forecast. Some form of forecast is almost always needed in the construction of an MPS, and it is important that the information used is updated regularly. In most companies sales forecasting is regarded as a hot potato; it is a tedious job which is impossible to do accurately, and which exposes the forecaster to criticism from all sides.

Forecasts are often confused with operational targets or sales budgets. Instead of being merely the best estimate of likely sales, they become goals which must be achieved. The effect is to give forecasting a political aspect. Front line sales people tend to produce low forecasts which they know they can beat, while sales managers produce high forecasts to spur on their subordinates. Some companies produce two forecasts; one to show the owner, or parent company, and another (rather higher) one which is used internally to measure performance and to motivate the sales force.

Under these circumstances it takes a bold person to volunteer to produce the demand forecast for the MPS. Often the forecast is produced by the master scheduler, simply because no-one else will do it. Also it is a sure way of getting the job done on time.

In fact there is no reason why the master scheduler should not carry out the statistical analysis involved in producing the forecast. The information needed is readily available within the IBS, and there may also be a forecasting module included in the software. Nevertheless it is essential that the raw statistical analysis is reviewed by sales and marketing people, to ensure that it makes commercial sense. Impending sales promotions, new product launches by key competitors, and planned price increases, are amongst the factors that could cause a forecast based solely on past demand to be highly unreliable.

Achieving an environment in which realistic forecasts can be produced regularly, free from political pressures and without acrimony, is a task for top management. Getting the environment right is far more important than spending time searching for that elusive mathematical forecasting technique which always produces the right answers. In reality no such technique exists, and complex methods do not necessarily produce the best results. A simple formula which can be manually adjusted when it looks wrong is usually better than a sophisticated technique that is difficult to understand,

and that people are therefore reluctant to override. This view is supported by research into the performance of different forecasting techniques. Vollmann, Berry and Whybark (1988) conclude that "Simple models usually outperform more complex procedures, especially for short-term forecasting." Short term, in this context, encompasses the forecasting horizons that most companies use for operations planning.

In addition to getting the environment for forecasting right, and finding an effective forecasting model, there are two further approaches to improving forecast accuracy which should be explored. The first is to introduce planning bills of material, as described in Chapter 2, for products that are available in many variants. The second way to improve forecast accuracy is to reduce the length of time over which forecasting is needed. In other words, to reduce the cumulative lead time of the product. This topic is discussed in the next section.

Even after all this work has been done, there may still be some products which cannot consistently be forecasted to acceptable levels of accuracy. Such products require very high levels of inventory, relative to their sales revenue, to achieve a reasonable level of availability. Since the cost of this inventory is not taken into account in the calculation of sales margin, the profitability of these products is frequently overstated.

Alternatively, if a high level of inventory is not used to ensure availability, these products cause customer dissatisfaction through unreliable delivery. This leads to complaints, which in turn cause senior managers to launch panic-mode expediting actions. The resulting disruption causes other orders to go late and costs to increase. Worst of all, the attempt to create a planning culture is undermined.

In either case, products that cannot be forecasted accurately do the company very little good. They should be redesigned to use materials and components that are common to other products, or are available on shorter lead times. If this is not possible, serious consideration should be given to dropping them from the sales catalogue. Unforecastability is not a technical problem for the statisticians; it is a warning sign to management that the product is not viable.

Lead time reduction

MRPII does not incorporate a process for reducing planning lead times. It works with the lead times it is given, launching new orders according to planned start date, and endeavouring to see that they are completed on their due date.

If these lead times are too long, orders will be launched earlier than necessary. The result will be to inflate work in progress, causing long queues at each work centre. These queues slow down the flow of work such that actual lead times turn out to be much the same as the planning lead times used by MRP. Put more simply, excessive lead times become a self-fulfilling prophecy.

Since MRPII does not automatically reduce lead times, and will operate quite happily with lead times that are unnecessarily long, management action is needed to remove the excess. The simplest way of doing this is through a progressive process of trial and error. An example of how this might work is as follows. Assume a manufacturing facility that is able to produce 100 units a day has work in progress of 700 units. Obviously it will take seven days to complete this existing workload, so the lead time for the next item entering the facility is seven days. A planning system using this lead time will ensure that the facility always contains seven days worth of work, so a steady state is maintained.

If a decision were taken to reduce the lead time to five days, the cycle would be broken. There is now no need to launch the next job, which is due to be completed in seven days time, for a further two days (any orders due in less than seven days have already been issued). By the time the job is launched, 200 units will have been completed from work in progress leaving a balance of 500 units. The output rate of 100 units a day is unchanged so the new order can be completed in five days, as planned.

This is a simplistic example, but the underlying logic is correct. Many planners, when faced with a manufacturing facility that is falling into arrears, attempt to correct the situation by increasing the lead time. All they are doing is ensuring that work is released into the shop even earlier, causing higher work in progress and compounding the arrears problem. The correct response is to stop releasing work into the shop until work in progress and lead time are back in balance. This is why input/output control, described in Chapter 6, is so important.

Clearly there must be a limit to the reduction that can be made to lead times before something starts to go wrong. Only the soft element of lead time, the queuing time, can be reduced in this way. The theoretical limit is reached when all the queuing time has been eliminated and there is only the hard element of lead time (transit, set-up and process time) left. In practice, as we saw in Chapter 5, scheduling problems will arise before this point is reached. The progressive trial and error process recognizes when this point is reached by monitoring due date adherence, and identifying the lead time at which a deterioration is evident. A lead time slightly greater than the point where due date adherence starts to deteriorate is the correct figure to use within MRP.

This is only the first stage of reducing lead time. Further improvements can be made by attacking the hard elements of lead time. This requires changes in shopfloor layout and in working practices, in order to:

- improve material flows, so that the remaining queuing time can be further reduced
- reduce transit time, through improved materials handling or by moving the operations closer together
- reduce lot sizes, so that total processing time is reduced
- reduce set-up time. This is unlikely to have much direct impact on lead times since most set-ups are measured in hours or minutes but it does

permit further reductions in lot size without reducing machine utilization.

Constant pressure on lead time reduction is needed. Shortening overall lead times, and hence the planning horizon, makes the MPS less reliant on forecasts of future demand. Other benefits include reduced work in progress inventory, enhanced responsiveness to customer demand, simplified shop-floor scheduling and control, and less requirement for storage space on the shopfloor.

The advantages of short lead times may seem obvious, yet it is surprising how many companies fall into the trap of never reviewing their lead times. A new computer system is installed and arbitrary lead time values are input, often with little management attention, in an initial crash exercise to set up the master data. Because these lead times seem to work (due to the self-fulfilling prophecy principle) no-one asks if they could be reduced. They become accepted as an unchangeable element of item master data. This tendency, where it exists, must be opposed. The rule is that lead times should always be justified, not assumed.

Target setting and performance monitoring

There is a well known adage that what gets measured gets done. It follows that if the wrong measurements are used, unproductive effort will be expended in making the numbers come right, and the real objectives of the business will suffer. Setting targets and monitoring performance are amongst the most important tasks that managers undertake. If the desired business results are to be achieved, managers need to set the right targets, and to monitor performance against them. As with so many other aspects of management, MRPII provides a distinctive perspective on the subject.

Management accounting

There is widespread concern in manufacturing industry about the relevance of traditional management accounting techniques such as absorption costing and variance analysis. These measures tend to encourage the creation of stock as a means of increasing reported profit and achieving high labour efficiency. In particular, the absolute importance of recovering overheads has long been the guiding principle of almost every production manager's working life. Traditional management accounting offers no balancing measures that expose the true cost of the inventory arising from such practices, or that encourage desirable goals such as speed of throughput and on-time delivery.

Unfortunately MRPII is very good at reinforcing traditional management accounting practices. Standard cost roll-up procedures happily support the use of absorption costing, while labour reporting facilities allow detailed variance analyses to be performed. It seems that the costing procedures implicit in MRPII are based upon a somewhat outdated concept of management accounting. This is not, however an inescapable feature of MRPII.

Costing for operations control

The standard cost roll-up procedure described in detail in Chapter 2 takes account of the material, labour and overhead costs incurred at each level of the bill of material. Production costs are calculated by processing each routing operation individually. At every operation the appropriate labour rates and overhead recovery rates are applied to the work done. These labour rates and overhead recovery rates can vary for each work centre, permitting tremendous sensitivity in the calculation of product manufacturing cost.

There are two ways in which overhead rates may be set for a work centre. The traditional approach is to allocate all overhead costs to individual work centres, based upon some arbitrary cost apportionment formula. Product standard costs calculated from these overhead rates include, or absorb, all overheads, hence the expression absorption costing. In reality, many overhead costs are time-based, and do not vary with the number or type of products produced. Instead they are incurred each month, no matter what the actual output. Yet absorption costing allows these costs to be carried into the future, rather than being charged against profit in the month they are incurred, by including them in inventory value.

Once these costs are hidden in inventory, the tendency is not to let them out again. Profits can be continually inflated by allowing inventory to rise. It is only when shipments to customers exceed production, and inventory falls, that these fixed overheads emerge as a charge against profit. The results can be dramatic. Some companies implementing JIT programmes have had to abandon their efforts because of the adverse short term effect on profit of massive reductions in inventory.

The alternative method of setting work centre overhead rates is to include only those items of overhead cost that arise when the production facility is actually used. These costs are called variable overheads. The remaining (fixed) overheads are those incurred each period regardless of production output. Instead of being included in the rolled-up costs of individual products, these fixed overheads are charged against profit in the period in which they arise. Product costs that include only material, labour and variable overhead are called marginal costs.

Because marginal costing does not involve the recovery of fixed overheads, it avoids the distortions that this procedure introduces. Marginal costing produces meaningful inventory valuations and it removes the pressure on production to recover overheads regardless of the consequences. Furthermore, marginal costing measures true production costs. These are the costs that can be directly influenced by the production, purchasing and engineering people. Fixed overheads are the responsibility of senior managers; these costs should not be included in the cost reports of managers who cannot control them.

MRPII can calculate either absorption costs or marginal costs, using the same cost roll-up mechanism. There is no bias in MRPII in favour of one type of costing or the other. It is the responsibility of top managers to decide the type of cost they want to use, and to configure the system accordingly.

Costing for strategic planning
Although marginal costing is the best approach for internal cost measurement, it is less helpful when it comes to strategic planning. Top managers are responsible for making many strategic decisions which require a detailed understanding of products costs. Marginal costs provide only part of the picture. For strategic decision making it is often necessary to know not just the direct production cost of a product, but the total cost of providing customers with a delivered product. This cost must include all manufacturing costs, including fixed overheads, as well as costs incurred in marketing and distribution. Clearly the total cost of a product will vary depending upon the market in which it is sold. A range of costs is therefore required for each product, one for each of those markets.

Without information on total product cost by market, it is impossible to identify which products are profitable, and where. This knowledge is essential in making decisions on, for example, product rationalization, new product development strategy, market development strategy, investment in new capacity (either at existing manufacturing sites or in regional markets), sub-contracting of non-strategic components or factoring of complete products, and the introduction of new manufacturing technology.

Generating product costs which include those overhead costs normally regarded as fixed may seem at odds with the argument used earlier, when discussing marginal costing. Then the point was made that fixed overheads should not be apportioned to individual products because they are incurred regardless of the volume or mix of products produced. In other words, they are time-based and constant.

This argument is valid for the short term management of operations, but in the longer term **all** costs are variable. This is what strategic decision making is all about. Capacity can be increased or decreased, technology can be changed and businesses can be restructured in response to longer term trends in product volumes and mix. These changes affect the on-going level of fixed overhead expenditure, even though that expenditure does not fluctuate in proportion to monthly activity levels. The question is, how do these costs that are usually treated as fixed actually vary in response to longer term shifts in the business?

According to Johnson and Kaplan (1987), "The goal of a good product cost system should be to make more obvious, more transparent, how costs currently considered to be fixed or sunk actually do vary with decisions made about product output, product mix and product diversity." They go on to say "By investigating in detail the demands placed on factory overhead departments, we will likely learn that cost drivers are more important than just physical volume of production. Among the cost drivers could be number of set-ups, hours of set-ups, number of orders placed, number of orders received, number of customer orders, number of shipments made, quantity of material ordered, number of parts, components and sub-assemblies in final products, amount of inventory, number of inspections, and number of engineering change orders." This idea that a whole range of cost drivers actually determine how fixed overheads vary has led to the development of activity based costing (ABC).

It is significant that all the potential cost drivers mentioned by Johnson and Kaplan can be extracted easily from an MRPII database. All these cost drivers are central to the way MRPII operates, and every transaction that is important in ABC is recorded in day-to-day MRPII operations. On reflection this is hardly surprising, since MRPII plans all manufacturing activities, while ABC seeks to measure costs by reference to those activities.

Cost roll-up techniques available in most IBS products do not use the cost drivers suggested by Johnson and Kaplan. Instead overhead costs are usually recovered by reference to operation labour hours, although sometimes the option of using machine hours or material costs is offered. The only one of the cost drivers listed above that is routinely used in calculating standard costs is hours of set-up.

There seems little doubt that as the potential of ABC is more widely understood, IBS products will increasingly offer a much greater range of possible cost drivers to be used in calculating costs. This will allow companies to design costing systems that reflect much more realistically the way that costs are incurred in their businesses. Even without special ABC software features, however, the information for ABC is readily available. All that is needed to produce ABC information is some judicious use of the 4GL query language.

ABC should be regarded as an additional tool, rather than a replacement for the more conventional form of standard costing. Marginal costs will continue to be used for internal control purposes, because they provide information that is relevant for operational measurement. The role of ABC is to help senior managers decide the longer term strategies for the business. MRPII can support both forms of costing.

Variance analysis: a flawed concept
Works order status reporting allows material and labour cost variances to be calculated for each operation of a works order. Labour variances can be aggregated to provide detailed departmental productivity statements. According to traditional management accounting theory, the resulting mass of data is a vital tool in managing labour productivity.

The reality is rather different. Shopfloor performance is rarely improved by raking over the coals to find out why excessive labour cost was incurred on manufacturing operations that were carried out some time ago. Most production operators, if asked why they had failed to produce at standard rates, could think of a hundred and one good reasons. The material was substandard, the tool was in need of re-grinding, the machine was faulty, and, of course, the allowed time was too tight anyway. Once the trail has gone cold it is impossible to establish the impact of these or other factors on the job in question.

Supervisors soon learn that to avoid these fruitless exchanges it is best to ensure that high levels of labour productivity are always recorded in the first place. This can be achieved by various ploys, including: scheduling work with loose time standards in preference to tighter jobs that are needed earlier; stockpiling work in progress to ensure there is always something to work on; keeping operators busy, whether or not the work is presently needed; avoiding training sessions or team meetings in works time, even though these may contribute to longer term performance improvements; maintaining large numbers of indirect workers (who are excluded from the variances) to service the directs; delaying recruitment and working excessive overtime instead, in case the work slackens off again, and many more. The common thread of these devices is that they are all harmful to the overall performance of the company.

Even without all these practical difficulties in using labour variances to manage productivity, the concept is still highly suspect. In most companies direct labour is a relatively small part of total production costs, and is declining further with continuing improvements in production technology. The use of labour variances tends to focus effort upon controlling the remaining manual tasks, whilst ignoring important and growing areas of indirect cost. This is truly an approach more fitted to the first decade of the twentieth century than the last.

In short, labour variances are of little use to anyone except, possibly, the management accountant. As an aid to improving company performance they are worse than useless. Most IBS software contains facilities for calculating labour variances, but that does not mean they have to be used. Operating an MRPII company requires performance measures that are relevant to the task in hand. It takes more than education and training to change attitudes and eliminate bad practice; obsolete measurement systems must be abandoned as well. Top management must be clear what they are asking their subordinates to achieve, and monitor success by using suitable measurement systems. If they fail to do this, they should not be surprised if the results are not what they wanted.

Material variances are different. Materials account for a high proportion of production costs and must be carefully managed. Unplanned wastage of material is readily identifiable through works order control and, unlike adverse labour variances, has a physical presence that is difficult to dispute. The calculation and monitoring of material variances enables quality improvement effort to be focused and measured. It is both necessary and straightforward.

Non-financial measures

Since the primary performance measuring tool of traditional management accounting, labour variances, no longer provides meaningful controls, some other metric is needed. One approach is to develop radical new accounting techniques that address the difficulties posed by traditional methods. An example is throughput accounting. Although the possibility of adopting new accounting techniques has been widely debated for some years, there has as yet been no large scale move to apply them. The alternative approach is to use non-financial measurements that relate more directly to the company's aims.

There are many non-financial measures that can be used to monitor operational performance. Examples of important targets that cannot be expressed in financial terms include, for example:

● inventory record accuracy
● forecast accuracy
● average time to process a customer order
● frequency of errors on order entry
● percentage achievement of the master production schedule
● frequency of stock-outs
● percentage of orders despatched on time
● number of overdue orders.

This is not intended to be a complete list, since the number of possible measures is almost limitless. Indeed one of the problems in using non-financial measures is identifying a manageable number of key targets which together ensure that the company is on course.

In an MRPII environment the task of selecting key performance measures is greatly simplified, because only one measure really matters, and that is **schedule adherence**.

Schedule adherence means providing the quantity of items ordered, at the time they are due, and to the quality specified. Schedule adherence applies equally to the delivery of goods from outside suppliers, the completion of internal works orders for individual components and for finished products, and the despatch of those products to the customer. It also covers supporting actions that are due for completion at predetermined times, such as engineering work needed to customize the product, or preparation of shipping documentation. If all these activities are completed according to the plan, the company has achieved all that it set itself to do.

In an MRPII company it would be quite perverse for top managers to apply additional measures of operational performance. Statistics such as plant and labour utilization, output volume and gross profit do not measure operational performance, since they are all predetermined by the plan. Top managers have already accepted when signing off the MPS that the best the company can achieve is to meet that plan. A failure to perform by operational managers can result in due dates being missed, but there is nothing they can do to improve on the plan. The supervisor who produces more than was planned is not helping the company, only producing surplus inventory.

This does not mean that all other measures are unnecessary. For example, continued success in achieving schedule adherence depends upon data accuracy remaining high, so regular data audits are still needed. Measures of plant activity levels are also important, not as a means of managing the plant but as an aid to producing better plans in the future.

Nevertheless, the single measure of schedule adherence is all that production managers, supervisors and team leaders need to be concerned with. In an MRPII environment there is no need for line managers to balance competing and incompatible targets, as is usual in companies that are not committed to management by planning. All they need to do is use the resources available to them to hit the schedule.

Organizing for MRPII

There are few aspects of a company that remain unaffected by the introduction of MRPII. From top management to the shopfloor people work in different ways to achieve different targets. It would not be unreasonable to assume that the formal organizational structure of the company may need to be changed to support the new ways of working.

Any discussion of organization structure must be qualified by the observation that, in this respect at least, all companies are different. Organizational structures are rarely determined solely by management theory or fashion. Instead they are largely a function of the particular talents of the individuals within the company and of the circumstances in which it finds itself at a point in time. When people and circumstances change, reporting lines may be readily adapted to the new situation. As there are no absolutes in the study of organizational structures, the subject can only be discussed in terms of trends.

Materials management

One definite trend associated with MRPII is the materials management form of organization. Materials management draws together production and inventory control, purchasing and stores under a single manager. Sometimes other activities are also included, particularly warehousing and distribution. The head of this function is sometimes called a logistics manager rather than a materials manager.

This form of organization can only exist in a meaningful way if it is based upon the use of information systems that are capable of integrating the various activities involved. A materials management form of organization truly exists only when departments which previously operated independently of each other start working together, by using shared systems and data.

During this transformation some jobs, such as manually posting stock balances and expediting production, disappear. New tasks need to be introduced, including the maintenance of planning lead times and safety stock levels, and the processing of MRP exception reports. Other jobs change in content, if not in name. For example the arrival of VDUs in the stockroom presents a significant new challenge to storekeepers, particularly those who were not previously responsible for stock recording. The role of purchasing also changes. Previously the emphasis was on the essentially clerical tasks of raising orders and expediting deliveries. MRPII allows much more opportunity to develop closer relationships with suppliers, based upon an ability to provide meaningful schedules of future requirements.

The materials management form of organization provides a unifying structure for bringing about all these changes. It is much more difficult to achieve efficient control of the materials used in the business if the functions making up materials management remain as separate departments throughout the MRPII implementation.

Master production scheduling

A key role in an MRPII company is that of master scheduler. Some companies implementing MRPII already have such a position, perhaps under a different name. Nevertheless the master production schedule takes on a greater significance once MRPII is implemented, and the scheduler will have a higher profile within the company. Whoever undertakes the role must have commercial awareness, understand production, be able to master complex computer-based tools, and be capable of justifying the resulting MPS to top management.

It is unlikely that the role of master scheduler will carry sufficient weight, or attract the right candidates, if it is positioned too far down the organizational structure. Often the position reports to the materials manager, who in turn reports to the manufacturing executive. This relatively lowly position tends to understate the importance of the MPS, and makes the task of producing it too remote from top management.

There is a further problem. The master scheduler must be seen as independent of any departmental prejudice. The MPS must not appear to favour the needs of production over those of sales, or vice versa. The MPS must be capable of gaining universal support and commitment from all parts of the organization.

One way of ensuring the independence of the MPS is by having the materials management department report directly to the chief executive. Such a structure emphasizes the pivotal role of material and capacity management in the planning culture of MRPII. It also removes a layer of management between the chief executive and the master scheduler, enabling top management to influence and identify with the MPS more readily.

Integrated businesses

Formal organizational structures may become less significant in the longer term. MRPII is a mechanism for integrating the disparate functions that exist within an organization. If all departments share the same data, use integrated processes and work to the same plan, the whole point of having specialist departments begins to evaporate. Future MRPII companies may be more loosely structured around multi-disciplinary teams. These teams may be set up permanently, to service the company's key business processes, or they may be short term problem solving teams. Few models of such an organization exist at present, but there seems little doubt that this is the evolutionary path. MRPII provides the central nervous system to support a much more dynamic form of organization than the traditional rigid, hierarchical model. Organic change, rather than organization structure, is the model for the future.

Total quality

Many companies have embarked upon TQM programmes in recent years. The objectives of these programmes may be stated in many different ways, but the ultimate intention is to change peoples' attitudes and expectations in relation to the quality of their work. In other words, to bring about a cultural change within the company. Under TQM, quality becomes the primary concern of everyone. Every task is seen to be a service carried out for a customer, whether that customer is outside the company or within it. The service provided must be to an agreed specification and at minimum cost. A simple definition of a TQM organization is one where the standard is zero defects, the task is continuous improvement and the goal is to delight the customer.

Companies that have been through a total quality programme successfully are well equipped to deal with an MRPII implementation. The focus on accuracy should prepare the company for the high standards of data integrity that MRPII requires. Familiarity with problem solving teams, which are widely used in TQM programmes, should enable MRPII task forces to carry out their work effectively. Good communication channels and educational processes created to support the TQM programme will be equally useful in the MRPII project. Finally, the flexibility and willingness to change that TQM fosters should help overcome any resistance to MRPII.

Of course it is quite possible to implement MRPII without first undertaking a TQM programme, but it is harder. MRPII is also about changing the culture, and much of what is done in implementing MRPII emulates TQM activities. In addition, though, the MRPII implementation is also concerned with extensive replacement of the company's operating systems.

A criticism of TQM could be that it creates the will for fundamental change without providing the means. TQM must prefer a planning culture to fire-fighting, integrated systems to departmental ones, shared information to fragmented data. Yet these changes will not come about simply because of an awareness that existing methods are wasteful and unreliable. Nor will the creation of narrowly focused improvement teams provide company-wide solutions. The awareness that improvement is needed must be supported by a framework for achieving that improvement. It is MRPII that supplies the planning methodology and systems integration needed to realize the TQM goals.

MRPII and TQM are therefore natural allies. In Chapter 6 we saw how JIT adds a further dimension to MRPII as a mechanism for continuous improvement on the shopfloor. On a broader front, TQM provides additional tools for company-wide process improvement, again by tapping the ability of the people in the business. Ideally a TQM programme would precede an MRPII implementation, although this may not always be possible. Even if a successful MRPII implementation has been completed, TQM is still relevant as a means of achieving further improvement.

Making MRPII stick

Once a company has undergone the trauma of a successful MRPII implementation its managers would find it difficult to imagine going back to the way things were. Yet companies do regress. MRPII is not irreversible; on the contrary, it needs constant attention to prevent decay setting in.

Once the initial education and training programme has been completed, MRPII begins to move out of the limelight. Other issues arise which take attention away from the new routines and working practices. As time passes, these routines start to seem less important than they did at first. Rules start getting bent to suit short term expediencies. The implementation team is disbanded, its members moving on to scale even greater heights elsewhere. Operations staff leave and their replacements are shown what to do, but not why to do it that way. So they devise their own 'improvements'.

A company can counter all these setbacks if the top management team retains its commitment. But even top managers are not there for ever. If the chief executive who originally sponsored the project leaves, the successor may not appreciate what has been achieved. Indeed it would not be surprising if a new chief executive decided to focus on other matters, if only to stamp a personal imprint on the company. Changes in other top managers, particularly the head of sales or manufacturing, could also undermine MRPII practices. It does not take a deliberate act of desecration, just an unwillingness to be bound by the MPS or a lack of interest in the regular data accuracy audit reports. The word soon spreads that MRPII does not matter any more.

Is it possible for a top management team to protect its work in perpetuity; to defend its creation from future neglect? It is not easy. An MRPII implementation is seen as a single project with an end date. In a company where things run reasonably smoothly the chaos and fire-fighting that preceded MRPII are soon forgotten. Newer personnel never experienced them. The current situation is regarded as the norm, not as something that has been fought hard for and is worth preserving. Gradually standards are allowed to slip. To overcome this drift into neglect there is a need for a mechanism that will continue to enforce the disciplines of MRPII, and make them inseparable from the way the company operates.

Such a mechanism can be provided by TQM. A total quality programme is not a transient project; it is for ever. Total quality requires that procedures are continually audited and kept up to date. Slippages in performance standards are not permitted. If training of new employees is inadequate, then this will be identified and corrected. Furthermore, the quality manager, the champion of the total quality programme, is probably the best person in the company to persuade a new chief executive of the dangers of abandoning MRPII disciplines. After all the quality manager is unbiased, independent of any conflict between production and sales. Also the position of quality manager confers upon its holder a responsibility that transcends the company's organizational hierarchy. The quality manager, then, must become the protector of the company's commitment to MRPII.

This idea is not so surprising as it may seem initially. The quality manager is responsible for ensuring that the company has a system that will deliver products to the required specification, at the right time and at minimum cost. MRPII provides much of that system. If MRPII decays, so does the company's ability to provide quality goods and services. It is quite clearly the role of the quality manager to ensure that no such decay occurs.

It is unlikely that the quality manager would also be the MRPII project manager, indeed it would be confusing to combine the two roles. A formal handover of responsibility should be made when the project team is wound up and the project manager moves on. In this handover the quality manager does not take over ownership of the project from the implementation team leader. Ownership is dispersed amongst the operational managers who use MRPII in performing their everyday work. It is these managers who are responsible for maintaining data integrity, training new staff, keeping manuals up to date and so on. The role of the quality manager is to be the protector of the company's commitment; the company conscience. This role is discharged through on-going auditing of adherence to operating procedures, counselling managers in the need for corrective action when slippages are identified, and escalating intractable problems to higher levels.

The MRPII culture

It should by now be very clear that MRPII is not simply a technical matter. MRPII is a strategy for integrated business planning and control. Only top management can create an environment in which MRPII can be implemented successfully, and sustained thereafter.

Top management commitment is not demonstrated by the presence of VDUs on executive desks, nor by a passive acquiescence to the MRPII project. Top managers must take a proactive role, changing the way they manage the business and accepting the constraints that MRPII places upon their freedom of action. Top managers who can combine this dynamic commitment to MRPII with a belief in total quality as their overriding concern will see their companies achieve true and sustained excellence.

8

Future directions

Continuing evolution

The story of MRPII has been one of continuing evolution. The original bill of material processors led the way to material requirements planning. MRP in turn developed into closed loop MRP, forming the framework around which integrated business systems were subsequently designed. In recent years IBS software has steadily accumulated more functionality and moved into new business areas.

While this was happening computers changed from big, slow, centralized mainframes into low cost PCs and multi-user mid-range systems. Batch systems were replaced by on-line processing. Proprietary software is now beginning to give way to open systems, while graphical user interfaces are changing the look and feel of the application software.

There is every reason to suppose that commercial IBS products will continue to evolve. Indeed the rate of change may increase. As the market for first time users shrinks, the competition between software suppliers for more modern replacement systems will be fierce. The combination of sophisticated users and a large population of system suppliers will ensure continuing pressure to introduce new concepts and facilities.

Furthermore, the environment within which manufacturing companies operate has also changed dramatically, and will continue to change in the future. MRPII has spanned a period that has seen the decline of mass production and the growth of customer focus and niche marketing. If MRPII is to continue to provide core business planning and control systems it must support the commercial pressures that are currently affecting manufacturing industry. These include the need for:

- faster and more flexible response to customer needs
- shorter product life-cycles and faster product development
- reduced waste and energy usage
- lean operation, using a minimum of administration and managerial staff

- lifetime product reliability
- dispersal of manufacturing facilities to the geographical markets in which the goods are sold (e.g. assembly of military and consumer products).

Companies will also be looking to their information systems to assist in managing new concerns, such as environmental care and product recyclability.

All these developments will cause companies to reassess the way they go about their business, the procedures they use and the management information systems they need. This reassessment will lead to more being asked of business planning and control systems, to enable ever higher standards of business performance to be achieved.

In response to these demands, future developments in business planning and control systems will focus upon three key issues. The first of these is the continued acceptability of traditional MRPII concepts and techniques, and the search for possible alternatives. The second is the emergence of enterprise resource planning (ERP). The third is the role of MRPII within CIM. The reactions of existing and potential MRPII companies, as well as those of software suppliers, to these issues will determine the future directions of MRPII. This chapter examines the likely impact of these three areas of development.

Room for improvement?

Many manufacturing companies use an IBS, and many of these would claim to be operating MRPII. Relatively few, however, have achieved the success they would wish. Yet in spite of the fact that MRPII has proved so difficult to implement successfully, no alternative methodology has emerged that offers serious competition.

One reason is that it is difficult to envisage any alternative methodology succeeding in companies that cannot maintain accurate data or create a realistic MPS. Yet it is problems as basic as this that cause many companies to fail with MRPII. A second reason for the pre-eminence of MRPII is that it dominates the software market. Even OPT, which comes nearest to posing a threat, is dependent upon integration with an IBS to provide data and supporting systems. Since MRPII can be defined very broadly, the resulting hybrid is merely MRPII by other means.

Companies that have seen JIT as an alternative to computer-based systems have mostly been disappointed. The central achievement of JIT has been to generate an awareness of the need to simplify the problem before applying technology-based solutions. At the level of shopfloor scheduling and control in particular, kanban can eliminate the need for expensive and complex data capture and scheduling systems in certain environments. Nevertheless, the need for higher level management planning and information systems remains. JIT is an execution system not a planning system, and it does not provide an alternative to the use of computers for planning purposes.

MRPII, it seems, is without serious rivals. Yet its acceptance by much of manufacturing industry has been grudging. Some companies have been reluctant to embark upon MRPII, or to attempt to revive failed implementations, because of a lack of faith in the MRPII philosophy. Criticism of MRPII (much of it, it must be said, biased and extremely ill-informed) has been widespread for many years. The more considered criticism tends to focus on two aspects of MRPII: the mechanics of the MRP/CRP concept and the centralized, autocratic nature of the overall methodology.

If these are real problems, and are limiting the acceptability and success of MRPII, then new methods should be found to overcome them. If, however, they are merely excuses for poor implementation then changing the approach will not help. Only better education and more positive publicity will move MRPII forward.

The case for replacing MRP/CRP

The basic MRP/CRP routine is about as simple a method for planning materials and capacity as could be imagined. Simplicity, however, is a double edged sword. It implies on the one hand robustness and ease of use, but on the other hand imprecision and limited applicability. Given that MRPII is often regarded as a complex solution to manufacturing planning and control, there is clearly virtue in its core techniques being comparatively straightforward. The relative lack of commercial success of OPT is, at least in part, due to the complexity and opaqueness of its scheduling algorithms. In contrast MRP/CRP is very easy to understand (although this may mislead people into thinking that MRPII is trivial, which it certainly is not).

The impact of the simplifications contained in the MRP/CRP routine were discussed in Chapter 5. The conclusion drawn there was that these simplifications are acceptable in medium and long term planning, but additional support may be necessary for short term production scheduling.

The possibility of a more sophisticated alternative to MRP/CRP remains, however. OPT is one such alternative, the merits of which were discussed in Chapter 6. OPT addresses some of the MRP/CRP disadvantages, such as fixed batch quantities and lead times, and it certainly deserves serious consideration. Even so, both MRP/CRP and OPT share a common assumption. Both techniques convert an assembly plan into manufacturing and purchasing schedules. They differ in the way the assembly plan is derived (MRP/CRP uses an MPS, whilst OPT develops an assembly schedule automatically, using finite capacity scheduling techniques). Nevertheless both techniques generate detailed schedules from the assembly plan which recognize capacity constraints but which assume that purchased materials can be obtained whenever they are needed. This assumption is not always valid.

The availability of a few critical materials could be taken into account in the creation of the MPS or, in the case of OPT, by treating those materials as constraints. Where large numbers of different purchased materials are used, each with its own delivery lead time, neither of these techniques is adequate. As a result, plans are often produced that violate normal supply lead times. Since the problem can be passed on to the supplier, who has to bear the brunt of endless last minute schedule changes, there is little incentive for the purchaser to improve the situation. In practice, of course, the supplier's efficiency is reduced, either through constant disruption to production or through the cost of carrying a high finished goods inventory. This inefficiency is ultimately passed on to the customer in the form of higher prices.

There seems to be no good reason why a production planning and scheduling system could not be developed that takes into account the availability of both materials and capacity. Computer technology has come a long way since the batch processing machines around which the MRP/CRP cycle was devised. Planning through sequential batch runs can no longer be regarded as state of the art. Interactive scheduling, considering all constraints (material as well as capacity) simultaneously, should now be the objective. Perhaps if there were a greater recognition of the need for efficient planning throughout the supply chain, rather than simply within individual companies, such systems would already be widely available.

Such a system would not need to rely upon arbitrary MPS time fences to minimize system nervousness and to control the extent of disruption caused by changes to the plan. Instead, any proposed changes could be explicitly modelled, the impact of each one on the company and its suppliers could be accurately assessed. Only then would the change be committed to MRP.

Perhaps such systems will be in common use one day, but they may not. In practice a well-managed MRPII implementation in a company that is sensitive to the problems of its suppliers will contribute very nearly as much as any conceivable planning system could. Whilst a greater choice in the core material and capacity planning techniques offered by software suppliers would be welcome, it is probable that most companies will prefer to stay with MRP/CRP.

Autocratic, or just structured and disciplined?

The hierarchical planning structure that is the foundation of MRPII is sometimes said to be too centralized and autocratic. The top management team decides the business strategy and MRPII methodology translates that strategy into specific tasks that must be carried out at predetermined times. There seems little opportunity for people lower down the organization to contribute their ideas and experience. Discussion of shopfloor scheduling and control in Chapter 6 stressed the desirability of local input, but even shopfloor scheduling must be carried out within limits set by the main planning system. In all other respects, MRPII is totally authoritarian. It forces disciplines and it structures everybody's work. Individual initiatives are discouraged because they may have unforeseen effects on other users of the data. Written procedures cover every eventuality, and training emphasizes the importance of working to the procedure.

People used to less rigid working methods may well resent this degree of regimentation. Yet MRPII is not alone in insisting upon working to procedure. JIT, which is generally seen as sympathetic to the human aspects of work, nevertheless stresses the need for standardized manufacturing operations. Every movement of each operation is expected to be carried out in the prescribed way every time it is performed. The reason is that standardization reduces the risk of errors, simplifies operator training and provides a sound basis for making further method improvements.

On a wider front, TQM also emphasizes the need for everyone in the company, not only the production workers, to follow procedures rigorously. In the past, new employees were often given only the most general instruction in the work required of them. They were then left to develop their own ways of carrying out the allotted tasks. The advantage of this style of management was that it could generate a feeling of personal satisfaction in, and ownership of, the job. Unfortunately it also led to considerable uncertainty, confusion, duplication, error and conflict. Companies that are committed to TQM will recognize that this approach is no longer acceptable. Thorough training is needed, both for new employees and existing ones, to ensure that all work is done in the correct way. This training must be supported by comprehensive written operating procedures.

This view of current trends in the workplace envisions a rather gloomy picture of conformity, repetition and a stifling of initiative. Yet such a working environment would be in no-one's interest. If people are bored and frustrated, their performance will deteriorate; if they are not allowed to contribute their ideas, the business is impoverished. Some form of counterpoint to the enforcement of standard procedures is needed to keep people motivated and creative.

The mechanism for combating mindless regimentation is the formation of continuous improvement teams. These teams, which are based upon natural work groups, meet frequently to discuss problems affecting their work and suggestions for improvement. For the teams to function properly they must be given training in problem solving techniques, and they must be provided with support services. On the shopfloor these support services would include process engineers and materials handling specialists. Teams in administration areas might need support from systems analysts, accountants and buyers.

It is not easy to establish a successful network of continuous improvement teams, as earlier attempts in the West to emulate Japanese-style quality circles proved. Management must commit the necessary training resource and support services, as well as providing the time for regular group meetings. Patience is also needed, since the teams will not immediately produce a steady stream of cost saving ideas.

Once the teams are established, and their role understood by the team members, the frustrations of repetitive working methods can be greatly reduced. Every aspect of the work that is awkward, error-prone, slow or unpleasant can be examined and improved by the team. Since a structure is in place which allows technical expertise to be brought in when needed, all the implications of the proposed change can be assessed without delay. If the proposal is accepted, procedures are rewritten immediately and the change implemented. The unrelenting rigidity of procedures that appeared to be so soul-destroying actually enables changes to be made quickly, and with certainty as to their wider implications.

Because improvements can be actioned quickly and easily, the rate of change can be high. Regular changes in working methods combat the onset of boredom, and the knowledge that the next team meeting is not far away stimulates people to think about further improvements while they are working. The contrast with undisciplined organizations is marked. In the latter it is almost impossible to change anything without numerous unforeseen problems emerging after the event. These problems require much fire-fighting effort, and create a resolve amongst the people affected not to risk changing anything else in the future, if they can avoid it.

The rigid style of running a business turns out to be the most responsive, adaptable and dynamic. Criticism that MRPII is too big, restrictive, and autocratic therefore misses the point. MRPII actually provides a disciplined, predictable environment within which continuous improvement can thrive. Management's task is to build the continuous improvement teams that can benefit from this environment.

A robust tool

Several real and apparent shortcomings of MRPII have been highlighted in this book. Some are relatively minor, others are fundamental to the whole concept. None of them has proved to be insurmountable. There are some drawbacks that fall into the category of things one has to learn to live with, as part of a commitment to MRPII. There are others that can be (and in some instances, have been) resolved by improved software. It always pays to shop around to see in detail what the system suppliers have to offer.

For the great majority of companies, MRPII offers far more positives than negatives. Managers considering a move to MRPII, therefore, should not be discouraged. The very many benefits of MRPII, not the least being real control of the business, perhaps for the first time, mean that such a move should not be delayed.

Enterprise resource planning (ERP)

Until recently IBS products have been designed solely for single site operation. Furthermore the computer hardware used to run this software usually takes the form of a central processor, with dedicated disk storage, to which VDUs and printers are connected, a form of architecture perfectly suitable for a single manufacturing site, but less appropriate in multi-site operations. Companies that wish to integrate the activities of several manufacturing sites have been unable to do so with standard software. Instead, each site has had to operate its own standalone system, a solution that prevents any real enterprise-wide integration.

In the past this lack of integration has not been a great problem. Multi-site companies were only too pleased if any of their sites achieved a successful MRPII implementation. The idea of attempting integrated MRPII across several sites would have been regarded as highly ambitious, to say the least. Differences in products or manufacturing technology persuaded many multi-site companies to allow each unit to select the software best suited to its specific requirements. This approach allowed greater ownership of the implementation within each unit, but made transfer of data between units, and with head office, even more difficult.

Other companies insisted upon all sites using the same software, a policy that some came to regret when the chosen system proved less than universally applicable. Even when this policy was successful there was still no mechanism for identical systems on different sites to share data or to co-ordinate plans across the enterprise.

Software suppliers are beginning to address the problems of multi-site companies through the development of new software products that are described as ERP systems.

What is ERP?

The term ERP is not easy to define, making it just as liable to be misunderstood as were MRP and MRPII before it. If ERP follows a similar path, unrealistic claims will be made for it, and ill-informed articles written. Some software suppliers will probably attempt to hi-jack the term to suit existing product features, in preference to changing their software. Different perceptions will thus be formed as to what ERP really means. Although it would be satisfying to forestall this potential confusion by producing a complete and incontestable definition of ERP, it is unrealistic to try. The final shape of ERP will only emerge when several of the market-leading software suppliers have launched their new products, and the market has given its verdict.

The overall objective of ERP is already clear. ERP is not a replacement for MRPII, it is an extension of it for businesses that comprise a number of semi-autonomous units. ERP may be considered as an umbrella strategy in which closed-loop MRP operates at individual unit level, while enterprise-wide integration allows co-ordination of activities between units. The extent to which the hierarchical planning process of MRPII is carried out centrally, rather than locally, will depend on the organization concerned. ERP software should, however, provide the option for corporate management to co-ordinate planning across multiple sites.

ERP is not simply about centralization of planning, however. Decentralization is also facilitated. Local managers are able to draw upon corporate information to assist them in making decisions within their own units.

Remote sales offices and distribution depots can be linked to the system, avoiding any fragmentation of information and control.

If ERP is to permit this form of operation, the old style central processor and database is no longer suitable. ERP systems must allow data to be distributed across several databases at different locations. These databases are connected by a network linking the sites. The user does not need to know where the data is held; the system retrieves the data that is needed from wherever it resides.

In order to operate as a true enterprise system, capable of supplying all the business systems needed by a large, multi-site company, ERP needs to satisfy a number of technical criteria. In particular ERP systems should:

- be based upon a relational database structure, and support a standard query language, such as SQL
- adopt open standards and be designed around a standard GUI, so that it may be fully integrated with other specialist applications used by the enterprise
- be multi-lingual, for companies operating within different countries
- incorporate a wide range of business applications, such as personnel systems, preventive maintenance, health and safety data and so on
- be suitable for a range of industry types, and not just be targeted at, for example, make-to-order businesses or process companies. This is important since different industry types may exist within a single enterprise.

Needless to say, the supplier should be capable of supporting the system in whatever location the user enterprise intends to install it.

Implications of ERP

The development of ERP systems will almost certainly be the main preoccupation of the major system suppliers during the mid-1990s. There will be intense competition to win lucrative business from large multi-site companies, although the cost of developing the high specification software will be considerable. Sales publicity will no doubt proclaim the death of MRPII, or at least attempt to consign it to a tactical, local role, rather than a strategic one.

To single-site companies, the ERP bandwagon may appear to have little relevance. This view may, however, turn out to be mistaken. There are implications of ERP which even single-site companies should take into account.

Out with the old, in with the new
The evolution of MRPII has reached its second discontinuity. The first was when batch processing was replaced by on-line systems. That marked the change from early MRP to integrated business systems. This new change will see distributed computing provide the means by which ERP will

succeed IBSs. The IBS products that have been developed and improved steadily since on-line systems first appeared will be replaced by completely new software written around ERP criteria. Even the more recent, Unix-based, IBS products may need extensive re-engineering to comply fully with ERP requirements.

The first discontinuous change affected only a small pool of existing users, while making MRPII viable for the first time for many other companies. This second change to ERP has the potential to affect large numbers of existing users, who will feel that they must migrate to newer software products in order to maintain their competitiveness.

Suppliers producing new ERP systems will not continue to develop their older products indefinitely. At some stage they will attempt to migrate all users, whether multi-site or single-site, to their new ERP systems. Since ERP software will be modular, and compatible with MRPII principles, companies should be able to make this transition without difficulty. Nevertheless there will be significant cost and upheaval involved, which the company may not consider to be justified by the benefits arising from the conversion. It is therefore important that any company proposing to acquire software incompatible with ERP standards should understand that it is probably buying an obsolescent product. The product may have quite a long useful life ahead of it, and the decision to acquire it may be sound, but a conscious evaluation of its life expectancy should be undertaken when making the choice.

ERP in single site companies

Many of the ERP features that have been described are as useful to a smaller, single-site company as they are to a Fortune 500 multi-national. Relational databases, SQL, and open systems are all valuable features. Furthermore, many single-site companies are dividing their operations into semi-autonomous business units, to gain the benefit of local responsibility and ownership. ERP would support local control of these business units while maintaining company-wide integration of information.

Some companies which are presently single-site may one day experience commercial or political pressures that force them into setting up overseas production units to service local markets. If such a development is possible, it would be unwise for a company to invest in an IBS that did not have ERP capability.

The extended enterprise

Single-site companies that consider ERP is not of interest to them should reflect on whether they really are as isolated as they think. Many organizations are beginning to link themselves more closely to their suppliers and their customers, using EDI networks. This trend will lead to companies sharing more information about their stock levels and produc-tion schedules, in order to integrate their logistics processes. The result will be supply chain MRPII, a concept that was introduced in Chapter 5.

Supply chain integration could go further. Increasing willingness to share information could lead to the creation of extended enterprises, informal associations of companies operating in successive tiers of the supply chain. The extended enterprise may decide to function as if it were a single, multi-site business. ERP would provide the means to co-ordinate planning throughout the extended enterprise, in order to synchronize the activities of the total supply chain.

What's in a name?

Some system suppliers may decide not to develop multi-site ERP systems, because of the high development costs, or because they are too small to provide adequate support for geographically dispersed customers. Even these suppliers will tend to develop new products that are truly open (if their existing products do not already fully comply with all the relevant standards) and which contain a wide range of functionality. Whether such systems will eventually be described as ERP remains to be seen.

It would be unfortunate if the term ERP displaced MRPII, because that would be to confuse the software with the management concept. ERP could more properly replace the expression IBS that has been used in this book, or the more common 'MRPII system' that has been avoided here. ERP represents a software specification rather than an alternative to MRPII. It is true that ERP offers companies new possibilities, but only by building firmly upon MRPII methodologies and disciplines.

Computer integrated manufacturing (CIM)

CIM is concerned with the integration of commercial, financial, engineering and production systems to improve responsiveness, quality, cost and competitiveness. CIM grew out of the recognition that standalone systems ('islands of automation') often failed to deliver any real business benefits, because the business environment in which they operated was unchanged.

The CIM vision is one of total business integration, with no local, departmental systems, no data that is duplicated unnecessarily, and no barriers between different functions. In the integrated business everyone is pursuing the same mission, everyone is working to the same plan, and everyone has access to the information they need to carry out their duties.

Achieving this vision requires far more than just computer technology. Integration is as much about creating the right culture as it is about installing systems. Implementing MRPII is a first step towards CIM, creating a planning culture and bringing integration of the core business processes. Nevertheless, it is only a first step.

The elements of CIM

The are several key business functions that are not generally regarded as part of an IBS, but which are certainly encompassed by CIM. Product design and development, production and process engineering, and plant maintenance are all examples of functions which gain little from an IBS (although they are expected to contribute data to it). These functions often have their own standalone systems, such as computer aided design and computer aided manufacturing (CAD/CAM), computer aided process planning (CAPP), and planned maintenance systems.

At the shopfloor level, considerable use is made of other non-IBS systems. One of the main uses of these systems is the control of manufacturing processes. For example, in the engineering industry CNC is widely used to operate individual metal cutting and forming machines. Groups of CNC machines can be made to operate as a flexible manufacturing system (FMS), by installing an automated materials handling system and using a cell controller to co-ordinate the whole unit. Process industry makes considerable use of programmable logic controllers (PLC) to adjust plant settings in response to input from sensors incorporated in the machinery. Ruggedized industrial PCs are used where greater processing power is required, and supervisory control and data acquisition (SCADA) systems are used to monitor complete stages of the production process.

The systems that are used to control shopfloor machinery and material handling equipment require even more responsive scheduling capabilities than that provided by a local finite scheduler. Real-time systems which can respond immediately to actual events are needed to sequence the activities of production machines and process plant. These event-driven systems represent yet another level in the planning hierarchy.

In a CIM environment, shopfloor process control systems would be linked to higher level planning systems so that work schedules could be passed down to the local controllers. These links would also allow feedback of actual events to be uploaded to the main planning system. Normally such links would be made via area controllers, which would have local scheduling and data capture capabilities; these area controllers would in turn be linked to the central IBS. Some of the issues arising in the linking of shopfloor devices to an IBS were discussed in Chapter 6.

Not all shopfloor systems are used for purposes connected with the scheduling and work tracking functions of MRPII. Examples of other types of shopfloor systems include operator time and attendance recording, statistical process control (SPC) and machine status monitoring. CIM incorporates all these systems that fall beyond the boundaries of MRPII, as well as the IBS itself. Documentation handling systems, electronic mail, executive information systems and many other systems may also be candidates for inclusion in a CIM strategy. It would be futile to attempt to provide a full list of all the functions that CIM might encompass. The final shape of a CIM strategy is determined solely by the needs and priorities of the company concerned.

In most cases, however, a CIM strategy is based upon an IBS. It is the IBS that provides the main commercial systems and generates the plans that drive the business. The IBS is surrounded by, and linked to, various engineering, production management and decision support systems, and to a hierarchy of scheduling, process control and data collection systems. The general structure is fairly well understood. The problem lies in bringing the vision to reality.

A CIM architecture

Companies wishing to implement a CIM strategy must consider how best to establish a communication system based upon one or more local area networks, and how to organize and manage the data required by the applications involved. In other words, they must design a CIM architecture. Clearly this architecture should be based upon open standards wherever possible. The qualification of 'wherever possible' is added because the development of open systems standards is still far from complete. Often there is no choice (or no economical choice) other than to use proprietary tools for at least part of the CIM strategy. Fortunately, as we saw in Chapter 3, some proprietary products are so widely used that they have become almost the equivalent of international standards.

Even if open systems are used it does not mean that different systems can be integrated simply by running a cable between them. Bespoke programming is always needed to link systems that were not specifically designed to be interfaced. Plug-compatible CIM, where modules from different suppliers can be integrated at will, is a concept that is still a very long way from realization.

Much of the data used within CIM applications is related in some way to the specification of products and their components, and to the processes used to make them. A CAD system, for example, contains basic item specifications for all manufactured parts. MRPII needs some of the CAD data, but adds to it the bill of material structure, lead times, inventory rules, and a host of other details. CAPP specifies in detail the operations involved in making the part. MRPII needs access to this information, for routing records, but generally only in summary form.

Many manufacturing companies have built interfaces between, in particular, CAD and IBS systems, and some suppliers offer in-built interfacing tools to assist this process. These links are usually unsophisticated in their objectives. They are intended merely to enable new product details to be transferred in batch mode from the CAD system to the IBS. Although such links can be useful, they do not constitute true integration. The problem is that the applications still do not share the same data. Each application holds the data it needs, and neither of the applications contains all the data needed by the other.

A development that should eventually simplify communication between different applications is the evolving ISO standard STEP (STandard for the

Exchange of Product model data). There have been several previous attempts to produce standards for the exchange of product definition data. Some, such as IGES (Initial Graphics Exchange Specification), are widely used. However, these standards have focused narrowly upon the transfer of product geometry and technical specification between different CAD systems. STEP promises to provide standards for the exchange of all product data, including planning, financial, quality and commercial data. When fully implemented, STEP will be an important enabler for CIM.

MRPII within CIM

The goal of systems integration is sometimes seen to be the provision of integrated data. In this narrow vision of CIM, all that is needed is unlimited access to data, supported by the means to extract and analyze information, and to present summaries in a form suitable for senior managers. The assumption is that because this access to timely information enables managers to know everything that is happening in the business, they are able to manage effectively; this is a very reactive vision of CIM. True CIM must be much more proactive, preventing problems rather than analyzing them.

The real aim of integration must be co-ordination and synchronization. Everybody working to the same plan, in the same timescales. This can only be achieved by using integration as a channel for communicating plans and schedules, and for receiving the feedback necessary to keep the plans meaningful. Data is important, but mainly in feeding the closed loop planning system. Management need to know performance against the targets established by the plans, but not the host of operational data used in constructing and monitoring the plans. Since closed loop planning is the core process of CIM, it follows that MRPII is central to CIM.

CIM is a slow, difficult, and often expensive journey. Nevertheless it is one which companies intending to survive into the twenty-first century will take. At present CIM means a great deal of bespoke programming and integration; there is no such thing as a CIM system that can be bought off the shelf. Probably there never will be, since there is so much variety between different companies at the level of detail in which CIM operates. Nevertheless the fact remains that much of the integration associated with CIM is not unique to individual companies. For example, integrating CAD with MRPII, and communicating works order information between MRPII and local scheduling systems are universal problems. There is no real reason why these particular wheels should have to be reinvented by every company that wants to roll forward on them.

IBS suppliers could do much to develop more CIM-friendly products. They could, for example, adopt standard terminology, formats and presentation of data. They could also develop more sophisticated shopfloor modules. If they do follow this route, the potential market could be huge. How many cars would there be on the roads now if potential motorists had to buy the engine from one supplier, the gearbox from another, the suspension and steering from a third, and then pay someone else to make the body and fit it all together? Probably very few. Yet this, in effect, is what manufacturers pursuing CIM have to do. CIM will always require a greater degree of customization than the average motorist would expect of a motor car, but it should be possible to start off with a reasonably specified base model.

The future for MRPII

This chapter has examined the future of MRPII by considering three issues. The first issue was the continuing relevance of MRPII in the face both of more recent production planning and control concepts, and of continued criticism of its underlying concepts from some quarters. The development of ERP was the second issue addressed. It seems that this will be the main focus for software development over the next few years. The third issue was CIM, a field in which there has been much interest but relatively little real progress.

From this analysis a number of conclusions about the future may be drawn. MRPII will continue to provide the planning framework and the core business systems for companies wishing to move towards business integration and lean production methods. Improved versions of MRP/CRP may emerge which are based upon more sophisticated scheduling method-ologies, and greater variety in this area would certainly be welcome. Nevertheless the position of traditional MRPII techniques is so well entrenched that most companies will continue to use them.

Software developers will concentrate upon ERP as their new marketing opportunity. ERP will be important to large, multi-site companies, but it is also relevant to smaller organizations. The aim of ERP is to create enterprise-wide information systems. Multi-company features are one aspect of this, but there are two others. Firstly ERP systems will attempt to provide a very wide range of applications modules within a single integrated framework. Secondly ERP will be based upon the use of truly open systems, so that specialized third party software can be readily integrated with the core system.

Both of these features are of importance to CIM. It is not yet clear whether system suppliers will include new engineering and shopfloor modules in their ERP systems, or whether they will concentrate initially upon additional commercial features. Nevertheless the ERP concept does seem to offer hope of more complete CIM products in the future. In the shorter term, the openness of ERP will simplify integration with third party shopfloor systems.

Conclusion

This book has ranged widely across the field of manufacturing manage-ment, as befits a work on a subject as broad as MRPII. In this final chapter we have considered how MRPII might change in the future, in response to a changing world. There seems little doubt that MRPII will continue to have a pivotal role in successful manufacturing companies, supported by more sophisticated software and greater systems integration. There is no sign of any fundamentally different form of manufacturing planning and control that will render basic MRPII concepts obsolete.

There are a few final conclusions to be drawn, particularly for those managers presently contemplating a move to MRPII, or struggling with a difficult implementation:

- MRPII is the only way to achieve real control of the business, so 'go for it'.
- Top managers must become more involved and must learn to run their businesses through MRPII.
- Implementing MRPII is most difficult in undisciplined and divided organizations, but for them the potential benefits are greatest.
- MRPII, like most aspects of management, is about people. It cannot be achieved without involving everyone in the business.

It would be unrealistic to believe that in the complex and challenging world in which we live, competitive manufacturing could be achieved without effort. For most companies, managing through MRPII is an essential part of maintaining and improving competitiveness. The effort involved is both necessary and worthwhile.

Bibliography

This bibliography contains books that I have found particularly helpful. Some are referred to in the text.

Browne, J., Harhen, J. and Shivnan, J. (1988) *Production Management Systems: A CIM Perspective*, Addison-Wesley Publishing Company

Christopher, M. (1986) *The Strategy of Distribution Management*, Butterworth-Heinemann, Oxford

Dixon, J.R., Nanni, A.J. and Vollman, T.E. (1990) *The New Performance Challenge: Measuring Operations for World-Class Competition*, Business One Irwin, Illinois

Goldratt, E.M. and Cox, J. (1984) *The Goal*, North River Press Inc, New York

Johnson, H.T. and Kaplan, R.S. (1987) *Relevance Lost: The Rise and Fall of Management Accounting*, Harvard Business School Press

Mather, H. (1988) *Competitive Manufacturing*, Prentice-Hall, New Jersey

Ohno, T. (1988) *Toyota Production System: Beyond Large-Scale Production*, English translation, Productivity Press, Massachusetts

Vollmann, T.E., Berry, W.L. and Whybark, D.C. (1988) *Manufacturing Planning and Control Systems*, 2nd edn, Irwin, Illinois

Wallace, T.F. (1990) *MRPII: Making it Happen*, 2nd edn, Oliver Wight Limited Publications Inc, Essex Junction

Weatherall, A. (1992) *Computer Integrated Manufacturing: A Total Company Competitive Strategy*, 2nd edn, Butterworth-Heinemann, Oxford

——— Index ———